VIRGINIA

GLENCOE

MATH

AUTHORS
Carter • Cuevas • Day • Malloy
Kersaint • Reynosa • Silbey • Vielhaber

Mc
Graw
Hill
Education

mheducation.com/prek-12

Send all inquiries to:
McGraw-Hill Education
8787 Orion Place
Columbus, OH 43240

ISBN: 978-0-07-682450-2
MHID: 0-07-682450-0

Printed in the United States of America.

2 3 4 5 6 QVS 21 20 19 18

CONTENTS IN BRIEF

Units organized by domain

Glencoe Math is organized into units based on groups of related standards called domains.
MP Mathematical Process Goals are embedded throughout the course.

MATHEMATICAL
PROCESS GOALS
HANDBOOK

Tetra Images/Getty Images

MP Mathematical Process Goals

Mathematical Process Goals Handbook

Everything you need,

anytime, anywhere.

With ConnectED, you have instant access to all of your study materials—anytime, anywhere. From homework materials to study guides—it's all in one place and just a click away. ConnectED even allows you to collaborate with your classmates and use mobile apps to make studying easy.

Resources built for you—available 24/7:

- Your eBook available wherever you are

- Personal Tutors and Self-Check Quizzes to help your learning

- An Online Calendar with all of your due dates

- eFlashcard App to make studying easy

- A message center to stay in touch

Go Mobile!

Visit mheonline.com/apps to get entertainment, instruction, and education on the go with ConnectED Mobile and our other apps available for your device.

Go Online!
connectED.mcgraw-hill.com

your Username

your Password

Vocab

Learn about new vocabulary words.

Watch

Watch animations and videos.

Tutor

See and hear a teacher explain how to solve problems.

Tools

Explore concepts with virtual manipulatives.

Sketchpad

Discover concepts using The Geometer's Sketchpad®.

Check

Check your progress.

eHelp

Get targeted homework help.

Worksheets
Access practice worksheets.

Chapter 1
Ratios and Proportional Reasoning

Essential Question

HOW can you show that two objects are proportional?

Real World
p. 43

Chapter 2
Percents

Real World
p. 119

Essential Question

HOW can percent help you understand situations involving money?

Chapter 3
Rational Numbers

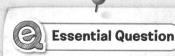

Essential Question

WHAT happens when you add, subtract, multiply, and divide fractions?

p. 251

Chapter 4
Expressions

e **Essential Question**

HOW can you use numbers and symbols to represent mathematical ideas?

Real World
p. 351

(t) Neil Overy/Getty Images, (b) ©Leo Fiedler/Royalty-Free/Corbis

Copyri... ...aw-Hill Education

ix

Chapter 5
Equations and Inequalities

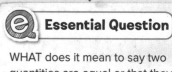

Essential Question

WHAT does it mean to say two quantities are equal or that they have a linear relationship?

Real World
p. 389

x

(t)Jupiterimages/Comstock Images/Getty Images; (b)Nicola Tree/Stockbyte/Getty Images   Copyright © McGraw-Hill Education

Chapter 6
Measure Figures

Essential Question

HOW do measurements help you describe real-world objects?

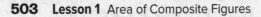

p. 503

xi

Chapter 7
Probability

e Essential Question

HOW can you predict the outcome of future events?

Real World
p. 627

Chapter 8
Statistics

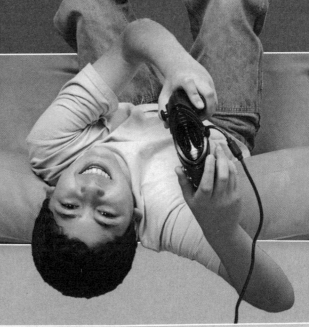

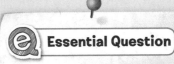

Essential Question

HOW do you know which type of graph to use when displaying data?

p. 697

Mathematical Process Goals Handbook

Essential Question

WHAT processes help me explore and explain mathematics?

Mathematical Process Goals

Mathematical Process Goals will help you become a successful problem solver and to use math effectively in your daily life.

What You'll Learn

MP Throughout this handbook, you will learn about each of these mathematical process goals and how they are integrated in the chapters and lessons of this book.

① **Focus on Mathematical Process Goals**
Mathematical Problem Solving

② **Focus on Mathematical Process Goals**
Mathematical Communication

③ **Focus on Mathematical Process Goals**
Mathematical Reasoning

④ **Focus on Mathematical Process Goals**
Mathematical Connections

⑤ **Focus on Mathematical Process Goals**
Mathematical Representations

Place a checkmark below the face that expresses how much you know about each Mathematical Process Goal. Then explain in your own words what it means to you.

😦 I have no clue.   😕 I've heard of it.   🙂 I know it!

Mathematical Process Goals				
Mathematical Process Goal	😦	😕	🙂	What it Means to Me
①				
②				
③				
④				
⑤				

What does it mean to persevere in solving problems?

Look up the word "persevere" in a dictionary. You might see "be persistent" or "follow something through to the end." When you persevere in solving math problems, you don't always stop at the first answer you get. You check if your solution is accurate, if it answers the problem, and if it makes sense!

Jared wants to paint his room. The dimensions of the room are 12 feet by 15 feet, and the walls are 9 feet tall. There are two windows, each with dimensions 6 feet by 5 feet. There are two doors, each with dimensions 30 inches by 6 feet. If a gallon of paint covers about 350 square feet, how many gallons of paint will he need to put two coats of paint on the wall?

1. **Understand** That's a lot of information! Go back and read the problem again. This time, circle the information given and underline what you are trying to find.

2. **Plan** Before you do ANY calculations, make a plan to solve the problem. List the steps you need to take.

   _____

   _____

   _____

3. **Solve** Apply your plan to solve the problem.

   Jared will need ⬚ gallons of paint.

4. **Check** Is your solution accurate? Does it make sense? Explain.

   _____

   _____

5. Did you feel like giving up at any point while solving the problem? Explain.

   _____

Solve each problem by using the four-step problem-solving model.

6. There are about 48,000 farms in Nebraska using approximately 45 million acres of land. This farmland covers about $\frac{9}{10}$ of the state. About how many acres are not made up of farmland?

Understand Circle the information you know and underline what you are trying to determine. Is there any information you will not use?

_____

Plan What strategy will you use to solve this problem?

_____

Solve Solve the problem. What is the solution?

_____

Check Does your answer make sense? Can you solve the problem another way to check your work?

_____

7. You and a friend went to the movies. You bought a student ticket and a drink. You split the cost of popcorn and a candy. You have $4.75 left. How much did you take with you? Show your steps below. Check your solution.

Student	$9	Popcorn	$6.50
Adult	$12	Candy	$5
Senior	$10	Drink	$4.50

_____

_____

_____

Find it in Your Book!

MP **Persevere with Problems**

Look in Chapter 1. Provide an example of where Mathematical Process Goal 1 is used. Explain why your example represents this process.

_____

_____

_____

Attend to Precision

What does it mean to communicate precisely?

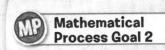

MP **Mathematical Process Goal 2**

Mathematical Communication

Communicating precisely is not just about giving the right answer. It also includes using terms, units, symbols, ideas, and procedures appropriately when discussing or solving problems.

Marlon drives his scooter to soccer practice every day. Each week, his scooter uses a quarter of a tank of gas. The practice field is 3 miles from his house and the gas tank holds 2.4 gallons of gas. He wants to find the unit rate per gallon of gas. Pair up with a classmate to discuss and answer the following.

1. In your own words, write the definitions for *ratio, equivalent ratio, bar diagram,* and *unit rate*.

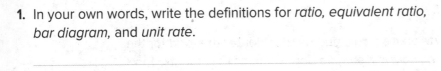

_____

_____

_____

2. How do the words from Exercise 1 relate to the problem?

_____

_____

3. Discuss with your partner the steps you will use to solve this problem. Summarize your discussion, and then solve the problem.

_____

_____

_____

4. What units of measure will describe the unit rate per gallon of gas?

_____

5. What is the unit rate per gallon for Marlon's scooter?

_____

Solve each problem.

The state of Colorado is shaped like a rectangle as shown in the map. The rate $\frac{1\ cm}{100\ km}$ can be used to find actual distances.

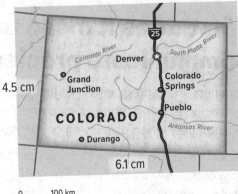

6. Use equivalent rates to find the actual distance x.

   a. $\frac{4.5\ cm}{x}$ b. $\frac{6.1\ cm}{x}$

7. What is the perimeter of the state on the map? the actual perimeter?

8. Claire is in charge of the 7th grade picnic and needs to order the food for the 90 students attending. She surveys a sample population of 18 students. Ten students chose hamburgers, 7 chose hot dogs, and 1 chose a veggie burger.

   a. Make a conjecture about how many students at the picnic will choose each type of food.

   b. Discuss with a partner if these numbers are exact or estimates. Then determine what problems Claire may have by using those numbers.

Find it in Your Book!

MP Attend to Precision

Look in Chapter 1. Provide an example of where Mathematical Process Goal 2 is used. Explain why your example represents this process.

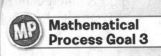

Reason Abstractly and Quantitatively

I need to double this recipe. How much flour do I need?

Suppose you want to double the ingredients from the recipe below. If you write an expression or an equation to figure out what you need, you are reasoning quantitatively. When you simplify the expression or solve the equation algebraically, you are reasoning abstractly.

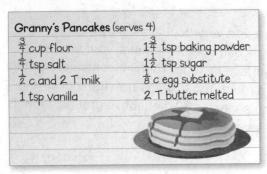

Granny's Pancakes (serves 4)

$\frac{3}{4}$ cup flour	$1\frac{3}{4}$ tsp baking powder
$\frac{1}{4}$ tsp salt	$1\frac{1}{2}$ tsp sugar
$\frac{1}{2}$ c and 2 T milk	$\frac{1}{8}$ c egg substitute
1 tsp vanilla	2 T butter, melted

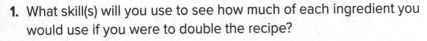

1. What skill(s) will you use to see how much of each ingredient you would use if you were to double the recipe?

_____

2. You planned for eight people to come for a pancake breakfast, but just found out that 10 people are coming! The recipe serves 4. Defne a variable and write an expression to determine the

amount of each ingredient to serve 10 people. _____

_____

3. Use the expression from Exercise 2 to complete the recipe card so that it serves 10 people. Is it appropriate to round any of the ingredients? Explain.

_____

_____

Granny's Pancakes (serves 10)

[ ] cup flour	[ ] tsp baking powder
[ ] tsp salt	[ ] tsp sugar
[ ] c and [ ] T milk	[ ] egg substitute
[ ] tsp vanilla	[ ] T butter, melted

It's Your Turn!

Reason abstractly or quantitatively to find a solution.

4. The graph shows the percent of people in different age groups that recently attended an amusement park. A total of 1.045 million people attended. How many of them were less than 25 years of age?

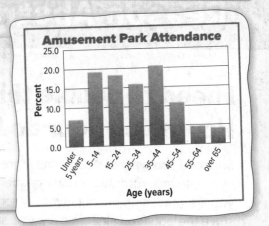

_____

_____

5. Cave exploration or spelunking is a very popular activity. Your family signs up for tours at a state park. On one of the tours, your brother is lowered 160 feet below the surface by rope. Then he continues another 70 feet below the surface to a room. You take the tree top tour where you climb to an adventure course that is 60 feet above ground. What is the difference between the elevations?

_____

_____

6. You and your family are traveling to a football game. You and your mother leave at 8:00 A.M. Your dad needs to wait for your sister to get home from dance practice, so he leaves at 9:30 A.M. If your mother drives at an average rate of 50 miles per hour, and your dad drives at an average rate of 65 miles per hour, when will he pass her? Suppose the game is 205 miles away. Who will get there first?

_____

_____

Find it in Your Book!

MP Reason Abstractly

Look in Chapter 1. Provide an example of where Process Goal 3 is used. Explain why your example represents this process.

_____

_____

_____

_____

Make Use of Structure

What is structure in mathematics?

Finding and making use of structure is important when solving problems. There is structure in writing and solving an equation or finding a pattern. We rely on being able to identify and use structure to sometimes find easier ways to solve problems.

At the Atlas Arcade, you can select a lunch combo from their new menu. First choose the type of sandwich. Then choose from a list of sides and a cookie.

Sandwich	Sides	Cookie
Chicken	Salad	Chocolate chip
Veggie	French fries	Oatmeal
Meatball	Onion rings	Raisin
	Soup	

1. Create a tree diagram or organized list that shows all of the possibilities for a veggie sandwich.

2. How many possible outcomes are there for a veggie sandwich?

3. How many total possibilities for all three types of sandwiches?

4. Can you think of another way to find the total number of outcomes?

5. Find a classmate that used a different method than you did and discuss the advantages and disadvantages of each method. Summarize your discussion.

It's Your Turn!

Describe the method you would use to solve each of the following.
Then solve.

6. Haney's scores on his science tests were 76%, 93%, 87%, 91%, and 83%. Haney wants a 90% test average for the term. If all tests are weighted the same, is it possible for him to get a 90% test average if there is only one more test? Explain.

7. You need to make a model of your bedroom for your art class. The scale is $\frac{3}{4}$-inch = 1 foot. What are the dimensions of your model?

8. A rectangle has a length of 4 centimeters and a width of 3 centimeters. The length and width are each multiplied by a factor of 3. Is the ratio $\frac{\text{area of new rectangle}}{\text{area of original rectangle}}$ equivalent to the ratio $\frac{\text{side length of new rectangle}}{\text{side length of original rectangle}}$? If not, explain how they are related.

Find it in Your Book!

MP **Make Use of Structure**

Look in Chapter 1. Provide an example of where Mathematical Process Goal 4 is used. Explain why your example represents this process.

Are you a visual person or do you prefer to use words?

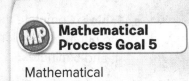

You might prefer to use diagrams or drawings when explaining ideas. Or you might prefer to use words. In math, we also use different ways to model the same idea. We can use words, graphs, tables, numbers, symbols, or diagrams.

1. Suppose you are selling T-shirts as a fundraiser for Key Club. The club makes a $6.30 profit for every T-shirt sold. Complete each model shown.

Words		Numbers	
		Profit ($)	**Number of shirts**
_____ per T-shirt		6.30	1
		12.60	
		18.90	
Symbols		**Graph**	
Let p = profit t = number of T-shirts sold $p = \boxed{}\, t$			

All of these model the same relationship between profit and number of T-shirts sold, just in different ways.

2. Which relationship would you prefer to use to determine the profit if 100 T-shirts were sold? Explain.

_____

_____

It's Your Turn!

Use the models shown to solve each problem.

3. A waterpark cycles about 24,000 gallons per minute through the local river.

a. **Tables** Complete the table to show the number of gallons used in 1, 2, 3, 4, and 5 minutes.

Time, x (minutes)	Gallons, y (thousand gallons)

b. **Graph** Graph the ordered pairs on the coordinate plane.

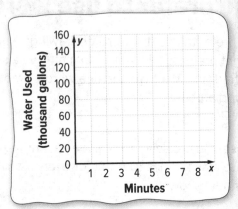

c. **Symbols** Write an equation to show the number of gallons of water y used in x minutes.

_____

4. Kitra is creating a treasure hunt for the school carnival. The scale on the map is 0.5 inch = 0.25 mile.

Map Length m (in.)	Distance d (mi)

a. **Tables** Complete the table to determine the actual distance for 0.5, 1, 1.5, 2, and 2.5 inches on the map.

b. **Symbols** Write an equation to determine the actual distance d for m inches on the map. _____

Find it in Your Book!

MP **Model with Mathematics**

Look in Chapter 5. Provide an example of where Mathematical Process Goal 5 is used. Explain why your example represents this process.

_____

_____

_____

_____

Use the Mathematical Processes

Solve.

The courtyard at Eastmoor Middle School is shaped like a rectangle that is 40.3 feet long. The width of the courtyard is 14.6 feet less than the length.

a. Draw and label a diagram of the school courtyard. What is the perimeter of the courtyard? _____

b. Student council wants to plant 14 trees so they are equally spaced around the courtyard. Draw a diagram showing where the trees should be planted. About how far apart are the trees? _____

Determine which mathematical process goals you used to determine the solution. Shade the circles that apply.

Which **MP** **Mathematical Process Goals** did you use? Shade the circle(s) that applies.

① Mathematical Problem Solving
② Mathematical Communication
③ Mathematical Reasoning

④ Mathematical Connections
⑤ Mathematical Representations

Reflect

 Answering the Essential Question

Use what you learned about the mathematical process goals to complete the graphic organizer. Write two different processes that you use for each category. Then describe how each process helps you explore and explain mathematics.

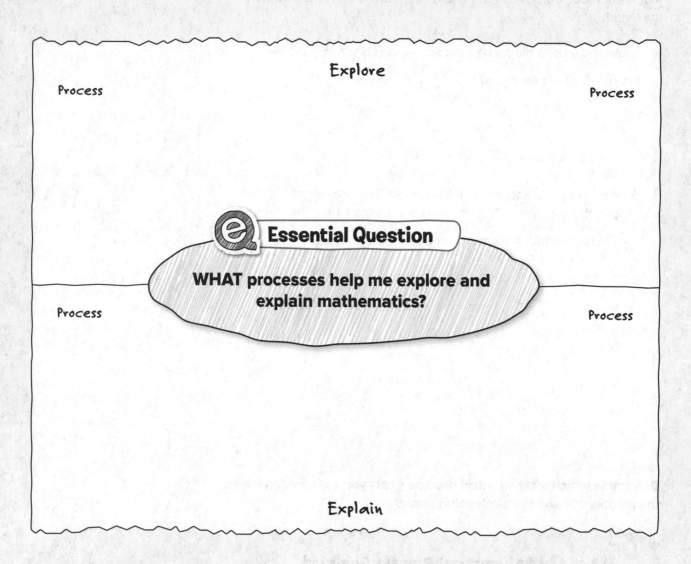

Explore

Process

Process

Essential Question

WHAT processes help me explore and explain mathematics?

Process

Process

Explain

 Answer the Essential Question. WHAT processes help me explore and explain mathematics?

Chapter 5
Equations and Inequalities

 Essential Question

WHAT does it mean to say two quantities are equal or that they have a linear relationship?

 Virginia Standards
7.10b, c, d; 7.12; 7.13

 Math in the Real World

Driving Suppose you live in a state where you must be at least 16 years of age to obtain a driver's license. Circle the statement that represents this age.

DRIVER LICENSE

NAME: Joan Smith
AGE: $a < 16$
       $a = 16$
       $a \geq 16$
ADDRESS:
   1234 Anyplace Dr.

 FOLDABLES®
Study Organizer

1 Cut out the Foldable in the back of the book.

 2 Place your Foldable on page 496.

 3 Use the Foldable to help you learn about equations and inequalities.

Vocabulary

Addition Property of Equality	equation	slope
Addition Property of Inequality	equivalent equation	slope-intercept form
coefficient	inequality	solution
constant rate of change	linear relationship	Subtraction Property of Equality
Division Property of Equality	Multiplication Property of Equality	Subtraction Property of Inequality
Division Property of Inequality	Multiplication Property of Inequality	two-step equation
	rise	y-intercept
	run	

Study Skill: Reading Math

Identify Key Information Have you ever tried to solve a word problem and didn't know where to start. Start by looking for key words in the text and images. Then write the important information in one sentence.

1. Highlight or circle key words in the following real-world problem.

   During a recent Super Bowl, millions of pounds of potato chips and tortilla chips were consumed. The number of pounds of potato chips consumed was 3.1 million pounds more than the number of pounds of tortilla chips. How many pounds of tortilla chips were consumed?

2. Write a sentence that summarizes the information provided. Include information from the text and the image. _____

12.4 million pounds   ? million pounds

Place a checkmark below the face that expresses how much you know about each concept. Then scan the chapter to find a definition or example of it.

☹ I have no clue.   ☹ I've heard of it.   ☺ I know it!

Equations and Inequalities				
Concept	☹	☹	☺	Definition or Example
inequalities				
solving one-step equations				
solving inequalities by addition or subtraction				
solving inequalities by multiplication or division				
solving two-step equations				
solving two-step inequalities				

When Will You Use This?

Here are a few examples of how equations are used in the real world.

Activity 1 Describe a situation when you only had a set amount of money to spend and you needed to buy a certain number of items. Then explain how you determined what you could buy.

_____

_____

Activity 2 Go online at **connectED.mcgraw-hill.com** to read the graphic novel **Movie Night**. How much does each DVD cost? How much money do they need for popcorn? _____

Seth, Marisol, and Jamar in
Movie Night

NEW RELEAS

Hey guys. Help me pick out some movies for movie night at school.

How much money can we spend?

Don't forget the popcorn.

Are You Ready?

Try the Quick Check below.
Or, take the Online Readiness Quiz.

Check ✓

Quick Review

Example 1

Write the phrase as an algebraic expression.

Phrase: five dollars more than Jennifer earned

Variable: Let d represent the number of dollars Jennifer earned.

Expression: $d + 5$

Example 2

Is 3, 4, or 5 the solution of the equation $x + 8 = 12$?

Value of x	$x + 8 = 12$	Are both sides equal?
3	$3 + 8 \overset{?}{=} 12$ $11 \neq 12$	no
4	$4 + 8 \overset{?}{=} 12$ $12 = 12$	yes ✓
5	$5 + 8 \overset{?}{=} 12$ $13 \neq 12$	no

The solution is 4 since replacing x with 4 results in a true sentence.

Quick Check

Words and Symbols Write the phrase as an algebraic expression.

1. 3 more runs than the Pirates scored

_____

2. a number decreased by eight

_____

3. ten dollars more than Grace has

_____

Show your work.

One-Step Equations Identify the solution of each equation from the list given.

4. $8 + w = 17$; 7, 8, 9 _____

5. $d - 12 = 5$; 16, 17, 18 _____

6. $6 = 3y$; 2, 3, 4 _____

7. $7 \div c = 7$; 0, 1, 2 _____

8. $a + 8 = 23$; 13, 14, 15 _____

9. $10 = 45 - n$; 35, 36, 37 _____

How Did You Do?

Which problems did you answer correctly in the Quick Check?
Shade those exercise numbers below.

 (1) (2) (3) (4) (5) (6) (7) (8) (9)

Inquiry **HOW can bar diagrams or algebra tiles help you solve an equation?**

In a recent year, 19 of the 50 states had a law banning the use of handheld cell phones while driving a school bus. Determine how many states did *not* have this law.

Hands-On Activity 1

You can represent this situation with an equation.

Step 1 The bar diagram represents the total number of states and the number of states that have passed a cell phone law. Fill in the missing information.

	states	
states with a law	**states that do not have a law**	
☐ states	?	

Step 2 Write an equation from the bar diagram. Let *x* represent the states that do not have a cell phone law for school bus drivers.

$$19 + x = 50$$

Step 3 Use the *work backward* strategy to solve the equation. Since $19 + x = 50$, $x = 50 - 19$. So, $x = \boxed{}$.

Check $19 + \boxed{} = 50$ ✔

So, $\boxed{}$ states did *not* have a law banning the use of cell phones by bus drivers.

Work with a partner to solve each problem.

1. Draw a bar diagram and write an addition equation to represent the following situation. Then solve the equation.

   The sum of a number and four is equal to 18.

   Equation: _____   Solution: $x =$ _____

2. **MP Use Math Tools** Jack collects postage stamps. He sold 7 of his stamps and had 29 stamps left. Complete the bar diagram below. Then write and solve a subtraction equation to find the number of stamps Jack had at the beginning.

   Equation: _____   Solution: $n =$ _____

   So, Jack had ▢ stamps at the beginning.

Analyze and Reflect

3. Suppose Jack sold 15 stamps and had 21 stamps left. How would the bar diagram change?

   _____

   _____

4. **MP Reason Abstractly** Suppose Jack had 40 stamps in the beginning and sold 7 of them. How would the bar diagram change? What equation could you write to represent the situation?

   _____

   _____

Hands-On Activity 2

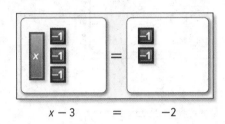 Tools

Solve $x - 3 = -2$ using algebra tiles.

Remember a 1-tile and −1 tile combine to make a *zero pair*. You can add or subtract zero pairs from either side of an equation without changing its value.

Step 1 | Model the equation.

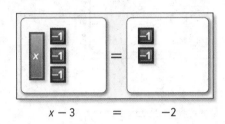

$$x - 3 \qquad = \qquad -2$$

Step 2 | Add three 1-tiles to the left side of the mat and _____ 1-tiles to the right side of the mat to form zero pairs on each side of the mat.

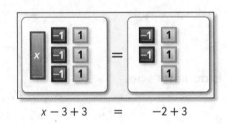

$$x - 3 + 3 \qquad = \qquad -2 + 3$$

Step 3 | Remove all of the zero pairs from each side. There is _____ 1-tile on the right side of the mat.

$$x \qquad = \qquad 1$$

Therefore, $x = \boxed{}$.

Check $\boxed{} - 3 = -2$ ✓

Investigate

MP Use Math Tools Work with a partner to solve each equation. Use algebra tiles. Show your work using drawings.

5. $x + 4 = 4$ $x =$ _____

6. $-2 = x + 1$ $x =$ _____

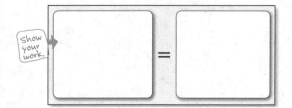

Show your work.

7. $x - 1 = -3$ $x =$ _____

8. $4 = x - 2$ $x =$ _____

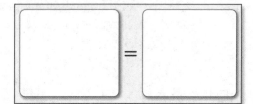

Analyze and Reflect

Work with a partner to complete the table. The first one is done for you.

	Equation	Related Equation
	$x + 3 = 4$	$x = 4 - 3$
9.	$6 + x = 10$	
10.	$x + 3 = -1$	
11.	$6 + x = -7$	

Create

On Your Own

12. **MP Construct an Argument** Write a rule that you can use to solve addition equations without using models or a drawing.

_____

_____

13. **Inquiry** HOW can bar diagrams or algebra tiles help you solve an equation?

_____

_____

Solve One-Step Addition and Subtraction Equations

Vocabulary Start-Up

 Tools Vocab

An **equation** is a sentence stating that two quantities are equal. The value of a variable that makes an equation true is called the **solution** of the equation.

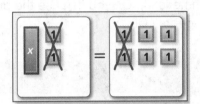

$$x + 2 = 6$$
$$-2 = -2$$
$$x = 4$$

The equations $x + 2 = 6$ and $x = 4$ are **equivalent equations** because they have the same solution, 4.

Circle the equations below that are equivalent to $x = 3$. **Use algebra tiles if needed.**

$x + 3 = 6$ $x + 1 = 6$ $x + 6 = 8$

$x + 3 = 3$ $x + 1 = 4$ $x + 2 = 5$

Real-World Link

Video Games Robyn had some video games, and then she bought 4 more games. Now she has 10 games. This scenario can be described using the equation $x + 4 = 10$.

1. What does x represent in the equation?

2. Write two different equations that are equivalent to $x + 4 = 10$.

Which MP Mathematical Process Goals did you use? Shade the circle(s) that applies.

① Mathematical Problem Solving   ④ Mathematical Connections

② Mathematical Communication   ⑤ Mathematical Representations

③ Mathematical Reasoning

Subtraction Property of Equality

Words   The **Subtraction Property of Equality** states that the two sides of an equation remain equal when you subtract the same number from each side.

Symbols   If $a = b$, then $a - c = b - c$.

You can use bar diagrams and the *work backward* problem-solving strategy to solve equations arithmetically. Or, you can use the properties of equality to solve equations algebraically.

Examples

Tutor

1. Solve $x + 6 = 4$. Check your solution.

$$x + 6 = 4 \qquad \text{Write the equation.}$$
$$\underline{-6 = -6} \qquad \text{Subtraction Property of Equality}$$
$$x = -2 \qquad \text{Simplify.}$$

Check $x + 6 = 4$ Write the original equation.

$$-2 + 6 \overset{?}{=} 4 \qquad \text{Replace } x \text{ with } -2.$$

$$4 = 4 \checkmark \qquad \text{The sentence is true.}$$

So, the solution is -2.

2. Solve $-5 = b + 8$. Check your solution.

$$-5 = b + 8 \qquad \text{Write the equation.}$$
$$\underline{-8 = \quad -8} \qquad \text{Subtraction Property of Equality}$$
$$-13 = b \qquad \text{Simplify.}$$

Check $-5 = b + 8$ Write the original equation.

$$-5 \overset{?}{=} -13 + 8 \qquad \text{Replace } b \text{ with } -13.$$

$$-5 = -5 \checkmark \qquad \text{The sentence is true.}$$

So, the solution is -13.

Got it? Do these problems to find out.

Solve each equation. Check your solution.

   a. $y + 6 = 9$ **b.** $x + 3 = 1$ **c.** $-3 = a + 4$

Work Zone

Solutions

Notice that your new equation, $x = -2$, has the same solution as the original equation, $x + 6 = 4$.

Show your work.

a. _____

b. _____

c. _____

Example

Watch | Tutor

3. An angelfish can grow to be 12 inches long. If an angelfish is 8.5 inches longer than a clown fish, how long is a clown fish?

Words	An angelfish is 8.5 inches longer than a clown fish.
Variable	Let c represent the length of the clown fish.
Equation	$12 \quad = \quad c \quad + \quad 8.5$

$12 \ = c + 8.5$ Write the equation.

$\underline{-\,8.5 = \quad -\,8.5}$ Subtraction Property of Equality

$3.5 = c$ Simplify.

A clown fish is 3.5 inches long.

Solve Arithmetically

You can use a bar diagram to solve an equation arithmetically.

-- angelfish, 12 inches --	
clown fish	
$-\!-c\!-\!+\!-\!-$ 8.5 inches $-\!-\!-$	

Work backward to solve for c.

$c = 12 - 8.5 = 3.5$

Got it? Do this problem to find out.

Show your work.

d. The highest recorded temperature in Warsaw, Missouri, is 118°F. This is 158° greater than the city's lowest recorded temperature. Find the lowest recorded temperature.

d. _____

Addition Property of Equality

Key Concept

Words	The **Addition Property of Equality** states that the two sides of an equation remain equal when you add the same number to each side.
Symbols	If $a = b$, then $a + c = b + c$.

Example

Tutor

4. Solve $x - 2 = 1$. Check your solution.

$x - 2 = \quad 1$ Write the equation.

$\underline{+\,2 = +\,2}$ Addition Property of Equality

$x \quad = \quad 3$ Simplify.

Show your work.

The solution is 3.   **Check** $3 - 2 = 1$ ✓

e. _____

f. _____

Got it? Do these problems to find out.

e. $y - 3 = 4$ **f.** $r - 4 = -2$ **g.** $q - 8 = -9$

g. _____

Models

A bar diagram can be used to represent this situation.

├------ jeans, j ------┤	
shoes	
├---- \$25 ----┤	-\$14 -┤

$j = 25 + 14 = 39$

Example

Tutor

5. **A pair of shoes costs \$25. This is \$14 less than the cost of a pair of jeans. Find the cost of the jeans.**

Shoes are \$14 less than jeans. Let j represent the cost of jeans.

$\quad 25 = j - 14$ Write the equation.

$\quad \underline{+\,14 = \;+\,14}$ Addition Property of Equality

$\quad\quad 39 = j$ Simplify.

The jeans cost \$39.

Got it? **Do this problem to find out.**

h. The average lifespan of a tiger is 17 years. This is 3 years less than the average lifespan of a lion. Write and solve an equation to find the average lifespan of a lion.

h. _____

Guided Practice

Check

Solve each equation. Check your solution. (Examples 1, 2, and 4)

1. $n + 6 = 8$

2. $7 = y + 2$

3. $-7 = c - 6$

Show your work.

4. Orville and Wilbur Wright made the first airplane flights in 1903. Wilbur's flight was 364 feet. This was 120 feet longer than Orville's flight. Write an equation to represent the flights. Use a bar diagram if needed. Then solve to find the length of Orville's flight. (Examples 3 and 5)

_____

5. @ **Building on the Essential Question** What are two methods for solving a real-world problem that can be represented by an equation?

_____

_____

Rate Yourself!

☐ I understand how to solve one-step addition and subtraction equations.

▶▶ Great! You're ready to move on!

☐ I still have some questions about solving equations.

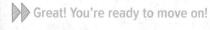 No Problem! Go online to access a Personal Tutor.

Tutor

Independent Practice

 Go online for Step-by-Step Solutions

Solve each equation. Check your solution. (Examples 1, 2, and 4)

1. $a + 3 = 10$

 Show your work.

2. $y + 5 = -11$

3 $s - 8 = 9$

4. $5 = x + 8$

5. $-2 = p - 1$

6. $14 = s + 7$

Use a bar diagram to solve arithmetically. Then use an equation to solve algebraically. (Examples 3 and 5)

7 Last week Tiffany practiced her bassoon a total of 7 hours. This was 2 hours more than she practiced the previous week. How many hours did Tiffany practice the previous week?

8. In a recent presidential election, Ohio had 18 electoral votes. This is 20 votes less than Texas had. How many electoral votes did Texas have?

9. **MP Multiple Representations** Use the table to solve.
  a. **Symbols** The difference in speeds of El Toro and T Express is 5 miles per hour. If El Toro has the greater speed, write and solve a subtraction equation to find its speed.

Tallest Wooden Roller Coasters	Height (feet)	Drop (feet)	Speed (mph)
Colossos	h	159	68
T Express	184	151	65
El Toro	181	176	s
Voyage	163	d	67

  b. **Diagram** Voyage has a drop that is 22 feet less than El Toro. Draw a bar diagram to the right and write an equation to find the height of Voyage.

 Show your work.

  c. **Words** Let h represent the height of the Colossos roller coaster. Explain why $h - 13 = 184$ and $h - 34 = 163$ are equivalent equations. Then explain the meaning of the solution.

10. The sum of the measures of the angles of a triangle is 180°. Write and solve an equation to find the missing measure.

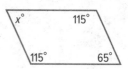

11. The sum of the measures of a quadrilateral is 360°. Write and solve an equation to find the missing measure.

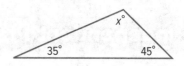

H.O.T. Problems Higher Order Thinking

12. (MP) **Reason Inductively** Write an addition equation and a subtraction equation that have 10 as a solution.

13. (MP) **Find the Error** Aisha is finding $b + 5 = -8$. Find her mistake and correct it.

14. (MP) **Reason Abstractly** Suppose $x + y = 11$ and the value of x increases by 2. If their sum remains the same, what must happen to the value of y? Justify your response

15. (MP) **Which One Doesn't Belong?** Identify the equation that does not belong with the other three. Explain your reasoning.

| $x + 4 = -2$ | $x + 5 = -1$ | $x + 2 = 8$ | $3 - x = 9$ |

16. (MP) **Reason Inductively** In the equation $x + y = 5$, the value for x is a whole number greater than 2 but less than 6. Find the possible solutions for y.

Extra Practice

Solve each equation. Check your solution.

17. $r + 6 = -3$

$$r + 6 = -3$$
$$\underline{ - 6 = -6}$$
$$r = -9$$

18. $w - 7 = 11$

19. $k + 3 = -9$

20. $-1 = q - 8$

21. $9 = r + 2$

22. $y + 15 = 11$

MP Use Math Tools Use a bar diagram to solve arthimetically. Then use an equation to solve algebraically.

23. The Miami Heat scored 79 points. This was 13 points less than the Chicago Bulls. How many points did the Chicago Bulls score?

24. Zach is $15\frac{1}{2}$ years old. This is 3 years younger than his brother Lou. How old is Lou?

25. The table shows a golfer's scores for four rounds of a recent U.S. Women's Open. Her total score was even with par. What was her score for the third round?

Round	Score
First	−1
Second	−3
Third	s
Fourth	+2

Copy and Solve Solve each equation. Check your solution. Show your work on a separate piece of paper.

26. $a - 3.5 = 14.9$

27. $b + 2.25 = 1$

28. $-\dfrac{1}{3} = r - \dfrac{3}{4}$

29. $x - 2.8 = 9.5$

30. $r - 8.5 = -2.1$

31. $z - 9.4 = -3.6$

32. $m + \dfrac{5}{6} = \dfrac{11}{12}$

33. $-\dfrac{5}{6} + c = -\dfrac{11}{12}$

34. $s - \dfrac{1}{9} = \dfrac{5}{18}$

35. The model represents the equation
$x - 2 = 5$. Determine if each statement
is true or false.

   a. To solve the equation, add 2 positive
   counters to each side of the equation mat. ☐ True ☐ False

   b. To solve the equation, add 5 negative
   to each side of the equation mat. ☐ True ☐ False

   c. The value of x is 7. ☐ True ☐ False

36. Britney practiced the piano a total of 7 hours this week. This is 3 hours
less than she practiced last week. Select the correct labels to complete
the bar diagram that is used to find the number of hours w Britney
practiced last week.

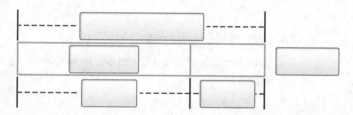

| this week |
| last week, w |
| 3 hours |
| 4 hours |
| 7 hours |
| 10 hours |

   How many hours did Britney practice the piano last week? ☐

Spiral Review

Multiply or divide.

37. $5(-4) =$ _____

38. $\dfrac{36}{-9} =$ _____

39. $(-10)(-6) =$ _____

40. $\dfrac{-42}{-7} =$ _____

41. $(-3)(12) =$ _____

42. $\dfrac{-54}{2} =$ _____

43. While playing a round of golf, Tina had a
score of three under par after the first three
holes. Write and solve an equation to find
Tina's average score per hole h after three
holes. _____

44. On Friday morning, the temperature dropped
2 degrees per hour for four hours. Write and
solve an equation to find the total number
of degrees d the temperature dropped on
Friday morning. _____

Inquiry HOW do you know which operation to use when solving an equation?

Sakiya tutors students to earn money to buy a new Blu-ray™ player that costs $63. She is able to tutor seven hours in a week. How much should she charge per hour to have enough money by the end of the week?

What do you know? _____

_____

What do you need to find? _____

_____

Hands-On Activity

Step 1 Draw a bar diagram that represents the money Sakiya needs to earn and the number of hours she is available to tutor that week.

hour 1	hour 2	hour 3	hour 4			

$\$\boxed{}$

?

Step 2 Write an equation from the bar diagram. Let x represent the amount she should charge each hour.

$$7x = 63$$

Step 3 Use the *work backward* strategy to solve the equation. Since

$7x = 63$, $x = 63 \div 7$. So, $x = \boxed{}$.

Check $7 \times \boxed{} = 63$ ✓

So, Sakiya should charge $\boxed{}$ per hour.

Investigate

Work with a partner to solve.

1. The screen on Lin's cell phone allows for 8 lines of text per message. The maximum number of characters for each message is 160. How many characters can each line hold? Complete the bar diagram below and write an equation. Then solve the equation.

Analyze and Reflect

Work with a partner to answer the following question.

2. **MP** **Make a Conjecture** Refer to Exercise 1. Suppose Lin's cell phone allows 4 lines of text and a maximum of 80 characters for each text message. How would the bar diagram and equation change?

Create

On Your Own

3. **MP** **Reason Abstractly** Keyani spent $70 for 4 hours of dance classes. How much did she spend per hour of dance class? Draw a bar diagram below and write an equation. Then solve the equation.

Show your work.

4. **Inquiry** HOW do you know which operation to use when solving an equation?

Multiplication and Division Equations

Vocabulary Start-Up

The expression 3x means *3 times the value of x*. The numerical factor of a multiplication expression like 3x is called a **coefficient**. So, 3 is the coefficient of x.

The figure below illustrates the multiplication equation $3x = 6$.

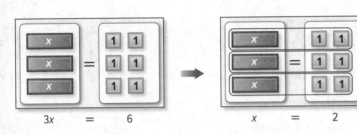

Since there are 3 xs, each x is matched with 2.

$$3x = 6 \qquad x = 2$$

The solution of $3x = 6$ is 2.

Write an equation that represents each of the models below. Identify the coefficient in your equation. Then solve.

1.

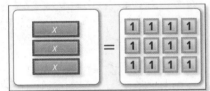

Equation: _____

Coefficient: ☐

Solution: ☐

2.

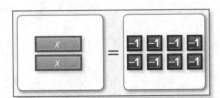

Equation: _____

Coefficient: ☐

Solution: ☐

Essential Question

WHAT does it mean to say two quantities are equal or that they have a linear relationship?

Vocabulary

coefficient
Division Property of Equality
Multiplication Property of Equality

Which 🅜🅟 **Mathematical Process Goals** did you use? Shade the circle(s) that applies.

① Mathematical Problem Solving

④ Mathematical Connections

② Mathematical Communication

⑤ Mathematical Representations

③ Mathematical Reasoning

Division Property of Equality

Work Zone

Words The **Division Property of Equality** states that the two sides of an equation remain equal when you divide each side by the same nonzero number.

Symbols If $a = b$ and $c \neq 0$, then $\frac{a}{c} = \frac{b}{c}$.

You can use the Division Property of Equality to solve multiplication equations.

Examples

Tutor

1. Solve $20 = 4x$. Check your solution.

$20 = 4x$ Write the equation.

$\dfrac{20}{4} = \dfrac{4x}{4}$ Division Property of Equality

$5 = x$ Simplify.

Check $20 = 4x$ Write the original equation.

$20 \overset{?}{=} 4(5)$ Replace x with 5.

$20 = 20$ ✓   This sentence is true.

So, the solution is 5.

2. Solve $-8y = 24$. Check your solution.

$-8y = 24$ Write the equation.

$\dfrac{-8y}{-8} = \dfrac{24}{-8}$ Division Property of Equality

$y = -3$ Simplify.

Check $-8y = 24$ Write the original equation.

$-8(-3) \overset{?}{=} 24$ Replace y with -3.

$24 = 24$ ✓   This sentence is true.

So, the solution is -3.

Show your work.

a. _____

b. _____

c. _____

Got it? Do these problems to find out.

Solve each equation. Check your solution.

   a. $30 = 6x$ **b.** $-6a = 36$ **c.** $-9d = -72$

Example

Tutor

3. **Lelah sent 574 text messages last week. On average, how many messages did she send each day?**

Let m represent the number of messages Lelah sent.

$574 = 7m$	Write the equation. There are 7 days in one week.
$\dfrac{574}{7} = \dfrac{7m}{7}$	Division Property of Equality
$82 = m$	Simplify.

Lelah sent 82 messages on average each day.

Got it? **Do this problem to find out.**

d. Mrs. Acosta's car can travel an average of 24 miles on each gallon of gasoline. Write and solve an equation to find how many gallons of gasoline she will need for a trip of 348 miles.

d. _____

Solve Arithmetically

You can use a bar diagram to solve an equation arithmetically.

text messages in 1 week, 574

m	m	m	m	m	m	m

├─┤
text messages in 1 day

Work backward to solve for m.

$m = 574 \div 7 = 82$

Show your work.

Multiplication Property of Equality

Key Concept

Words   The **Multiplication Property of Equality** states that the two sides of an equation remain equal if you multiply each side by the same number.

Symbols   If $a = b$, then $ac = bc$.

You can use the Multiplication Property of Equality to solve division equations.

Example

Tutor

4. **Solve $\dfrac{a}{-4} = -9$.**

$\dfrac{a}{-4} = -9$	Write the equation.
$\dfrac{a}{-4}(-4) = -9(-4)$	Multiplication Property of Equality
$a = 36$	Simplify.

e. _____

f. _____

Got it? **Do these problems to find out.**

e. $\dfrac{y}{-3} = -8$ **f.** $\dfrac{m}{5} = -7$ **g.** $30 = \dfrac{b}{-6}$

g. _____

Example

 Tutor

5. The distance *d* Tina travels in her car while driving 60 miles per hour for 3 hours is given by the equation $\frac{d}{3} = 60$. How far did she travel?

$$\frac{d}{3} = 60 \qquad \text{Write the equation.}$$

$$\frac{d}{3}(3) = 60(3) \qquad \text{Multiplication Property of Equality}$$

$$d = 180 \qquad \text{Simplify.}$$

Tina traveled 180 miles.

Distance Formula

The distance formula, distance = rate × time, can be written as $d = rt$, $r = \frac{d}{t}$, or $t = \frac{d}{r}$.

Guided Practice

 Check ✓

Solve each equation. Check your solution. (Examples 1, 2, and 4)

1. $6c = 18$

2. $24 = -8x$

3. $7m = -28$

 Show your work.

4. $\frac{p}{9} = 9$

5. $\frac{a}{12} = -3$

6. $\frac{n}{-10} = -4$

7. Antonia earns $6 per hour helping her grandmother. Write and solve an equation to find how many hours she needs to work to earn $48. (Example 3) _____

8. A shark can swim at an average speed of 25 miles per hour. At this rate, how far can a shark swim in 2.4 hours? Use $r = \frac{d}{t}$. (Example 5) _____

9. **Building on the Essential Question** How is the process for solving multiplication and division one-step equations like solving one-step addition and subtraction equations?

_____

_____

_____

Rate Yourself!

How confident are you about solving one-step multiplication and division equations? Check the box that applies.

☐ ☐ ☐ ☐ ☐

For more help, go online to access a Personal Tutor. **Tutor**

Independent Practice

Go online for Step-by-Step Solutions eHelp

Solve each equation. Check your solution. (Examples 1, 2, and 4)

1. $7a = 49$

 Show your work.

2. $-6 = 2x$

3. $-32 = -4b$

4. $\dfrac{u}{6} = 9$

5. $-8 = \dfrac{c}{-10}$

6. $54 = -9d$

7. $-12y = 60$

8. $\dfrac{r}{20} = -2$

9. $\dfrac{g}{10} = -9$

10. Brandy wants to buy a digital camera that costs \$300. Suppose she saves \$15 each week. In how many weeks will she have enough money for the camera? Use a bar diagram to solve arithmetically. Then use an equation to solve algebraically. (Example 3) _____

 Show your work.

11. A race car can travel at a rate of 205 miles per hour. At this rate, how far would it travel in 3 hours? Use $r = \dfrac{d}{t}$. Write an equation and then solve.
(Example 5)

12. A certain hurricane travels at 20.88 kilometers per hour. The distance from Cuba to Key West is 145 kilometers. Write and solve a multiplication equation to find about how long it would take the hurricane to travel from Cuba to Key West.

13. **Multiple Representations** Kennedy saves $5.50 for each hour she works. She needs to save an additional $44 to buy an E-reader. How many more hours does Kennedy need to work to pay for the E-reader?

   a. Diagram Draw a bar diagram that represents the situation.

Show your work.

   b. Algebra Write an equation that represents the situation.

   c. Words Describe the process you would use to solve your equation. Then solve.

🔥 H.O.T. Problems Higher Order Thinking

14. **Reason Abstractly** Describe a real-world situation in which you would use a division equation to solve a problem. Write your equation and then solve your problem.

Situation: _____

_____

_____

Equation: _____ Solution: _____

15. **Identify Structure** *True* or *false*. To solve the equation $5x = 20$ you can use the Multiplication Property of Equality. Explain your reasoning.

_____

_____

16. **Persevere with Problems** Solve $3|x| = 12$. Explain your reasoning.

_____

_____

17. **Persevere with Problems** Explain how you would solve $\frac{-30}{x} = 6$. Then solve the equation.

_____

_____

Extra Practice

Solve each equation. Check your solution.

18. $-4j = 36$

> Homework Help

$$-4j = 36$$
$$\frac{-4j}{-4} = \frac{36}{-4}$$
$$j = -9$$

19. $-4s = -16$

20. $63 = -9d$

21. $\frac{m}{10} = 7$

$$\frac{m}{10} = 7$$
$$\frac{m}{10}(10) = 7(10)$$
$$m = 70$$

22. $\frac{h}{-3} = 12$

23. $\frac{g}{12} = -10$

24. The width of a computer monitor is 1.25 times its height. Find the height of the computer monitor at the right. Use a bar diagram to solve arithmetically. Then use an equation to solve algebraically. _____

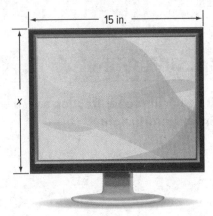

15 in.

x

25. A dragonfly, the fastest insect, can fly a distance of 50 feet at a speed of 25 feet per second. Find the time in seconds. Write the equation in the form $d = rt$, then solve.

26. **MP Find the Error** Raul is solving $-6x = 72$. Find his mistake and correct it.

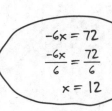

$$-6x = 72$$
$$\frac{-6x}{6} = \frac{72}{6}$$
$$x = 12$$

27. The formula $A = bh$ can be used to find the area A of a parallelogram with base b and height h. The parallelogram shown has an area of 56 square inches.

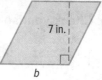

7 in.

b

What is the length of the base? [   ]

28. The table shows the prices of different satellite radio plans. Mrs. Freedman paid $99 for m months of satellite radio under Plan A. Fill in each box to write a multiplication equation to represent the situation.

[   ] × [   ] = [   ]

m	16.50
11.99	99
14.35	

Satellite Radio Plans	
Plan	Cost per Month ($)
A	16.50
B	14.35
C	11.99

How many months of service did Mrs. Freedman purchase? [   ]

Spiral Review

Write each improper fraction as a mixed number and each mixed number as an improper fraction.

29. $\dfrac{10}{3} =$ _____

30. $\dfrac{40}{7} =$ _____

31. $\dfrac{101}{100} =$ _____

32. $2\dfrac{2}{7} =$ _____

33. $3\dfrac{1}{4} =$ _____

34. $10\dfrac{5}{9} =$ _____

Divide.

35. $6 \div 1.5 =$ _____

36. $3.6 \div 0.4 =$ _____

37. $2.73 \div 1.3 =$ _____

Multiply. Write in simplest form.

38. $\dfrac{2}{9} \times \dfrac{7}{5} =$ _____

39. $\dfrac{3}{4} \times 7 =$ _____

40. $\dfrac{5}{8} \times \dfrac{4}{15} =$ _____

HOW can you use bar diagrams to solve equations with rational coefficients?

Two thirds of Chen's homeroom class plan to participate in the school talent show. If 16 students from the class plan to participate, how many students are in the homeroom class?

What do you know? _____

_____

What do you need to find? _____

_____

Hands-On Activity

You can represent the situation above with an equation.

Step 1 Draw a bar diagram that represents the total number of students in the class and how many plan to participate.

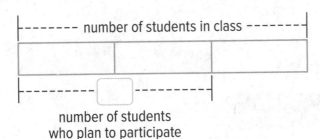

Step 2 Write an equation from the bar diagram. Let c represent the total number of students in the class. _____

Step 3 Find the number of students represented by the sections of the bar. Write that number in each section of the bar in Step 1.

Since each section represents 8 students, there are 8 × 3 or ☐ students in the class.

Check $\frac{2}{3} \times 24 = \frac{2}{3} \times \frac{24}{1}$

$\qquad\qquad = \frac{48}{3}$ or 16 ✓

Investigate

Work with a partner to solve the following problem.

1. Eliana is spending $\frac{3}{5}$ of her monthly allowance on a costume for the talent show. She plans to spend $24. Draw a bar diagram to represent the situation. Then write and solve an equation to find the amount of Eliana's monthly allowance.

Equation: _____   Solution: _____

Analyze and Reflect

Work with a partner to answer the following question.

2. **MP Make a Conjecture** Suppose Eliana planned on spending $\frac{3}{4}$ of her monthly allowance on a costume. How would the diagram and equation be different?

_____

_____

Create

3. **MP Model with Mathematics** Write a real-world problem that could be represented by the equation $\frac{2}{3}x = 12$. Then solve the equation.

_____

_____

_____

4. **Inquiry** HOW can you use bar diagrams to solve equations with rational coefficients?

_____

_____

_____

Solve Equations with Rational Coefficients

Real-World Link

WHAT does it mean to say two quantities are equal or that they have a linear relationship?

Essential Question

Social Networks Three-fourths of the students in Aaliyah's class belong to a social network. There are 15 students in her class that belong to a social network.

1. Create a bar diagram and shade $\frac{3}{4}$, or 0.75, of it.

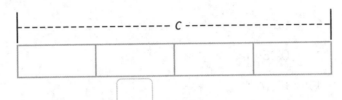

Label 15 along the bottom to show the amount of the bar that represents 15 students.

2. Based on the diagram, (circle) the equation that can be used to find c, the number of students in Aaliyah's class.

$$15c = \frac{3}{4}$$ $$0.75c = 15$$ $$4c = 15$$

3. Based on what you know about solving equations, explain how you could solve the equation you circled in Exercise 2.

_____

4. How many students are in Aaliyah's class?

_____

Which **MP** **Mathematical Process Goals** did you use? Shade the circle(s) that applies.

① Mathematical Problem Solving

② Mathematical Communication

③ Mathematical Reasoning

④ Mathematical Connections

⑤ Mathematical Representations

Decimal Coefficients

If the coefficient is a decimal, divide each side by the coefficient.

Example

1. **Solve $16 = 0.25n$. Check your solution.**

$16 = 0.25n$ Write the equation.

$\dfrac{16}{0.25} = \dfrac{0.25n}{0.25}$ Division Property of Equality

$64 = n$ Simplify.

Check $16 = 0.25n$ Write the original equation.

$16 \stackrel{?}{=} 0.25 \cdot 64$ Replace n with 64.

$16 = 16$ ✓   This sentence is true.

The solution is 64.

Division with Decimals

$$
\begin{array}{r}
64. \\
0.25\overline{)16.00} \\
-\underline{150} \\
100 \\
-\underline{100} \\
0
\end{array}
$$

Show your work.

a. _____

Got it? Do these problems to find out.

a. $6.4 = 0.8m$ **b.** $-2.8p = 4.2$ **c.** $-4.7k = -10.81$

b. _____

c. _____

Real World Example

2. **Jaya's coach agreed to buy ice cream for all of the team members. Ice cream cones are $2.40 each. Write and solve an equation to find how many cones the coach can buy with $30.**

Let n represent the number of cones the coach can buy.

$2.4n = 30$ Write the equation; $\$2.40 = 2.4$.

$\dfrac{2.4n}{2.4} = \dfrac{30}{2.4}$ Division Property of Equality

$n = 12.5$ Simplify.

Since the number of ice cream cones must be a whole number, there is enough money for 12 ice cream cones.

Got it? Do this problem to find out.

d. _____

d. Suppose the ice cream cones cost $2.80 each. How many ice cream cones could the coach buy with $42?

Fraction Coefficients

Recall that two numbers with a product of 1 are called multiplicative inverses, or reciprocals. If the coefficient in a multiplication equation is a fraction, multiply each side by the reciprocal of the coefficient.

Examples

Tutor

3. Solve $\frac{3}{4}x = \frac{12}{20}$.

$$\frac{3}{4}x = \frac{12}{20}$$ Write the equation.

$$\left(\frac{4}{3}\right) \cdot \frac{3}{4}x = \left(\frac{4}{3}\right) \cdot \frac{12}{20}$$ Multiply each side by the reciprocal of $\frac{3}{4}$, $\frac{4}{3}$.

$$\overset{1}{\cancel{\frac{4}{3}}} \cdot \overset{1}{\cancel{\frac{3}{4}}}x = \overset{1}{\cancel{\frac{4}{3}}} \cdot \overset{4}{\cancel{\frac{12}{20}}}{\scriptstyle 5}$$ Divide by common factors.

$$x = \frac{4}{5}$$ Simplify. Check the solution.

Fractions as Coefficients

The expression $\frac{3}{4}x$ can be read as $\frac{3}{4}$ of x, $\frac{3}{4}$ multiplied by x, $3x$ divided by 4, or $\frac{x}{4}$ multiplied by 3.

4. Solve $-\frac{7}{9}d = 5$. Check your solution.

$$-\frac{7}{9}d = 5$$ Write the equation.

$$\left(-\frac{9}{7}\right) \cdot \left(-\frac{7}{9}\right)d = \left(-\frac{9}{7}\right) \cdot 5$$ Multiply each side by the reciprocal of $-\frac{7}{9}$, $-\frac{9}{7}$.

$$\left(-\frac{9}{7}\right) \cdot \left(-\frac{7}{9}\right)d = \left(-\frac{9}{7}\right) \cdot \frac{5}{1}$$ Write 5 as $\frac{5}{1}$.

$$\left(-\overset{1}{\cancel{\frac{9}{7}}}\right) \cdot \left(-\overset{1}{\cancel{\frac{7}{9}}}\right)d = \left(-\frac{9}{7}\right) \cdot \frac{5}{1}$$ Divide by common factors.

$$d = -\frac{45}{7} \text{ or } -6\frac{3}{7}$$ Simplify.

Check $-\frac{7}{9}d = 5$ Write the original equation.

$$-\frac{7}{9}\left(-\frac{45}{7}\right) \overset{?}{=} 5$$ Replace d with $-\frac{45}{7}$.

$$\frac{315}{63} \overset{?}{=} 5$$ Simplify.

$$5 = 5 \checkmark$$ This sentence is true.

Show your work.

Got it? Do these problems to find out.

e. $\frac{1}{2}x = 8$ **f.** $-\frac{3}{4}x = 9$ **g.** $-\frac{7}{8}x = -\frac{21}{64}$

e. _____

f. _____

g. _____

Example

Bar Diagrams

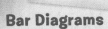

A bar diagram can be used to represent this situation.

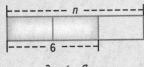

$$n = 6 \div \frac{2}{3} = \frac{6}{1} \times \frac{3}{2} = 9$$

5. Valerie needs $\frac{2}{3}$ yard of fabric to make each hat for the school play. **Write and solve an equation to find how many hats she can make with 6 yards of fabric.**

Write and solve a multiplication equation. Let n represent the number of hats.

$$\frac{2}{3}n = 6 \qquad \text{Write the equation.}$$

$$\left(\frac{3}{2}\right) \cdot \frac{2}{3}n = \left(\frac{3}{2}\right) \cdot 6 \qquad \text{Multiply each side by } \frac{3}{2}.$$

$$n = 9 \qquad \text{Simplify.}$$

So, Valerie can make 9 hats.

Guided Practice

 Check ✓

Solve each equation. Check your solution. (Examples 1, 3, and 4)

1. $1.6k = 3.2$

2. $-2.5b = 20.5$

3. $-\frac{1}{2} = -\frac{5}{18}h$

 Show your work.

Write and solve an equation. (Examples 2 and 5)

4. The average growth of human hair is 0.5 inch per month. Find how long it takes a human to grow 3 inches of hair.

Equation: _____ Solution: _____

5. Three fourths of the fruit in a refrigerator are apples. There are 24 apples in the refrigerator. How many pieces of fruit are in the refrigerator?

Equation: _____ Solution: _____

6. ⓔ **Building on the Essential Question** What is the process for solving a multiplication equation with a rational coefficient?

_____

_____

_____

_____

Rate Yourself!

Are you ready to move on? Shade the section that applies.

YES   ?   NO

For more help, go online to access a Personal Tutor. Tutor

Independent Practice

Go online for Step-by-Step Solutions

Solve each equation. Check your solution. (Examples 1, 3, and 4)

1. $1.2x = 6$

 show your work.

2. $14.4 = -2.4b$

3 $-3.6h = -10.8$

4. $\frac{2}{5}t = \frac{12}{25}$

5. $-3\frac{1}{3} = -\frac{1}{2}g$

6. $-\frac{7}{9}m = \frac{11}{6}$

7 **Financial Literacy** Dillon deposited $\frac{3}{4}$ of his paycheck into the bank. The deposit slip shows how much he deposited. Write and solve an equation to find the amount of his paycheck. (Example 2)

Equation: _____   Solution: _____

DEPOSIT   CHECKS | 4 6 . 5 0
Name: Dillon Gates
Date: 9/22
Great Savings Bank
Transaction #
•543345890•3221•8755P   DEPOSIT $ 4 6 . 5 0

8. Twenty-four students brought their permission slips to attend the class field trip to the local art museum. If this represented eight tenths of the class, how many students are in the class? Use a bar diagram to solve arithmetically. Then use an equation to solve algebraically. (Example 5)

Equation: _____   Solution: _____

9. **MP** **Justify Conclusions** Seventy-five percent, or 15, of the students in Emily's homeroom class are going on a field trip. Two thirds, or 12, of the students in Santiago's homeroom class are going on the field trip. Which class has more students? Justify your answer. _____

_____

_____

_____

10. **⑩ Reason Abstractly** Nora and Ryan are making stuffed animals for a toy drive. The table shows the fabric purchases they made. Who purchased the more expensive fabric?

Explain your reasoning. _____

_____

_____

_____

Purchaser	Amount Purchased (yd)	Amount Paid ($)
Nora	$\frac{2}{3}$	4
Ryan	0.8	6

 H.O.T. Problems Higher Order Thinking

11. **⑩ Reason Inductively** Complete the statement: If $8 = \frac{m}{4}$, then

$m - 12 = $ ■. Explain. _____

_____

12. **⑩ Which One Doesn't Belong?** Identify the pair of numbers that does

not belong with the other three. Explain. _____

_____

$$\frac{9}{6}, \frac{6}{9}$$ $$4, \frac{1}{4}$$ $$\frac{3}{5}, 5$$ $$\frac{2}{7}, \frac{7}{2}$$

13. **⑩ Persevere with Problems** The formula for the area of a trapezoid is

$A = \frac{1}{2}h(b_1 + b_2)$, where b_1 and b_2 are both bases and h is the height. Find the

value of h in terms of A, b_1, and b_2. Justify your answer.

_____

_____

_____

14. **⑩ Model with Mathematics** Write a real-world problem that can be

represented by the equation $224 = 3.5r$. Then solve the problem and explain

the solution.

_____

_____

_____

_____

Extra Practice

Solve each equation. Check your solution.

15. $0.4d = 2.8$

Homework Help →

$$0.4d = 2.8$$
$$\frac{0.4d}{0.4} = \frac{2.8d}{0.4}$$
$$d = 7$$

16. $-5w = -24.5$

17. $-22.8 = 6n$

18. $\frac{7}{8}k = \frac{5}{6}$

$$\frac{7}{8}k = \frac{5}{6}$$
$$\left(\frac{8}{7}\right) \cdot \frac{7}{8}k = \left(\frac{8}{7}\right) \cdot \frac{5}{6}$$
$$k = \frac{40}{42} \text{ or } \frac{20}{21}$$

19. $-6\frac{1}{4} = \frac{3}{5}c$

20. $-\frac{4}{7}v = -8\frac{2}{3}$

21. The Mammoth Cave Discovery Tour includes an elevation change of 140 feet. This is $\frac{7}{15}$ of the elevation change on the Wild Cave Tour. What is the elevation change on the Wild Cave Tour? Use a bar diagram to solve arithmetically. Then use an equation to solve algebraically.

Equation: _____   Solution: _____

22. **MP** **Model with Mathematics** Refer to the graphic novel frame below. Write and solve an equation to find how many movies they have time to show.

Equation: _____   Solution: _____

23. Which of the following high speed trains are traveling at a rate of 150 miles per hour? Select all that apply.

☐ a train that travels 100 miles in $\frac{2}{3}$ hour ☐ a train that travels 160 miles in $\frac{5}{6}$ hour

☐ a train that travels 125 miles in $\frac{4}{5}$ hour ☐ a train that travels 90 miles in $\frac{3}{5}$ hour

24. The table shows the results of a survey. Of those surveyed, 275 students said they prefer pop music.

Write an equation that could be used to find the total number of students s who were surveyed.

How many students were surveyed?

Music Preference	
Type	Fraction of Students
Jazz	$\frac{1}{8}$
Pop	$\frac{5}{8}$
Rap	$\frac{1}{4}$

Spiral Review

Use the order of operations to evaluate each expression.

25. $6 \times 4 - 2 =$ _____

26. $70 - 5 \times 4 =$ _____

27. $18 \div 2 - 7 =$ _____

28. Write *add, divide, multiply,* and *subtract* in the correct order to complete the following sentence.

When using the order of operations to evaluate an expression,

always _____ and _____ before you _____

and _____ .

Write and evaluate an expression for each situation.

29. Used paperback books are $0.25, and hardback books are $0.50. If you buy 3 paperback books and 5 hardback books, how much money do you spend?

Expression: _____ Solution: _____

30. Suppose you order 2 pizzas, 2 garlic breads, and 1 order of BBQ wings. How much change would you receive from $30?

Expression: _____ Solution: _____

Item	Cost
14" pizza	$8
garlic bread	$2
BBQ wings	$4

Inquiry HOW can a bar diagram or algebra tiles help you solve a real-world problem?

 **Virginia Standards**
7.12

Latoya plays basketball and tennis. She has two basketballs and three tennis balls that weigh a total of 48 ounces. Each tennis ball weighs 2 ounces. What is the weight of a basketball?

Hands-On Activity 1

You can use a bar diagram to represent the situation.

Step 1 Draw a bar diagram that represents the total weight.

← 48 oz →				
basketball			tennis	tennis	
--------?--------	--------?--------	2 oz	2 oz	□

Step 2 Write an equation that is modeled by the bar diagram. Let x represent the weight of a basketball.

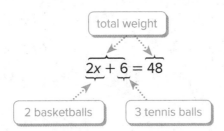

total weight

$$2x + 6 = 48$$

2 basketballs   3 tennis balls

Step 3 Use the bar diagram to solve the equation. Subtract the weight of the tennis balls, □ ounces, from the total weight, □ ounces.

The two basketballs together weigh □ − □, or □ ounces.

Divide the weight by □ to find the weight of one basketball.

So, $x =$ □. The weight of one basketball is □ ÷ □, or □ ounces.

Check $2 \cdot$ □ $+ 6 = 48$ ✓

The weight of one basketball is □ ounces.

You can use algebra tiles to model and solve the equation $4x - 2 = 10$.

Step 1 Model the equation.

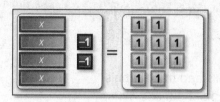

$4x - 2 = 10$

Step 2 Add ☐ 1-tiles to each side of the mat to form zero pairs on the left side.

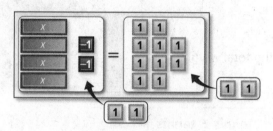

$4x - 2 + 2 = 10 + 2$

Step 3 Remove both zero pairs from the left side so that the variable is by itself.

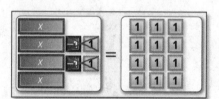

$4x = 12$

Step 4 Divide the remaining tiles into ☐ equal groups.

$\dfrac{4x}{4} = \dfrac{12}{4}$

So, $x = $ ☐.

Check $4 \cdot$ ☐ $- 2 = 10$ ✓

Investigate

Collaborate

Work with a partner to solve the following problem.

1. **MP Reason Abstractly** Ryan is saving money to buy a skateboard that costs $85. He has already saved $40. He plans to save the same amount each week for three weeks. Draw a bar diagram. Then write an equation. How much should Ryan save each week?

Show your work.

Work with a partner to solve each equation. Use algebra tiles. Show your work using drawings.

2. $2x + 1 = 5$ $x =$ _____

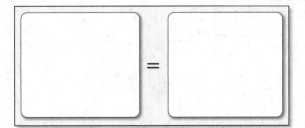

3. $3x + 2 = 11$ $x =$ _____

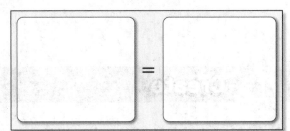

4. $4x + 3 = -5$ $x =$ _____

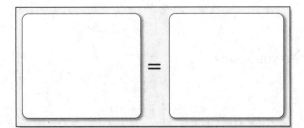

5. $2x - 1 = 7$ $x =$ _____

6. $5x - 2 = -7$ $x =$ _____

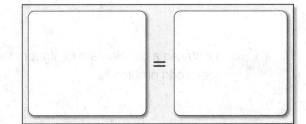

7. $3x - 4 = 5$ $x =$ _____

Analyze and Reflect

8. **MP** **Reason Inductively** Work with a partner. Read the steps to model and solve an equation using algebra tiles. Then (circle) each correct equation.

Steps to Solve	Choices of Equation		
• Add three 1-tiles to each side of the mat. • Divide tiles into two equal groups.	$2x + 3 = 15$	$3x + 2 = 15$	$2x - 3 = 15$
• Add four 1-tiles to each side of the mat. • Divide tiles into three equal groups.	$3x - 4 = 11$	$3x + 4 = 11$	$4x - 3 = 11$
• Remove seven 1-tiles from each side of the mat. • Divide tiles into three equal groups.	$7x + 3 = 10$	$3x + 7 = 10$	$3x - 7 = 10$
• Add two —1-tiles to each side of the mat. • Remove two zero pairs from the left side of the mat. • Divide tiles into five equal groups.	$5x - 2 = -8$	$5x + 2 = -8$	$2x + 5 = -8$

9. **MP** **Construct an Argument** What did you observe while choosing the correct equations in the table above?

_____

_____

Create

10. **MP** **Model with Mathematics** Write a real-world problem and an equation that the bar diagram below could represent. Then solve your problem.

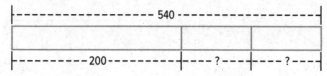

_____

_____

_____

_____

11. **inquiry** HOW can a bar diagram or algebra tiles help you solve a real-world problem?

_____

_____

Solve Two-Step Equations

Balloons A company charges $2 for each balloon in an arrangement and a $3 delivery fee. You have $9 to spend. The equation $2x + 3 = 9$, where x is the number of balloons, represents the situation. Work backward to solve for x.

 Essential Question

WHAT does it mean to say two quantities are equal or that they have a linear relationship?

Vocabulary

two-step equation

Virginia Standards
7.12

Start with the amount of money you have to spend.　[ ] →(Subtract the $3 delivery fee.)→ [ ] →(Since each balloon is $2, divide by two.)→ [ ]

So, you can purchase [ ] balloons.

Check your work by substituting your solution into the equation.

$$2\left(\boxed{}\right) + 3 \stackrel{?}{=} 9.$$

$$\boxed{} + 3 \stackrel{?}{=} 9$$

$$\boxed{} = 9$$

1. How many balloons could you have purchased if there was a $1 delivery charge?

_____

Start with the amount of money you have to spend.　[ ] →(Subtract the $1 delivery fee.)→ [ ] →(Since each balloon is $2, divide by two.)→ [ ]

Which MP Mathematical Process Goals did you use? Shade the circle(s) that applies.

① Mathematical Problem Solving
② Mathematical Communication
③ Mathematical Reasoning
④ Mathematical Connections
⑤ Mathematical Representations

Solve Two-Step Equations

Recall that the *order of operations* ensures that numerical expressions, such as 2 · 5 + 3, have only one value. To reverse the operations, undo them in reverse order.

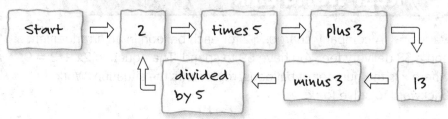

A **two-step equation**, such as 2x + 3 = 9, has two different operations, multiplication and addition. To solve a two-step equation, undo the operations in reverse order of the order of operations.

> This equation is written as px + q = r, where p, q, and r are rational numbers.

| Step 1 | Undo the addition or subtraction first. |

| Step 2 | Undo the multiplication or division. |

Examples

1. Solve 2x + 3 = 9. **Check your solution.**

$2x + 3 =$	9	Write the equation.
$-3 = -3$		Undo the addition first by subtracting 3 from each side.
$2x =$	6	
$\dfrac{2x}{2} =$	$\dfrac{6}{2}$	Next, undo the multiplication by dividing each side by 2.
$x =$	3	Simplify.

Check $2x + 3 = 9$ Write the original equation.

$2(3) + 3 \stackrel{?}{=} 9$ Replace x with 3.

$9 = 9 \checkmark$ The sentence is true.

The solution is 3.

> **STOP and Reflect**
>
> What are the two operations you would perform to solve 3x – 4 = 8? Write your answer below.

2. Solve $3x + 2 = 23$. **Check your solution.**

$3x + 2 = 23$ Write the equation.

$\underline{\quad -2 = -2\quad}$ Undo the addition first by subtracting 2 from each side.

$3x \quad = 21$

$\dfrac{3x}{3} = \dfrac{21}{3}$ Division Property of Equality

$x = 7$ Simplify.

Check $3x + 2 = 23$ Write the original equation.

$3(7) + 2 \overset{?}{=} 23$ Replace x with 7.

$23 = 23 \checkmark$ The sentence is true.

The solution is 7.

---

3. Solve $-2y - 7 = 3$. **Check your solution.**

$-2y - 7 = 3$ Write the equation.

$\underline{\quad +7 = +7\quad}$ Undo the subtraction first by adding 7 to each side.

$-2y = 10$

$\dfrac{-2y}{-2} = \dfrac{10}{-2}$ Division Property of Equality

$y = -5$ Simplify.

The solution is -5.   Check the solution.

---

4. Solve $4 + \dfrac{1}{5}r = -1$. **Check your solution.**

$4 + \dfrac{1}{5}r = -1$ Write the equation.

$\underline{-4 \qquad = -4}$ Undo the addition first by subtracting 4 from each side.

$\dfrac{1}{5}r = -5$

$5 \cdot \dfrac{1}{5}r = 5 \cdot (-5)$ Multiplication Property of Equality

$r = -25$ Simplify.

The solution is -25.   Check the solution.

> **Got it?** Do these problems to find out.

Solve each equation. Check your solution.

a. $2x + 4 = 10$ **b.** $3x + 5 = 14$ **c.** $5 = 2 + 3x$

d. $4x + 5 = 13$ **e.** $-5s + 8 = -2$ **f.** $-2 + \dfrac{2}{3}w = 10$

Equations

Remember, solutions of the new equation are also solutions of the original equation.

Show your work.

a. _____

b. _____

c. _____

d. _____

e. _____

f. _____

Example

 Tutor

5. Toya had her birthday party at the movies. It cost $27 for pizza and $8.50 per friend for the movie tickets. How many friends did Toya have at her party if she spent $78?

Words	Cost of pizza	plus	Cost of 1 friend	times	number of friends	equals $78.
Variable	Let n represent the number of friends.					
Equation	27	+	8.50	$\cdot$	n	= 78

Solve Arithmetically

You can use a bar diagram to solve an equation arithmetically.

$78	
pizza	tickets
$-$27	$-$8.50n

Subtract 27 from 78. Then divide by 8.5.

$78 - 27 = 51; 51 \div 8.5 = 6$

$$27 + 8.50n = 78 \qquad \text{Write the equation.}$$
$$\underline{-27 \qquad\qquad = -27} \qquad \text{Subtract 27 from each side.}$$
$$8.50n = 51$$
$$\frac{8.50n}{8.50} = \frac{51}{8.50} \qquad \text{Division Property of Equality}$$
$$n = 6 \qquad \text{Simplify.}$$

Toya can have 6 friends at her party.

Guided Practice

 Check ✓

Solve each equation. Check your solution. (Examples 1–4)

1. $13 = 1 + 4s$

2. $-3y - 5 = 10$

3. $-7 = 1 + \frac{2}{3}n$

 Show your work.

4. Syreeta wants to buy some CDs that each cost $14, and a DVD that costs $23. She has $65. Write and solve an equation to find how many CDs she can buy. (Example 5)

Equation: _____

Solution: _____

5. **Building on the Essential Question** When solving an equation, explain why it is important to perform identical operations on each side of the equals sign.

_____

_____

_____

Rate Yourself!

How well do you understand solving two-step equations? Circle the image that applies.

Clear   Somewhat   Not So
          Clear   Clear

For more help, go online to access a Personal Tutor. Tutor

FOLDABLES Time to update your Foldable!

Independent Practice

Go online for Step-by-Step Solutions
eHelp

Solve each equation. Check your solution. (Examples 1–4)

1. $3x + 1 = 10$

Show your work.

2. $-3 + 8n = -5$

3. $4h - 6 = 22$

4. $-8s + 1 = 33$

5. $-4w - 4 = 8$

6. $5 + \frac{1}{7}b = -2$

7. **MP Reason Abstractly** Cristiano is saving money to buy a bike that costs $189. He has saved $99 so far. He plans on saving $10 each week. In how many weeks will he have enough money to buy the bike? Use a bar diagram to solve arithmetically. Then use an equation to solve algebraically. (Example 5)

Show your work.

Solve each equation. Check your solution.

8. $2r - 3.1 = 1.7$

9. $4t + 3.5 = 12.5$

10. $8m - 5.5 = 10.1$

11 Temperature is usually measured on the Fahrenheit scale (°F) or the Celsius scale (°C). Use the formula $F = 1.8C + 32$ to convert from one scale to the other.

   a. Convert the temperature for Alaska's record low in July to Celsius. Round to the nearest degree.

Alaska Record Low Temperatures (°F) by Month	
January	−80
April	−50
July	16
October	−48

   b. Hawaii's record low temperature is −11°C. Find the difference in degrees Fahrenheit between Hawaii's record low temperature and the record low temperature for Alaska in January.

12. **MP Model with Mathematics** Refer to the graphic novel frame below. Jamar figured that they will spend $39 for popcorn. Each movie cost $19. Write and solve an equation to find how many movies they can purchase.

_____

_____

 H.O.T. Problems Higher Order Thinking

13. **MP Reason Inductively** Refer to Exercise 11. Is there a temperature in the table at which the number of degrees Celsius is the same as the number of degrees Fahrenheit? If so, find it. If not, explain why not.

_____

_____

14. **MP Persevere with Problems** Suppose your school is selling magazine subscriptions. Each subscription costs $20. The company pays the school half of the total sales in dollars. The school must also pay a one-time fee of $18. Write and solve an equation to determine the fewest number of subscriptions that can be sold to earn a profit of $200.

_____

15. **MP Model with Mathematics** Write a real-world problem that can be represented by the equation $\dfrac{(12 + 14) \times h}{2} = 52$. Then solve the problem.

_____

_____

Extra Practice

Solve each equation. Check your solution.

16. $5x + 4 = 19$

Homework
Help →

$5x + 4 = 19$
$\quad -4 = -4$
$\dfrac{5x}{5} = \dfrac{15}{5}$
$\quad x = 3$

17. $6m + 1 = -23$

18. $5 + 4d = 37$

19. $-7y + 3 = -25$

20. $25 + \dfrac{11}{12}b = 47$

21. $15 - \dfrac{1}{2}b = -3$

22. It costs $7.50 to enter a petting zoo. Each cup of food to feed the animals is $2.50. If you have $12.50, how many cups can you buy? Use a bar diagram to solve arithmetically. Then use an equation to solve algebraically.

Show your work.

23. **MP** **Multiple Representations** The perimeter of a rectangle is 48 centimeters. Its length is 16 centimeters. What is the width *w*?

a. Draw a bar diagram that represents this situation.

b. Write and solve an equation that represents this situation.

_____

c. How does solving the equation arithmetically compare to solving an equation algebraically?

_____

_____

24. Admission to an amusement park costs $15 and game tickets cost $0.50 each. Craig has $22 to pay for admission and game tickets. Select the correct labels to complete the bar diagram that can be used to find the number of game tickets t that Craig can purchase.

admission
game tickets
0.50
15
22
0.50t
t

How many game tickets can Craig purchase? [   ]

25. A rental car company charges a fixed fee of $30 plus $0.05 per mile. Let c represent the total cost of renting a car and driving it m miles.

Write an equation that could be used to find the total cost of renting a car and driving it any number of miles. [   ]

The Boggs family paid $49.75 for their car rental. How many miles did they drive? [   ]

Spiral Review

Use the Distributive Property to rewrite each expression.

26. $2(x + 7) =$

27. $6(10 + n) =$

28. $5(k - 4) =$

Factor each expression.

29. $5x + 5 \cdot 7 =$ _____

30. $4n + 4 \cdot 2 =$ _____

31. $10t + 10 \cdot 3 =$ _____

32. $7v + 7 \cdot 8 =$ _____

Inquiry HOW are equations in $p(x + q) = r$ form different from $px + q = r$ equations?

 Virginia Standards
7.12

Mark has two summer jobs. He babysits and helps with the gardening. He works at each job three days a week and earns a total of $240. The table shows his earnings each day. How much does he earn each day babysitting?

Job	Daily Earnings ($)
Babysitting	x
Gardening	30

What do you know? _____

_____

What do you need to find? _____

_____

Hands-On Activity 1

Step 1 Draw a bar diagram that represents the situation.

$x + \$30$	$x + \$30$	$x + \$30$
earnings each day	earnings each day	earnings each day

Step 2 Write an equation that is modeled by the bar diagram.

$3(\$x + \$30) = \boxed{}$

From the diagram, you can see that one third of Mark's total earnings

is equal to $x + \$30$. So, $x + \$30 = \dfrac{\$240}{3}$ or $\boxed{}$.

Mark earns $\boxed{}$ − $30, or $\boxed{}$ each day babysitting.

Vijay and his brother bought two hamburgers and two lemonades. The hamburgers cost $6 each. They spent a total of $16. How much did each lemonade cost?

Hands-On Activity 2

Tools

Use algebra tiles to model the situation described above.

Step 1 Model $2(x + 6) = 16$ using algebra tiles. Use ☐ groups of $(x + 6)$ tiles.

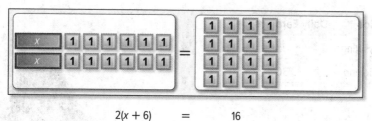

$$2(x + 6) \quad = \quad 16$$

Step 2 Divide the tiles into ☐ equal groups on each side of the mat.

Remove ☐ group from each side.

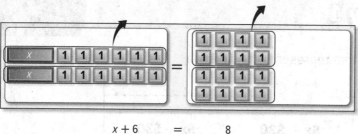

$$x + 6 \quad = \quad 8$$

Step 3 Remove the same number of 1-tiles from each side.

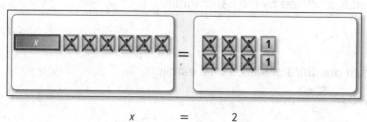

$$x \quad = \quad 2$$

So, $x =$ ☐. Each lemonade costs ☐.

Work with a partner to model and solve each equation. Use a bar diagram for Exercises 1 and 2. Use algebra tiles for Exercises 3–6.

1. $3(x + 5) = 21$ $x =$ _____

2. $2(x - 3) = 10$ $x =$ _____

3. $4(x + 1) = 8$ $x =$ _____

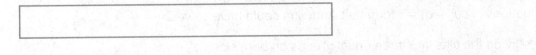

4. $3(x + 2) = -12$ $x =$ _____

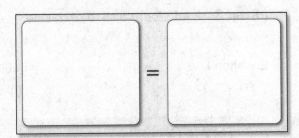

5. $2(x - 1) = 6$ $x =$ _____

6. $3(x - 4) = -3$ $x =$ _____

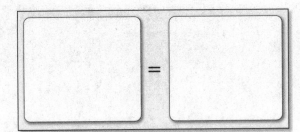

Work with a partner to write and solve an equation that represents each problem.

7. Refer to Activity 1. If Mark worked four days a week and made $360, how much did he earn babysitting each day?

_____

8. Refer to Activity 2. If Vijay and his brother spent a total of $15, how much did each lemonade cost?

_____

9. (MP) **Reason Inductively** After modeling an equation using algebra tiles, Angelina used the steps shown below to solve the equation. Write two different equations in $p(x + q) = r$ form that Angelina could have solved.

| Step 1 | Divide the tiles into three equal groups on both sides of the mat. |

| Step 2 | Remove two groups from each side. |

| Step 3 | Add four 1-tiles to each side. |

Equation 1: _____   Equation 2: _____

Create

On Your Own

10. (MP) **Model with Mathematics** Write a real-world problem that can be represented by the equation $4(x + 15) = 140$. Then solve the problem.

_____

_____

_____

_____

11. **inquiry** HOW are equations in $p(x + q) = r$ form different from $px + q = r$ equations?

_____

_____

More Two-Step Equations

Real-World Link

Watch ▶

Essential Question

WHAT does it mean to say two quantities are equal or that they have a linear relationship?

Virginia Standards
7.12

Museums A new exhibit about dinosaurs is being constructed. The exhibit is a rectangle that is 36 feet long. It has a perimeter of 114 feet. Follow the steps to write an equation that can be used to find the width of the museum exhibit.

Step 1 Draw a diagram to help visualize the exhibit.

Label the length and width. Let w represent the width.

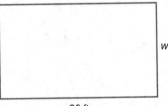

w

36 ft

Step 2 Write an expression that represents the sum of the length and width of the exhibit. _____

Step 3 Write an expression that represents twice the sum of the length and width. _____

Step 4 Write an equation that represents the perimeter of the exhibit. _____

Which **MP** **Mathematical Process Goals** did you use? Shade the circle(s) that applies.

① Mathematical Problem Solving   ④ Mathematical Connections

② Mathematical Communication   ⑤ Mathematical Representations

③ Mathematical Reasoning

Solve Two-Step Equations

An equation like $2(w + 36) = 114$ is in the form $p(x + q) = r$. It contains two factors, p and $(x + q)$, and is considered a two-step equation. Solve these equations using the properties of equality.

Examples

Tutor

1. Solve $3(x + 5) = 45$.

Method 1 Solve arithmetically.

← ———————— 45 ———————— →
x + 5	x + 5	x + 5
← ? →

Draw a bar diagram. From the diagram, you can see that $x + 5 = 45 \div 3$ or 15. So, $x = 15 - 5$ or 10.

Method 2 Solve algebraically.

$3(x + 5) = 45$ Write the equation.

$\dfrac{3(x + 5)}{3} = \dfrac{45}{3}$ Division Property of Equality

$x + 5 = 15$ Simplify.

$\underline{-5 = -5}$ Subtraction Property of Equality

$x = 10$ Simplify.

2. Solve $5(n - 2) = -30$.

$5(n - 2) = -30$ Write the equation.

$\dfrac{5(n - 2)}{5} = \dfrac{-30}{5}$ Division Property of Equality

$n - 2 = -6$ Simplify.

$\underline{+2 = +2}$ Addition Property of Equality

$n = -4$ Simplify. Check the solution.

Check Your Work

Remember to plug your solution back into the original equation to see if it makes a true statement.

Show your work.

Got it? Do these problems to find out.

a. $2(x + 4) = 20$ **b.** $3(b - 6) = 12$ **c.** $-7(6 + d) = 49$

a. _____

b. _____

c. _____

Equations with Rational Coefficients

Sometimes the factor p, in $p(x + q)$, will be a fraction or decimal.

Examples

3. Solve $\frac{2}{3}(n + 6) = 10$. **Check your solution.**

$\frac{2}{3}(n + 6) = 10$ Write the equation.

$\frac{3}{2} \cdot \frac{2}{3}(n + 6) = \frac{3}{2} \cdot 10$ Multiplication Property of Equality

$(n + 6) = \frac{3}{2} \cdot \left(\frac{\overset{5}{\cancel{10}}}{1}\right)$ $\frac{2}{3} \cdot \frac{3}{2} = 1$; write 10 as $\frac{10}{1}$.

$n + 6 = 15$ Simplify.

$\underline{-6 = -6}$ Subtraction Property of Equality

$n = 9$ Simplify.

Check $\frac{2}{3}(n + 6) = 10$ Write the original equation.

$\frac{2}{3}(9 + 6) \overset{?}{=} 10$ Replace n with 9. Is this sentence true?

$10 = 10 \checkmark$ The sentence is true.

---

4. Solve $0.2(c - 3) = -10$. **Check your solution.**

$0.2(c - 3) = -10$ Write the equation.

$\frac{0.2(c - 3)}{0.2} = -\frac{10}{0.2}$ Division Property of Equality

$c - 3 = -50$ Simplify.

$\underline{+3 = +3}$ Addition Property of Equality

$c = -47$ Simplify.

Check $0.2(c - 3) = -10$ Write the original equation.

$0.2(-47 - 3) \overset{?}{=} -10$ Replace c with -47. Is this sentence true?

$-10 = -10 \checkmark$ The sentence is true.

Got it? Do these problems to find out.

d. $\frac{1}{4}(d - 3) = -15$ **e.** $0.75(6 + d) = 12$ **f.** $(t + 3)\frac{5}{9} = 40$

> **Reciprocals**
> The product of a number and its reciprocal is 1.

Show your work.

d. _____

e. _____

f. _____

Example

5. Jamal and two cousins received the same amount of money to go to a movie. Each boy spent $15. Afterward, the boys had $30 altogether. Write and solve an equation to find the amount of money each boy received.

Let m represent the amount of money each boy received.

$$3(m - 15) = 30 \qquad \text{Write the equation.}$$
$$\frac{3(m - 15)}{3} = \frac{30}{3} \qquad \text{Division Property of Equality}$$
$$m - 15 = 10 \qquad \text{Simplify.}$$
$$\underline{+15 = +15} \qquad \text{Addition Property of Equality}$$
$$m = 25 \qquad \text{Simplify.}$$

So, each boy received $25.

STOP and Reflect

Solve the problem in Example 5 arithmetically. How does the arithmetic solution compare to the algebraic solution? Write your answer below.

Guided Practice

Solve each equation. Check your solution. (Examples 1–4)

1. $2(p + 7) = 18$

2. $(4 + g)(-11) = 121$

3. $(v + 5)\left(-\dfrac{1}{9}\right) = 6$

4. $0.8(m - 5) = 10$

5. Mr. Singh had three sheets of stickers. He gave 20 stickers from each sheet to his students and has 12 total stickers left. Write and solve an equation to find how many stickers were originally on each sheet. (Example 5)

Equation: _____

Solution: _____

6. ⓔ **Building on the Essential Question** What is the difference between $px + q = r$ and $p(x + q) = r$?

_____

_____

_____

_____

Rate Yourself!

Are you ready to move on?
Shade the section that applies.

I have a few questions.

I'm ready to move on.

I have a lot of questions.

For more help, go online to access a Personal Tutor.

Tutor

FOLDABLES Time to update your Foldable!

Independent Practice

Go online for Step-by-Step Solutions eHelp

Solve each equation. Check your solution. (Examples 1–4)

1. $8(s + 3) = 72$

2. $-7(z - 6) = -70$

3. $(t + 8)(-2) = 12$

4. $\frac{8}{11}(n - 10) = 64$

5. $-0.6(r + 0.2) = 1.8$

6. $\left(w - \frac{4}{9}\right)\left(-\frac{2}{3}\right) = -\frac{4}{5}$

7. The length of each side of an equilateral triangle is increased by 5 inches, so the perimeter is now 60 inches. Write and solve an equation to find the original length of each side of the equilateral triangle. (Example 5)

Equation: _____   Solution: _____

8. **MP Multiple Representations** Miguel and three of his friends went to the movies. They originally had a total of $40. Each boy had the same amount of money and spent $7.50 on a ticket. How much money did each boy have left after buying his ticket?

a. Model Draw a bar diagram that represents the situation.

b. Algebra Write and solve an equation that represents the situation.

_____

c. Words Explain how you solved your equation.

_____

_____

d. Words Compare the arithmetic solution and the algebraic solution.

_____

_____

9. Mrs. Sorenstam bought one ruler, one compass, and one mechanical pencil at the prices shown in the table for each of her 12 students.

Item	Price ($)
compass	1.49
mechanical pencil	0.59
ruler	0.49

a. Suppose Mrs. Sorenstam had 36 cents left after buying the school supplies. Write an equation to find the amount of money Mrs. Sorenstam initially had to spend on each student.

_____

b. Describe a two-step process you could use to solve your equation. Then solve the equation.

_____

_____

 H.O.T. Problems Higher Order Thinking

10. **Model with Mathematics** Write a real-world situation that can be represented by the equation $2(n + 20) = 110$.

_____

_____

_____

11. **MP** **Find the Error** Marisol is solving the equation $6(x + 3) = 21$. Find her mistake and correct it.

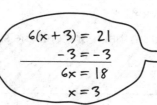

$$6(x + 3) = 21$$
$$\underline{-3 = -3}$$
$$6x = 18$$
$$x = 3$$

12. **MP** **Persevere with Problems** Solve $p(x + q) = r$ for x.

_____

13. **MP** **Use Math Tools** Write an equation to represent the bar diagram at the right. Then write a real-world problem that can be represented by the equation and the diagram.

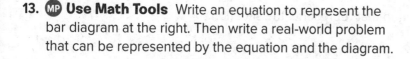

_____

_____

_____

_____

Extra Practice

Solve each equation. Check your solution.

14. $0.25(3 + a) = 0.5$

Homework Help

$0.25(3 + a) = 0.5$

$\dfrac{0.25(3 + a)}{0.25} = \dfrac{0.5}{0.25}$

$3 + a = 2$

$a = -1$

15. $12(x - 20) = -48$

16. $-28 = 7(n + 3)$

17. $(t + 9)20 = 140$

18. $\dfrac{5}{9}(8 + c) = -20$

19. $(d - 3)\dfrac{2}{5} = 30$

20. **MP Reason Abstractly** Anne bought a necklace for each of her three sisters. She paid $7 for each necklace. Suppose she had $9 left. Write and solve an equation to find how much money Anne had initially to spend on each sister.

Equation: _____

Solution: _____

Solve each equation. Check your solution.

21. $1\dfrac{3}{5}(t - 6) = -0.4$ _____

22. $\left(x + 5\dfrac{1}{2}\right)0.75 = \dfrac{5}{8}$ _____

23. Mr. Gomez bought fruit to make fruit salad. He bought $2\dfrac{1}{2}$ pounds of apples and spent $4.50 on apples and oranges. Write and solve an equation to determine the number of pounds of oranges Mr. Gomez bought.

_____

Fruit	Price per Pound ($)
apples	1.20
bananas	0.50
grapes	1.50
oranges	1.20

24. A rectangular classroom is 32 feet long and has a perimeter of 120 feet. Label the drawing with the correct values to represent the situation. Let *w* represent the width of the classroom.

Write an expression that represents the sum of the length and width. ⬚

Write an expression that represents twice the sum of the length and width. ⬚

Write an equation you could use to find the perimeter of the classroom. ⬚

What is the width of the classroom? ⬚

⬚ ft

⬚ ft $P =$ ⬚ ft   ⬚ ft

⬚ ft

25. Which of the following are operations that you should use to solve the equation $p(x - q) = r$ for x? Select all that apply.

☐ Subtract q from both sides.   ☐ Multiply both sides by p.

☐ Divide both sides by p.   ☐ Add q to both sides.

Spiral Review

Solve each equation.

26. $x + 3 = 5$

27. $x - 2 = -6$

28. $4x = 12$

29. $-6x = -24$

30. $\frac{x}{2} = -1$

31. $\frac{x}{-3} = 1$

Write the number or numbers from the set $\{-3, -2, -1, 0, 1, 2, 3\}$ that make each statement true.

32. $4m = 12$ _____

33. $y - 1 = 1$ _____

34. $v > 0$ _____

35. $r \leq 0$ _____

Case #1 Yard Work

Mike earned extra money by doing yard work for his neighbor. Then he spent $5.50 at the convenience store and four times that amount at the bookstore. Now he has $7.75 left.

How much money did Mike have before he went to the convenience store and the bookstore?

Understand *What are the facts?*

You know Mike has $7.75 left. You need to find the amount before his purchases.

Plan *What is your strategy to solve this problem?*

Start with the end result and work backward.

Solve *How can you apply the strategy?*

He has $7.75 left.
Undo the four times $5.50 spent at the bookstore.
Since $5.50 × 4 is $22, add $7.75 and $22.

	$7.75
	+ $22.00
	$29.75

Undo the $5.50 spent at the convenience store.

	+ $5.50

Add $5.50 and ⬚. $35.25

So, Mike's starting amount was ⬚.

Check *Does the answer make sense?*

Assume Mike started with $35.25. He spent $5.50 and $22. He had

$35 − $5.50 − $22 or ⬚ left. So, $35.25 is correct. ✓

Analyze the Strategy

MP Construct an Argument Describe how to solve a problem by working

backward. _____

_____

_____

Marisa spent $8 on a movie ticket. Then she spent $5 on popcorn and one half of what was left on a drink. She had $2 left.

How much did she have initially?

Understand

Read the problem. What are you being asked to find?

I need to find _____.

Underline key words and values. What information do you know?

I know Marisa has ☐ left and that she spent ☐ , ☐ , and

_____.

Is there any information that you do *not* need to know?

I do not need to know _____.

Plan

Choose a problem-solving strategy.

I will use the _____ strategy.

Solve

Use your problem-solving strategy to solve the problem.
Marisa has $2 left.

Undo the half-of-what-was-left   _____
amount. Multiply by 2.

Undo the spent $5. Add $5.   _____

Undo the spent $8. Add $8.   _____

So, Marisa had ☐ initially.

Check

Use information from the problem to check your answer.

Marisa's initial amount: _____

Amount after spending $8:   _____

Amount after spending $5:   _____

Amount after spending half of what was left: _____

Work with a small group to solve the following cases. Show your work on a separate piece of paper.

Case #3 Waterfalls

Angel Falls in Venezuela is 3,212 feet high. It is 29 yards higher than 2.5 times the architectural height of the Empire State Building.

Find the architectural height, in feet, of the Empire State Building.

Case #4 Number Theory

Travis works at a kite factory. He checks all the kites before they are packaged. Travis discovered that of the 28 kites that he inspected, 7 kites did not pass: 4 kites did not have tails, and 3 kites had the wrong colors.

Of the 476 kites Travis examined, how many did not have tails and how many had the wrong colors?

Case #5 Time

Timothy's morning schedule is shown.

At what time does Timothy wake up if he arrives at school at 7:35 A.M.?

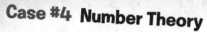

Timothy's Schedule	
Activity	**Time**
Wake up	■
Get ready for school — $\frac{3}{4}$ h	■
Walk to school — $\frac{5}{12}$ h	7:35 A.M.

Use any strategy!

Case #6 Money

Antonio has saved $28 to spend at the arcade.

If he has 5 bills, how many of each kind of bill does he have?

Mid-Chapter Check

Vocabulary Check

1. Define *equation*. Give an example of two equivalent equations.

_____

_____

2. Fill in the blank with the correct term.

A _____ is the numerical factor of a multiplication expression like 3*x*.

Skills Check and Problem Solving

Solve each equation. Check your solution.

3. $21 + m = 33$

4. $a - 5 = -12$

5. $5f = -75$

6. $15 = \dfrac{b}{15}$

7. $19 = 4p + 5$

8. $3(n - 7) = -30$

9. Cameron has 11 adult Fantail goldfish. This is 7 fewer Fantail goldfish than his friend Julia has. Write and solve a subtraction equation to determine the number of Fantail goldfish *g* that Julia has.

Equation: _____   Solution: _____

10. **MP** **Persevere with Problems** The pentagon shown is a regular pentagon, so each side has the same length. The perimeter of the pentagon is 22.5 centimeters. What is the value of *x*? _____

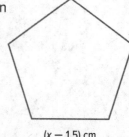

$(x - 1.5)$ cm

inquiry **HOW is an inequality like an equation? How is it different?**

Virginia Standards
7.13

Mr. Numkena volunteered to drive Hinto and his friends to the school dance. The car can carry up to 5 people, including the driver. How many friends can ride in the car with Hinto?

What do you know? _____

_____

What do you need to find? _____

_____

Hands-On Activity 1

Tools

The real-world situation described above can be represented by the inequality $x + 2 \leq 5$. Let x represent the friends that can ride with Hinto.

$$x + 2 \leq 5$$

Mr. Numkena, Hinto, and friends

Maximum number of people

You can use a balance to model and solve the inequality $x + 2 \leq 5$.

Step 1 On one side of a balance, place a paper bag and ☐ cubes to model $x + 2$.

Step 2 On the other side of a balance, place ☐ cubes.

Add one cube to the bag at a time. Then complete the table.

Number of Friends, x	$x + 2$	Less than or equal to 5?
1	3	yes
2		
3		
4		

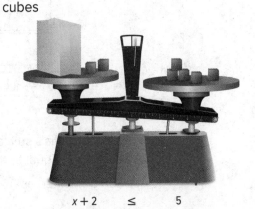

$x + 2$ $\leq$ 5

So, up to ☐ friends can ride with Hinto to the school dance.

An *inequality* is a mathematical sentence that compares quantities. The table shows two examples of inequalities.

Words	Symbols
x is less than two	$x < 2$
x is greater than or equal to four	$x \geq 4$

To solve an inequality means to find values for the variable that make the sentence true. You can use bar diagrams to solve inequalities.

Hands-On Activity 2

An airline charges for checked luggage that weighs more than 50 pounds. Mia's suitcase currently weighs 35 pounds and she still needs to pack her shoes. Find the maximum amount her shoes can weigh so Mia will not be charged a fee.

Step 1 In the bar diagram, write the maximum weight Mia's luggage can be without a fee. Label the weight of Mia's luggage without her shoes.

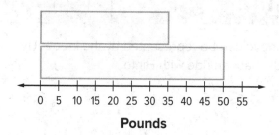

Pounds

Step 2 In the bar diagram, write an *x* beside the bar that represents the weight of Mia's luggage.

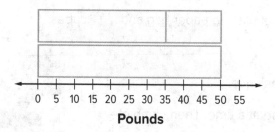

Pounds

The weight of Mia's suitcase plus the weight of her shoes must be less than or equal to the maximum luggage weight.

This can be written as $35 + x \leq 50$.

Using the bar diagram, Mia's shoes cannot weigh more than $50 - 35$ or ⬚ pounds.

Investigate

Work with a partner to solve the following problems.

MP Reason Inductively For Exercises 1–3, assume the paper bag is weightless. Write the inequality represented by each balance. Then write the different possible numbers of cubes in the paper bag if the sides of each balance remain unlevel.

1.

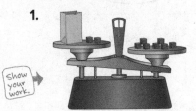

Show your work.

Inequality: _____

Number of Cubes: _____

2.

Inequality: _____

Number of Cubes: _____

3.

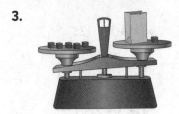

Inequality: _____

Number of Cubes: _____

4. **MP Reason Abstractly** At an amusement park, roller coaster riders are required to be at least 48 inches tall. Last year, Myron was 42 inches tall. Complete the bar diagram to determine the number of inches *x* Myron needed to grow this year to be able to ride the roller coaster. Then write an inequality to represent the situation.

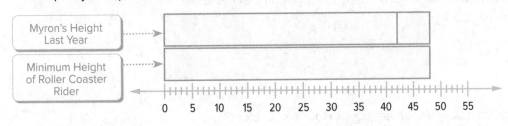

Myron's Height Last Year

Minimum Height of Roller Coaster Rider

0   5   10   15   20   25   30   35   40   45   50   55

So, Myron needed to grow at least _____ inches.

Inequality: _____

Analyze and Reflect

Collaborate

Work with a partner to circle the correct inequality for each situation. The first one is done for you.

Real-World Situation	Inequalities	
Yolanda wants to score at least 84% on the next history test.	$x \leq 84$	$\boxed{x \geq 84}$
5. To see a certain movie, you must be at least 13 years old.	$n \leq 13$	$n \geq 13$
6. Kai has \$4.99 left on a music download gift card. She has a download costing \$1.99 in her online shopping cart. How much money does Kai have left to spend?	$x + 1.99 \leq 4.99$	$x + 1.99 > 4.99$
7. In some states, teens must be at least 16 years old to obtain a driver's license.	$x < 16$ $x \leq 16$	$x > 16$ $x \geq 16$
8. The Walter family budgets a maximum amount of \$125 per week for groceries. Mr. Walter already spent \$40. How much more can the Walter family spend on groceries?	$x + 40 < 125$ $x + 40 \leq 125$	$x + 40 > 125$ $x + 40 \geq 125$
9. Miles pays \$30 for a ticket to an amusement park. He cannot spend more than \$50. How much more money can Miles spend at the amusement park?	$x + 30 < 50$ $x + 30 \leq 50$	$x + 30 > 50$ $x + 30 \geq 50$

Create

On Your Own

10. **MP Model with Mathematics** Write a real-world situation that could be represented by $x + 20 \geq 50$.

_____

_____

11. **Inquiry** HOW is an inequality like an equation? How is it different?

_____

_____

_____

Solve Inequalities by Addition or Subtraction

Real-World Link

Mail A first class stamp can be used for letters and packages weighing thirteen ounces or less. Fisher is mailing pictures to his grandmother, and only has a first class stamp. His envelope weighs 2 ounces. Follow the steps to determine how much the pictures can weigh so that Fisher can use the stamp.

Step 1 Let x represent the weight of the pictures. Write and solve an equation to find the maximum weight of the pictures.

weight of the envelope		weight of the pictures		maximum weight of the package
☐	**+**	x	**=**	☐

Solve for x.

So, the maximum weight of the pictures is ☐ ounces.

Step 2 Replace the equals sign in your equation with the less than or equal to symbol, $\leq$.

$$2 + x \;\boxed{}\; 13$$

Refer to Step 2. Name three possible values of x that will result in a true sentence.

Which 🆆 **Mathematical Process Goals** did you use? Shade the circle(s) that applies.

① Mathematical Problem Solving

② Mathematical Communication

③ Mathematical Reasoning

④ Mathematical Connections

⑤ Mathematical Representations

Essential Question

WHAT does it mean to say two quantities are equal or that they have a linear relationship?

Vocabulary

Subtraction Property of Inequality
Addition Property of Inequality
inequality

Virginia Standards
7.13

Solve Inequalities

Words	You can solve inequalities by using the **Addition Property of Inequalities** and the **Subtraction Property of Inequalities**. When you add or subtract the same number from each side of an inequality, the inequality remains true.
Symbols	For all numbers a, b, and c, **1.** if $a > b$, then $a + c > b + c$ and $a - c > b - c$. **2.** if $a < b$, then $a + c < b + c$ and $a - c < b - c$.
Examples	$$\begin{array}{r} 2 < 4 \\ +3 \quad +3 \\ \hline 5 < 7 \end{array} \qquad \begin{array}{r} 6 > 3 \\ -4 \quad -4 \\ \hline 2 > -1 \end{array}$$

Work Zone

An **inequality** is a mathematical sentence that compares quantities. Solving an inequality means finding values for the variable that make the inequality true.

The table below gives some examples of the words you might use when describing different inequalities.

	Inequalities			
Words	• is less than • is fewer than	• is greater than • is more than • exceeds	• is less than or equal to • is no more than • is at most	• is greater than or equal to • is no less than • is at least
Symbols	$<$	$>$	$\leq$	$\geq$

Examples

Tutor

1. Solve $x + 3 > 10$.

$$\begin{array}{ll} x + 3 > 10 & \text{Write the inequality.} \\ \underline{-3 \quad -3} & \text{Subtract 3 from each side.} \\ x > 7 & \text{Simplify.} \end{array}$$

Therefore, the solution is $x > 7$.

You can check this solution by substituting a number greater than 7 into the original inequality. Try using 8.

$$\begin{array}{ll} \textbf{Check} \quad x + 3 > 10 & \text{Write the inequality.} \\ 8 + 3 \overset{?}{>} 10 & \text{Replace } x \text{ with 8. Is this sentence true?} \\ 11 > 10 & \text{This is a true statement. } \checkmark \end{array}$$

2. Solve $-6 \geq n - 5$.

$-6 \geq n - 5$ Write the inequality.

$\underline{+5 \qquad +5}$ Add 5 to each side.

$-1 \geq n$ Simplify.

The solution is $-1 \geq n$ or $n \leq -1$.

You can check this solution by substituting -1 or a number less than -1 into the original inequality.

Got it? Do these problems to find out.

Solve each inequality.

a. $a - 3 < 8$ **b.** $0.4 + y \geq 7$

Show
your
work.

a. _____

b. _____

Tutor

Example

3. Solve $a + \dfrac{1}{2} < 2$. Graph the solution set on a number line.

$a + \dfrac{1}{2} < 2$ Write the inequality.

$\dfrac{-\dfrac{1}{2} \quad -\dfrac{1}{2}}{}$ Subtract $\dfrac{1}{2}$ from each side.

$a < 1\dfrac{1}{2}$ Simplify.

The solution is $a < 1\dfrac{1}{2}$.   Check your solution.

Graph the solution.

> Place an open dot at $1\dfrac{1}{2}$. Draw a line and an arrow to the left.

$$\xleftarrow{\hspace{2cm}} \quad \overset{\oplus}{\underset{-1 \quad 0 \quad 1 \quad 2 \quad 3 \quad 4}{|\quad|\quad|\quad|\quad|\quad|}}$$

Open and Closed Dots

When graphing inequalities, an open dot is used when the value should not be included in the solution, as with > and < inequalities. A closed dot indicates the value is included in the solution, as with ≤ and ≥ inequalities.

Got it? Do these problems to find out.

Solve each inequality. Graph the solution set on the number line provided.

c. $h + 4 > 4$ **d.** $x - 6 \leq 4$

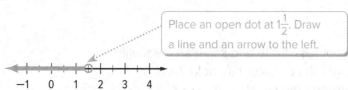

c. _____

d. _____

Write Inequalities

Inequalities can be used to represent real-world situations. You will want to first identify a variable to represent the unknown value.

Example

4. Dylan has **$18** to ride go-karts and play games at the state fair. Suppose the go-karts cost **$5.50**. Write and solve an inequality to find the most he can spend on games.

Words	Cost of go-kart	plus	cost of games	must be less than or equal to	total amount.
Symbols	Let x = the cost of the games.				
Inequality	5.5	+	x	$\leq$	18

$$5.5 + x \leq 18 \quad \text{Write the inequality. } (5.50 = 5.5)$$
$$\underline{-5.5 \qquad -5.5} \quad \text{Subtract 5.5 from each side.}$$
$$x \leq 12.5 \quad \text{Simplify.}$$

So, the most Dylan can spend on games is $12.50.

Guided Practice

Solve each inequality. Graph the solution set on a number line. (Examples 1–3)

1. $6 + h \geq 12$ _____

2. $14 + t > 5$ _____

 Show your work.

3. An elevator can hold 2,800 pounds or less. Write and solve an inequality that describes how much more weight the elevator can hold if it is currently holding 2,375 pounds. Interpret the solution. (Example 4)

_____

_____

4. Ⓔ **Building on the Essential Question** Explain when you would use addition and when you would use subtraction to solve an inequality. _____

_____

_____

Rate Yourself!

Are you ready to move on? Shade the section that applies.

YES ? NO

For more help, go online to access a Personal Tutor.

Independent Practice

Go online for Step-by-Step Solutions eHelp

Solve each inequality. (Examples 1 and 2)

1. $h - 16 \leq -24$ _____

2. $y + 6 \geq -13$ _____

3 $-3 < n - 8$ _____

 Show your work.

4. $3 \leq m + 1.4$ _____

5. $x + 0.7 > -0.3$ _____

6. $w - 8 \geq 5.6$ _____

Solve each inequality. Graph the solution set on a number line. (Example 3)

7. $m + 5 \geq -1$ _____

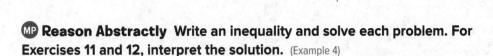

8. $-11 > t + 7$ _____

MP Reason Abstractly Write an inequality and solve each problem. For Exercises 11 and 12, interpret the solution. (Example 4)

9 Four more than a number is more than 13.

10. The sum of a number and 19 is at least 8.2.

Inequality: _____

Inequality: _____

Solution: _____

Solution: _____

11. The high school soccer team can have no more than 26 players. Write and solve an inequality to determine how many more players can make the team if the coach has already chosen 17 players.

Inequality: _____

Solution: _____

Interpretation: _____

12. Lalo has 1,500 minutes per month on his cell phone plan. How many more minutes can he use if he has already talked for 785 minutes?

Inequality: _____

Solution: _____

Interpretation: _____

13. Refer to the diagram below.

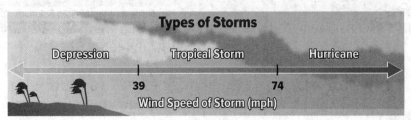

a. A hurricane has winds that are at least 74 miles per hour. Suppose a tropical storm has winds that are 42 miles per hour. Write and solve an inequality to find how much the winds must increase before the storm becomes a hurricane.

Inequality: _____   Solution: _____

b. A *major storm* has wind speeds that are at least 110 miles per hour. Write and solve an inequality that describes how much greater these wind speeds are than the slowest hurricane.

Inequality: _____   Solution: _____

 H.O.T. Problems Higher Order Thinking

14. (MP) **Reason Inductively** Compare and contrast the solutions of $a - 3 = 15$ and $a - 3 \geq 15$. _____

_____

_____

15. (MP) **Model with Mathematics** Write an addition inequality for the solution set graphed below.

_____

16   18   20   22   24

16. (MP) **Persevere with Problems** Solve $x + b > c$ for x.

_____

17. (MP) **Reason Inductively** Does the graph shown at the right show the solution set of the inequality $x + 3 \geq 2$? If not, explain how you

would change the graph to show the actual solution set. _____

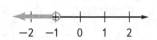

−2   −1   0   1   2

_____

_____

Extra Practice

Solve each inequality.

18. $10 < b - 8$ ___$18 < b$___

$$10 < b - 8$$
$$\underline{+8 \qquad +8}$$
$$18 < b$$

Homework Help

19. $1.2 + m \le 5.5$ _____

20. $c - 1\frac{1}{4} > -2\frac{1}{2}$ _____

MP **Model with Mathematics** Solve each inequality. Graph the solution set on a number line.

21. $-21 < a - 16$ _____

22. $t - 6.2 < 4$ _____

Write an inequality and solve each problem.

23. Eight less than a number is less than 10.

Inequality: _____

Solution: _____

24. The difference between a number and $21\frac{1}{2}$ is no more than $14\frac{1}{4}$.

Inequality: _____

Solution: _____

25. There were a total of 125 cars at a car dealership. A salesperson sold 68 of the cars in one month. Write and solve an inequality that describes how many more cars, at most, the salesman has left to sell. Interpret the solution.

Inequality: _____   Solution: _____

Interpretation: _____

Copy and Solve Solve each inequality. Graph the solution set on a number line. Show your work on a separate sheet of paper.

26. $n - \frac{1}{5} \le \frac{3}{10}$

27. $6 > x + 3\frac{1}{3}$

28. $c + 1\frac{1}{4} < 5$

29. $9 \le m - 2\frac{1}{5}$

30. $\frac{3}{4} + d > 4\frac{1}{2}$

31. $-\frac{7}{8} \le n + 3\frac{5}{16}$

32. Joaquin can send up to 250 text messages each month. So far this month, he has sent 141 text messages. Let t represent the number of text messages Joaquin can send during the rest of the month.

Write an inequality to model the situation

Solve the inequality for t.

Graph the solution on the number line.

Interpret the solution to the inequality. Explain your reasoning.

33. Which inequality has the solution set shown in the number line below? Select all that apply.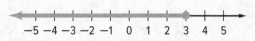

-5 -4 -3 -2 -1 0 1 2 3 4 5

☐ $x + 4 \leq 7$ ☐ $12 > x + 9$ ☐ $x + 1 \leq 2$ ☐ $-7 \geq x - 10$

Spiral Review

Solve each equation. Then graph each solution on the number line below.

34. $x + 2 = 1$

35. $x - 1 = -5$

36. $2x = 10$

37. $-2x = 4$

38. $\frac{x}{2} = 1$

39. $\frac{x}{-2} = 3$

Solve Inequalities by Multiplication or Division

 Real-World Link

 Essential Question

WHAT does it mean to say two quantities are equal or that they have a linear relationship?

Vocab
abc **Vocabulary**

Multiplication Property of Inequality

Division Property of Inequality

🪐 **Virginia Standards**
7.13

Science An astronaut in a space suit weighs about 300 pounds on Earth, but only 50 pounds on the Moon.

weight on Earth		weight on Moon
300 lb	>	50 lb

1. If the astronaut and space suit each weighed half as much, would the inequality still be true?

$$\frac{300}{2} > \frac{50}{2}$$  Divide each side by 2.

   $\boxed{} > \boxed{}$

   Is the inequality still true? Circle yes or no.

   Yes   No

2. Is the weight of one astronaut greater on Pluto or Earth? Would the weight of 5 astronauts be greater on Pluto or on Earth? Explain by using an inequality.

Location	Weight of Astronaut (lb)
Earth	300
Moon	50
Pluto	67
Jupiter	796

_____

3. Is the weight of one astronaut greater on Jupiter or on Earth? Would the weight of 5 astronauts be greater on Jupiter or on Earth? Explain by using an inequality.

_____

📌 Which **MP** **Mathematical Process Goals** did you use? Shade the circle(s) that applies.

① Mathematical Problem Solving   ④ Mathematical Connections

② Mathematical Communication   ⑤ Mathematical Representations

③ Mathematical Reasoning

Multiplication and Division Properties of Inequality, Positive Number

STOP and Reflect

What does the inequality $c > 0$ mean? Explain below.

Words The **Multiplication Property of Inequality** and the **Division Property of Inequality** state that an inequality remains true when you multiply or divide each side of an inequality by a positive number.

Symbols For all numbers a, b, and c, where $c > 0$,

1. if $a > b$, then $ac > bc$ and $\frac{a}{c} > \frac{b}{c}$.
2. if $a < b$, then $ac < bc$ and $\frac{a}{c} < \frac{b}{c}$.

These properties are also true for $a \geq b$ and $a \leq b$.

You can solve inequalities by using the Multiplication Property of Inequality and the Division Property of Inequality.

Examples

Tutor

1. Solve $8x \leq 40$.

$8x \leq 40$ Write the inequality.

$\dfrac{8x}{8} \leq \dfrac{40}{8}$ Divide each side by 8.

$x \leq 5$ Simplify.

The solution is $x \leq 5$. You can check this solution by substituting 5 or a number less than 5 into the inequality.

2. Solve $\dfrac{d}{2} > 7$.

$\dfrac{d}{2} > 7$ Write the inequality.

$2\left(\dfrac{d}{2}\right) > 2(7)$ Multiply each side by 2.

$d > 14$ Simplify.

The solution is $d > 14$. You can check this solution by substituting a number greater than 14 into the inequality.

Got it? Do these problems to find out.

Show your work.

a. _____

b. _____

a. $4x < 40$

b. $6 \geq \dfrac{x}{7}$

Multiplication and Division Properties of Inequality, Negative Number

Words   When you multiply or divide each side of an inequality by a negative number, the inequality symbol must be reversed for the inequality to remain true.

Symbols   For all numbers a, b, and c, where $c < 0$,

1. if $a > b$, then $ac < bc$ and $\frac{a}{c} < \frac{b}{c}$.

2. if $a < b$, then $ac > bc$ and $\frac{a}{c} > \frac{b}{c}$.

Examples

$$7 > 1$$

$$-2(7) < -2(1) \quad \text{Reverse the symbols.}$$

$$-14 < -2$$

$$-4 < 16$$

$$\frac{-4}{-4} > \frac{16}{-4}$$

$$1 > -4$$

These properties are also true for $a \geq b$ and $a \leq b$.

STOP and Reflect

What does the inequality $c < 0$ mean? Expain below.

Examples

Tutor

3. Solve $-2g < 10$. Graph the solution set on a number line.

$$-2g < 10 \qquad \text{Write the inequality.}$$

$$\frac{-2g}{-2} > \frac{10}{-2} \qquad \text{Divide each side by } -2 \text{ and reverse the symbol.}$$

$$\qquad\qquad\quad \text{Simplify.}$$

$$g > -5$$

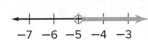

−7 −6 −5 −4 −3

4. Solve $\frac{x}{-3} \leq 4$. Graph the solution set on a number line.

$$\frac{x}{-3} \leq 4 \qquad\qquad \text{Write the inequality.}$$

$$-3\left(\frac{x}{-3}\right) \geq -3(4) \qquad \text{Multiply each side by } -3 \text{ and reverse the symbol.}$$

$$x \geq -12 \qquad\qquad \text{Simplify.}$$

−16   −14   −12   −10   −8   −6

Got it?   Do these problems to find out.

c. $\frac{k}{-2} < 9$

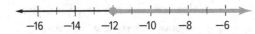

c. _____

 ## Example

 Tutor

5. Ling earns $8 per hour working at the zoo. Write and solve an inequality that can be used to find how many hours she must work in a week to earn at least $120. Interpret the solution.

Words	Amount earned per hour	times	number of hours	is at least	amount earned each week.
Variable	Let x represent the number of hours.				
Inequality	8	•	x	$\geq$	120

$8x \geq 120$ Write the inequality.

$\dfrac{8x}{8} \geq \dfrac{120}{8}$ Divide each side by 8.

$x \geq 15$ Simplify.

So, Ling must work at least 15 hours.

Guided Practice

 Check ✓

Solve each inequality. Graph the solution set on a number line. (Examples 1–4)

1. $-3n \leq -22$ _____

2. $\dfrac{t}{-4} < -11$ _____

3. At a baseball game you can get a single hot dog for $2. You have $10 to spend. Write and solve an inequality to find the number of hot dogs you can buy. Interpret the

solution. (Example 5) _____

4. **Building on the Essential Question** Explain when you should reverse the inequality symbol when solving

an inequality. _____

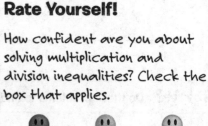

Rate Yourself!

How confident are you about solving multiplication and division inequalities? Check the box that applies.

For more help, go online to access a Personal Tutor.

Independent Practice

Go online for Step-by-Step Solutions

Solve each inequality. (Examples 1 and 2)

1. $6y < 18$ _____

2. $-3s \geq 33$ _____

3 $60 \leq \dfrac{m}{3}$ _____

4. $\dfrac{t}{-2} < 6$ _____

5. $\dfrac{m}{-14} \leq -4$ _____

6. $-56 \leq -8x$ _____

7. $12n \leq 54$ _____

8. $\dfrac{h}{9} > \dfrac{1}{4}$ _____

9. $\dfrac{w}{-5} \geq 9$ _____

Solve each inequality. Graph the solution set on a number line. (Examples 3 and 4)

10. $4x \geq 36$ _____

11 $20 < 5t$ _____

12. $\dfrac{s}{-6} > -16$ _____

13. $\dfrac{x}{-4} \geq 8$ _____

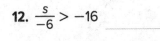

14. A pool charges $4 each visit, or you can buy a membership. Write and solve an inequality to find how many times a person should use the pool so that a membership is less expensive than paying each time. Interpret the solution. (Example 5)

Inequality: _____ Solution: _____

Interpretation: _____

_____

Solving a two-step linear inequality is similar to solving a two-step linear equation.

$$2 - 5x < 17$$
$$\underline{-2 \qquad -2} \qquad \text{Subtract 2 from each side.}$$
$$-5x < 15$$
$$\frac{-5x}{-5} > \frac{15}{-5} \qquad \text{Divide each side by } -5 \text{ and reverse the symbol.}$$
$$x > -3$$

Solve each inequality.

15. $4y - 6 > 12$

16. $-5h + 6 < -14$

17. $3(n - 6) < 18$

H.O.T. Problems Higher Order Thinking

18. **MP** **Identify Structure** Write two different inequalities that have the solution $y > 6$. One inequality should be solved using multiplication properties, and the other should be solved using division properties.

19. **MP** **Persevere with Problems** You score 15, 16, 17, 14, and 19 points out of 20 possible points on five tests. What must you score on the sixth test to have an average of at least 16 points?

20. **MP** **Reason Inductively** The inequalities $3x > 2$ and $9x > 6$ are equivalent inequalities. Write another inequality that is equivalent to $3x > 2$ and $9x > 6$.

21. **MP** **Persevere with Problems** Consider the inequalities $b \geq 4$ and $b \leq 13$.

a. Graph each inequality on the number line.

b. Do the solution sets of the two inequalities overlap? If so, what does this overlapping area represent?

c. A compound inequality is an inequality that combines two inequalities. Write a compound inequality for the situation.

d. Look back at the graph of the solutions for both inequalities. Make another graph that shows only the solution of the compound inequality.

Extra Practice

Solve each inequality.

22. $-10n > -20$ $n < 2$

$$-10n > -20$$
$$\frac{-10n}{-10} < \frac{-20}{-10}$$
$$n < 2$$

Homework Help ➡

23. $-7y < 35$ _____

24. $15 < 3r$ _____

25. $12p \geq -72$ _____

26. $\frac{t}{-7} > 10$ _____

27. $-8 < \frac{y}{5}$ _____

Solve each inequality. Graph the solution set on a number line.

28. $\frac{h}{5} \leq -12$ _____

29. $-3w < -39$ _____

30. $15 < 4x$ _____

31. $10 \leq \frac{t}{-2}$ _____

32. **MP Reason Abstractly** Each game at a carnival costs $0.50, or you can pay $15 and play an unlimited amount of games. Write and solve an inequality to find how many times you should play a game so that the unlimited game play is less expensive than paying each time. Interpret the solution.

Inequality: _____ Solution: _____

Interpretation: _____

Write an inequality for each sentence. Then solve the inequality.

33. The product of a number and 4 is at least -12.

Inequality: _____

Solution: _____

34. Five times a number is less than -45.

Inequality: _____

Solution: _____

35. Caitlin earns $7 per hour babysitting. She wants to earn at least $105 for a camping trip. Determine if each statement is true or false.

a. The inequality $\frac{h}{7} \geq 105$ models how many hours Caitlin must babysit to earn at least $105.

☐ True   ☐ False

b. The inequality $7h \geq 105$ models how many hours Caitlin must babysit to earn at least $105.

☐ True   ☐ False

c. Caitlin must babysit up to 15 hours in order to earn at least $105.

☐ True   ☐ False

36. Soccer balls cost $24 each at Sports Emporium. Coach Neville can spend at most $120 on equipment for the soccer team. Let b represent the number of soccer balls Coach Neville can buy.

Write an inequality to model the situation.

Solve the inequality for b.

Graph the solution on the number line.

How many soccer balls can Coach Neville buy? List all of the possible answers.

Spiral Review

Solve each equation. Check your solution.

37. $5k + 6 = 16$

38. $-14 = 2x - 8$

39. $-4n + 3 = 13$

40. $25 = 7m + 4$

41. $10.5 + h = 22.5$

42. $14n - 32 = 22$

Linear Relationships

 Real-World Link

Music Marcus can download two songs from the Internet each minute. This is shown in the table below.

Time (minutes), x	0	1	2	3	4
Number of Songs, y	0	2	4	6	8

1. Compare the change in the number of songs y to the change in time x. What is the rate of change?

_____

_____

2. Graph the ordered pairs from the table on the graph shown. Label the axes. Then describe the pattern shown on the graph.

_____

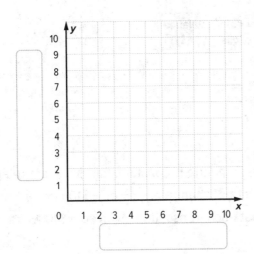

Essential Question

WHAT does it mean to say two quantities are equal or that they have a linear relationship?

 Vocabulary

linear relationship

 Virginia Standards
7.10a

Which **MP** **Mathematical Process Goals** did you use? Shade the circle(s) that applies.

① Mathematical Problem Solving

② Mathematical Communication

③ Mathematical Reasoning

④ Mathematical Connections

⑤ Mathematical Representations

Linear Relationships

Relationships that have straight-line graphs, like the one on the previous page, are called **linear relationships**. Notice that as the number of songs increases by 2, the time in minutes increases by 1.

+2 +2 +2 +2

Number of Songs, y	0	2	4	6	8
Time (minutes), x	0	1	2	3	4

+1 +1 +1 +1

Rate of Change

$\dfrac{2}{1} = 2$ songs per minute

The rate of change between any two points in a linear relationship is the same or *constant*. A linear relationship has a constant rate of change.

Example

Tutor

1. The balance in an account after several transactions is shown. Is the relationship between the balance and number of transactions linear? If so, find the constant rate of change. If not, explain your reasoning.

Show your work.

Number of Transactions	Balance ($)
3	170
6	140
9	110
12	80

+3 (between 3 and 6) −30
+3 (between 6 and 9) −30
+3 (between 9 and 12) −30

As the number of transactions increases by 3, the balance in the account decreases by $30.

Since the rate of change is constant, this is a linear relationship. The constant rate of change is $\dfrac{-30}{3}$ or −$10 per transaction. This means that each transaction involved a $10 *withdrawal*.

Got it? Do these problems to find out.

a. _____

b. _____

a.
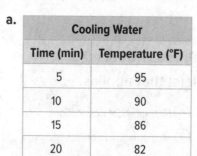

Cooling Water	
Time (min)	Temperature (°F)
5	95
10	90
15	86
20	82

b.
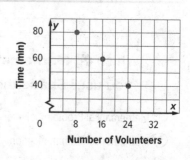

Proportional Linear Relationships

Key Concept

Words	Two quantities a and b have a proportional linear relationship if they have a constant ratio and a constant rate of change.
Symbols	$\frac{b}{a}$ is constant and $\frac{\text{change in } b}{\text{change in } a}$ is constant.

To determine if two quantities are proportional, compare the ratio $\frac{b}{a}$ for several pairs of points to determine if there is a constant ratio.

Example

Watch | Tutor

2. **Use the table to determine if there is a proportional linear relationship between a temperature in degrees Fahrenheit and a temperature in degrees Celsius. Explain your reasoning.**

> **Proportional Relationships**
> Two quantities are proportional if they have a constant ratio.

+5 +5 +5 +5

Degrees Celsius	0	5	10	15	20
Degrees Fahrenheit	32	41	50	59	68

+9 +9 +9 +9

Constant Rate of Change

$\frac{\text{change in } °F}{\text{change in } °C} = \frac{9}{5}$

Since the rate of change is constant, this is a linear relationship.

To determine if the two scales are proportional, express the relationship between the degrees for several columns as a ratio.

$\frac{\text{degrees Fahrenheit}}{\text{degrees Celsius}} \longrightarrow \frac{41}{5} = 8.2 \qquad \frac{50}{10} = 5 \qquad \frac{59}{15} \approx 3.9$

Since the ratios are not the same, the relationship between degrees Fahrenheit degrees Celsius is *not* proportional.

Check: Graph the points on the coordinate plane. Then connect them with a line.

The points appear to fall in a straight line so the relationship is linear. ✔

The line connecting the points does not pass through the origin so the relationship is not proportional. ✔

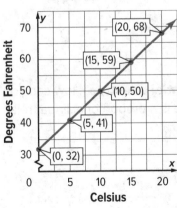

Got it? Do this problem to find out.

c. _____

c. Use the table to determine if there is a proportional linear relationship between mass of an object in kilograms and the weight of the object in pounds. Explain your reasoning.

Weight (lb)	20	40	60	80
Mass (kg)	9	18	27	36

Guided Practice

Check ✓

1. The amount of paint y needed to paint a certain amount of chairs x is shown in the table. Is the relationship between the two quantities linear? If so, find the constant rate of change. If not, explain your reasoning. (Example 1)

_____

_____

_____

Paint Needed for Chairs

Chairs, x	Cans of Paint, y
5	6
10	12
15	18

2. The altitude y of a certain airplane after a certain number of minutes x is shown in the graph. Is the relationship linear? If so, find the constant rate of change. If not, explain your reasoning. (Example 1)

_____

_____

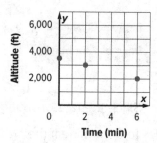

3. Determine whether a proportional relationship exists between the two quantities shown in Exercise 1. Explain your reasoning. (Example 2)

_____

_____

_____

4. **ⓔ Building on the Essential Question** How can you use a table to determine if there is a proportional linear relationship between two quantities?

_____

_____

_____

Rate Yourself!

Are you ready to move on?
Shade the section that applies.

YES ? NO

For more help, go online to access a Personal Tutor.

Tutor

Independent Practice

Determine whether the relationship between the two quantities shown in each table or graph is linear. If so, find the constant rate of change. If not, explain your reasoning. (Example 1)

1.

Cost of Electricity to Run Personal Computer	
Time (h)	Cost (¢)
5	15
8	24
12	36
24	72

Show your work.

_____

_____

2.

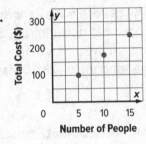

Distance Traveled by Falling Object				
Time (s)	1	2	3	4
Distance (m)	4.9	19.6	44.1	78.4

_____

_____

_____

3.

Italian Dressing Recipe				
Oil (c)	2	4	6	8
Vinegar (c)	$\frac{3}{4}$	$1\frac{1}{2}$	$2\frac{1}{4}$	3

_____

_____

_____

4.

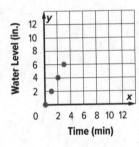

_____

_____

_____

5.

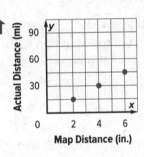

_____

_____

_____

6.

_____

_____

_____

Determine whether a proportional relationship exists between the two quantities shown in the following Exercises. Explain your reasoning. (Example 2)

7. Exercise 1

_____

_____

_____

8. Exercise 3

_____

_____

_____

9. Exercise 5

_____

_____

_____

10. **Use Math Tools** Match each table with its rate of change.

2.4 ft/min

Time (minutes)	20	30	40
Altitude (feet)	170	162	154

10 ft/min

Time (minutes)	1	2	3
Distance (feet)	20	30	40

−0.8 ft/min

Time (minutes)	4	6	8
Height (feet)	1	1.5	2

0.25 ft/min

Time (minutes)	5	10	15
Depth (feet)	12	24	36

H.O.T. Problems Higher Order Thinking

11. **MP Persevere with Problems** A dog starts walking, slows down, and then sits down to rest. Sketch a graph of the situation to represent the different rates of change. Label the *x*-axis "Time" and the *y*-axis "Distance".

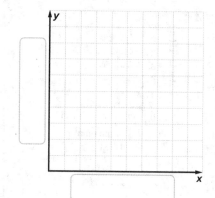

12. **MP Model with Mathematics** Describe a situation with two quantities that have a proportional linear relationship.

_____

_____

_____

13. **MP Justify Conclusions** Each table shows a relationship with a constant rate of change. Is each relationship proportional? Justify your reasoning.

a.
Cost of Play Tickets ($)			
t	1	2	3	4
c	3.50	4.00	4.50	5.00

b.
Cost of Play Tickets ($)			
t	1	2	3	4
c	2.50	5.00	7.50	10.00

_____

_____

_____

Extra Practice

Determine whether the relationship between the two quantities shown in each table is linear. If so, find the constant rate of change. If not, explain your reasoning.

14.

Sale Price Comparison	
Retail Price ($)	Sale Price ($)
0	0
10	5
20	10
30	15
40	20
50	25
60	30

+10 / +5

Yes; the rate of change between the sale price and retail price is a constant value of $\frac{1}{2}$.

15.

Total Number of Customers Helped at Jewelry Store	
Time (h)	Total Helped
1	12
2	24
3	36
4	60

_____

_____

_____

16. Determine whether a proportional relationship exists between the two quantities in Exercise 14. Explain your reasoning. _____

_____

_____

MP Reason Abstractly Find the constant rate of change for each graph and interpret its meaning.

17.

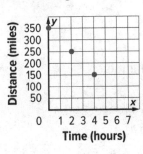

Time (hours)

18.

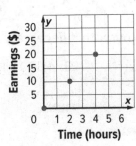

Time (hours)

19.

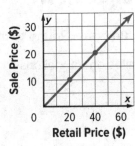

Retail Price ($)

20. The table shows the amount of money in Will's savings account. Graph the points on the coordinate plane and connect them with a straight line.

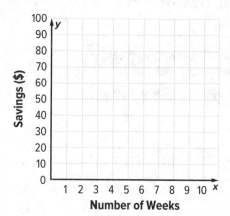

Week	Savings ($)
1	40
2	55
3	70
4	85
5	100

What is the constant rate of change?

21. The graph shows the distance Bianca traveled on her 2-hour bike ride. Determine if each statement is true or false.

a. She traveled at a constant speed of 12 miles per hour for the entire ride. ☐ True ☐ False

b. She traveled at a constant speed of 12 miles per hour for the first hour. ☐ True ☐ False

c. She traveled at a constant speed of 4 miles per hour for the last hour. ☐ True ☐ False

Spiral Review

Find the unit rate. Round to the nearest hundredth if necessary.

22. 60 miles on 2.5 gallons _____

23. 4,500 kilobytes in 6 minutes _____

24. 10 red peppers for $5.50 _____

25. 72.6 meters in 11 seconds _____

Inquiry HOW can you use a graphing calculator to determine the rate of change?

At the school store, tickets to the football game are sold for $5 each. The equation $y = 5x$ can be used to find the total cost y of any number of tickets x. Find the rate of change.

What do you know? _____

What do you need to find? _____

Hands-On Activity

Recall that a rate of change is a rate that describes how one quantity changes in relation to another.

Step 1 Enter the equation. Press $\boxed{Y=}$ 5 $\boxed{X,T,\theta,n}$.

Step 2 Graph the equation in the standard viewing window. Press $\boxed{Zoom}$ 6.

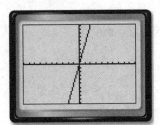

Step 3 Press $\boxed{2nd}$ $\boxed{TblSet}$ $\boxed{\blacktriangledown}$ $\boxed{\blacktriangledown}$ $\boxed{ENTER}$ $\boxed{\blacktriangledown}$ $\boxed{ENTER}$ to generate the table automatically. Press $\boxed{2nd}$ $\boxed{Table}$ to access the table. Choose any two points on the line and find the rate of change.

$$\frac{\text{change in total cost}}{\text{change in number of tickets}} = \frac{\$\left(\boxed{} - \boxed{}\right)}{\left(\boxed{} - \boxed{}\right) \text{ tickets}}$$

$$= \frac{\boxed{}}{\boxed{} \text{ ticket}}$$

So, the rate of change, or unit rate, is _____ .

Investigate

Work with a partner. School T-shirts are sold for $10 each and packages of markers are sold for $2.50 each.

1. For each item, write an equation that can be used to find the

   total cost *y* of *x* items. _____

2. Graph the equations in the same window as the equation from the Activity. Copy your calculator screen on the blank screen shown.

Analyze and Reflect

3. Refer to Exercises 1 and 2. Find each rate of change. Is there a relationship between the steepness of the lines on the graph and the rates of change?

   Explain. _____

   _____

   _____

   _____

Create

4. **MP Reason Inductively** Without graphing, write the equation of a line that is steeper than $y = \frac{1}{3}x$. Explain your reasoning.

   _____

   _____

5. **inquiry** HOW can you use a graphing calculator to determine the rate of change?

   _____

   _____

   _____

Using Slope

Vocabulary Start-Up

Recall that the **slope** of a line is the ratio of the **rise,** or the change in *y*, to the **run,** or the change in *x*.

Complete the graphic organizer.

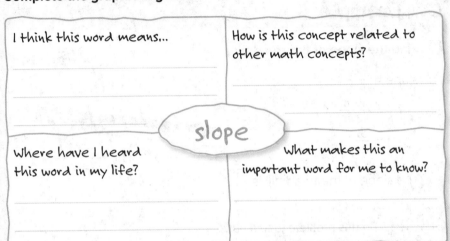

I think this word means...

How is this concept related to other math concepts?

slope

Where have I heard this word in my life?

What makes this an important word for me to know?

 Essential Question

WHAT does it mean to say two quantities are equal or that they have a linear relationship?

Virginia Standards
7.10a

Real-World Link

A ride at an amusement park rises 8 feet every horizontal change of 2 feet. How could you determine the slope of the ride?

Which **MP** **Mathematical Process Goals** did you use? Shade the circle(s) that applies.

① Mathematical Problem Solving
② Mathematical Communication
③ Mathematical Reasoning
④ Mathematical Connections
⑤ Mathematical Representations

Find Slope Using a Graph or Table

Slope is a rate of change. It can be positive (slanting upward) or negative (slanting downward).

$$slope = \frac{rise}{run}$$ ← vertical change between any two points
← horizontal change between the same two points

Example

1. **Find the slope of the treadmill.**

$slope = \frac{rise}{run}$ Definition of slope

$= \frac{10 \text{ in.}}{48 \text{ in.}}$ rise = 10 in., run = 48 in.

$= \frac{5}{24}$ Simplify.

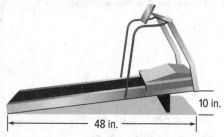

10 in.

48 in.

The slope of the treadmill is $\frac{5}{24}$.

 Show your work.

Got it? Do this problem to find out.

a. A hiking trail rises 6 feet for every horizontal change of 100 feet. What is the slope of the hiking trail?

a. _____

Examples

Tutor

Translating Rise and Run

up	→ positive
down	→ negative
right	→ positive
left	→ negative

2. **The graph shows the cost of muffins at a bake sale. Find the slope of the line.**

Choose two points on the line. The vertical change is 2 units and the horizontal change is 1 unit.

$slope = \frac{rise}{run}$ Definition of slope

$= \frac{2}{1}$ rise = 2, run = 1

The slope of the line is $\frac{2}{1}$ or 2.

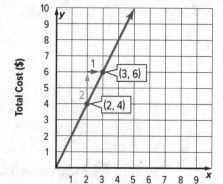

Total Cost ($)

Muffins Purchased

(3, 6)

(2, 4)

3. The table shows the number of pages Garrett has left to read after a certain number of minutes. The points lie on a line. Find the slope of the line.

Time (min), x	Pages left, y
1	12
3	9
5	6
7	3

Choose any two points from the table to find the changes in the x- and y-values.

$\text{slope} = \dfrac{\text{change in } y}{\text{change in } x}$ Definition of slope

$= \dfrac{9 - 12}{3 - 1}$ Use the points (1, 12) and (3, 9).

$= \dfrac{-3}{2} \text{ or } -\dfrac{3}{2}$ Simplify.

To check, choose two different points from the table and find the slope.

Check $\text{slope} = \dfrac{\text{change in } y}{\text{change in } x}$

$= \dfrac{3 - 6}{7 - 5}$

$= \dfrac{-3}{2} \text{ or } -\dfrac{3}{2}$ ✓

> **Slope**
>
> In linear relationships, no matter which two points you choose, the slope, or rate of change, of the line is always constant.

> Show your work.

Got it? Do these problems to find out.

Find the slope of each line.

b.

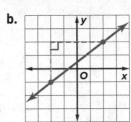

c.

x	−6	−2	2	6
y	−2	−1	0	1

b. _____

c. _____

Slope Formula

Key Concept

Words	The slope m of a line passing through points (x_1, y_1) and (x_2, y_2) is the ratio of the difference in the y-coordinates to the corresponding difference in the x-coordinates.
Model	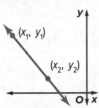
Symbols	$m = \dfrac{y_2 - y_1}{x_2 - x_1}$, where $x_2 \neq x_1$

It does not matter which point you define as (x_1, y_1) and (x_2, y_2).
However the coordinates of both points must be used in the same order.

Using the Slope Formula

To check Example 4, let $(x_1, y_1) = (-4, 3)$ and $(x_2, y_2) = (1, 2)$. Then find the slope.

d. _____

e. _____

Example

4. Find the slope of the line that passes through $R(1, 2)$, $S(-4, 3)$.

$m = \dfrac{y_2 - y_1}{x_2 - x_1}$ Slope formula

$m = \dfrac{3 - 2}{-4 - 1}$ $(x_1, y_1) = (1, 2)$
               $(x_2, y_2) = (-4, 3)$

$m = \dfrac{1}{-5}$ or $-\dfrac{1}{5}$ Simplify.

Got it? Do these problems to find out.

d. $A(2, 2)$, $B(5, 3)$ **e.** $J(-7, -4)$, $K(-3, -2)$

Guided Practice

Check ✓

1. Find the slope of the storage shed's roof. (Example 1)

_____

3 ft | 15 ft

Find the slope of each line. (Examples 2 and 3)

2. 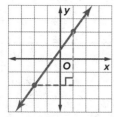 _____

3.

x	0	1	2	3
y	1	3	5	7

_____

Find the slope of the line that passes through each pair of points. (Example 4)

4. $A(-3, -2)$, $B(5, 4)$ _____

5. $E(-6, 5)$, $F(3, -3)$ _____

6. **Building on the Essential Question** In any linear relationship, explain why the slope is always the same.

_____

_____

Rate Yourself!

How well do you understand slope? Circle the image that applies.

Clear   Somewhat Clear   Not So Clear

For more help, go online to access a Personal Tutor. Tutor

Independent Practice

 Go online for Step-by-Step Solutions

1 Find the slope of a ski run that descends 15 feet for every horizontal change of 24 feet. (Example 1)

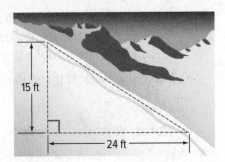

15 ft

24 ft

_____

Find the slope of each line. (Example 2)

2.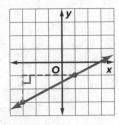

3.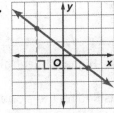

The points given in the table lie on a line. Find the slope of each line.

(Example 3)

4.

x	0	2	4	6
y	9	4	−1	−6

5.

x	0	1	2	3
y	3	5	7	9

Find the slope of the line that passes through each pair of points. (Example 4)

6. A(0, 1), B(2, 7) _____

7 C(2, 5), D(3, 1) _____

8. E(1, 2), F(4, 7) _____

9. **MP** **Justify Conclusions** Wheelchair ramps for access to public buildings are allowed a maximum of one inch of vertical increase for every one foot of horizontal distance. Would a ramp that is 10 feet long and 8 inches tall meet this guideline? Explain your reasoning to a classmate.

_____

_____

10. **MP** **Multiple Representations** For working 3 hours, Sofia earns $30.60. For working 5 hours, she earns $51. For working 6 hours, she earns $61.20.

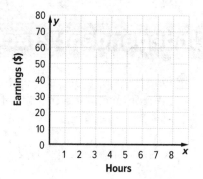

a. **Graphs** Graph the information with hours on the horizontal axis and money earned on the vertical axis. Draw a line through the points.

b. **Numbers** What is the slope of the line?

_____

c. **Words** What does the slope of the line represent?

How does the slope relate to the unit rate? _____

_____

H.O.T. Problems Higher Order Thinking

11. **MP** **Find the Error** Jacob is finding the slope of the line that passes through $X(0, 2)$ and $Y(4, 3)$. Circle his mistake and correct it.

_____

_____

_____

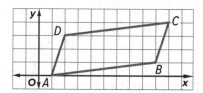

12. **MP** **Persevere with Problems** Two lines that are parallel have the same slope. Determine whether quadrilateral $ABCD$ is a parallelogram. Justify your reasoning.

_____

_____

_____

_____

_____

13. **MP** **Model with Mathematics** Give three points that lie on a line with each of the following slopes.

a. 5 _____

b. $\frac{1}{5}$ _____

c. -5 _____

Extra Practice

14. Find the slope of a road that rises 12 feet for every horizontal change of 100 feet.

$\dfrac{3}{25}$

15. Wyatt is flying a kite in the park. The kite is a horizontal distance of 24 feet from Wyatt's position and a vertical distance of 72 feet.

Find the slope of the kite string. _____

 Homework Help

$\text{slope} = \dfrac{\text{rise}}{\text{run}}$ Definition of slope

$= \dfrac{12 \text{ ft}}{100 \text{ ft}}$ rise = 12 ft, run = 100 ft

$= \dfrac{3}{25}$ Simplify.

Find the slope of each line.

16.

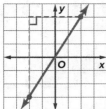

17.

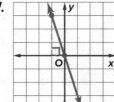

MP Use Math Tools The points given in the table lie on a line. Find the slope of each line.

18.

x	−3	3	9	15
y	−3	1	5	9

19.

x	−2	−1	1	2
y	−4	−2	2	4

Find the slope of the line that passes through each pair of points.

20. $M(-2, 3), N(7, -4)$ _____

21. $G(-6, -1), H(4, 1)$ _____

22. $J(-9, 3), K(2, 1)$ _____

23. Line *AB* represents a steep hill.

The coordinates of point *A* are [　　　] and the coordinates of point *B* are [　　　]. The slope of the hill is [　　　].

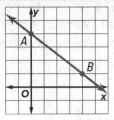

24. Lionel charted the growth of his puppy for several weeks and plotted the values on a graph. Draw a line that passes through the points (2, 4) and (10, 20).

What is the slope of the line? What does this slope represent?

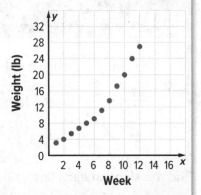

Spiral Review

25. The wait time to ride the Thunder boats is 30 minutes when 180 people are in line. Write and solve a proportion to find the wait time when 240 people are in line.

Solve each proportion.

26. $\dfrac{5}{7} = \dfrac{a}{35}$

27. $\dfrac{12}{p} = \dfrac{36}{45}$

28. $\dfrac{3}{9} = \dfrac{21}{k}$

29. $\dfrac{n}{15} = \dfrac{17}{34}$

30. $\dfrac{-7}{10} = \dfrac{3.5}{j}$

31. $\dfrac{12}{18} = \dfrac{-40}{x}$

Slope-Intercept Form

 Real-World Link Watch

Football An interception in football is when a defensive player catches a pass made by an offensive player.

In a nonproportional linear relationship, the graph passes through the point (0, *b*) or the *y*-intercept. The **y-intercept** of a line is the *y*-coordinate of the point where the line crosses the *y*-axis.

Complete the steps to derive the equation for a nonproportional linear relationship by using the slope formula.

$$\frac{\boxed{}}{\boxed{}} = \boxed{}$$ Slope formula

$(x_1, y_1) = (0, b)$

$\dfrac{y - b}{x - 0} = m$ $(x_2, y_2) = (x, y)$

$\dfrac{\boxed{}}{\boxed{}} = m$ Simplify.

$y - b = \boxed{} \cdot \boxed{}$ Multiplication Property of Equality

$y = \boxed{} + \boxed{}$ Addition Property of Equality

slope ⟶   ⟵ **y-intercept**

$$y = mx + b$$

Graph: y-axis and x-axis with line passing through (0, b) and (x, y); origin (0, 0).

How can knowing about an interception in football help you remember the definition of *y*-intercept?

_____

_____

Copyright © McGraw-Hill Education   PCN Photography/Alamy

Essential Question

WHAT does it mean to say two quantities are equal or that they have a linear relationship?

Vocabulary

y-intercept
slope-intercept form

Virginia Standards
7.10b, c, d

I got it!

Which ⓂⓅ **Mathematical Process Goals** did you use? Shade the circle(s) that applies.

① Mathematical Problem Solving   ④ Mathematical Connections

② Mathematical Communication   ⑤ Mathematical Representations

③ Mathematical Reasoning

Slope-Intercept Form of a Line

Nonproportional linear relationships can be written in the form $y = mx + b$. This is called the **slope-intercept form**. When an equation is written in this form, m is the slope and b is the y-intercept.

Examples

1. State the slope and the y-intercept of the graph of the equation $y = \frac{2}{3}x - 4$.

$y = \frac{2}{3}x + (-4)$ Write the equation in the form $y = mx + b$.

$y = mx + b$ $m = \frac{2}{3}, b = -4$

The slope of the graph is $\frac{2}{3}$, and the y-intercept is -4.

a. _____

b. _____

c. _____

Got it? Do these problems to find out.

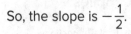

a. $y = -5x$ **b.** $y = \frac{1}{4}x - 6$ **c.** $y = -x + 5$

Examples

2. Write an equation of a line in slope-intercept form with a slope of -3 and a y-intercept of 0.

$y = mx + b$ Slope-intercept form

$y = -3x + 0$ Replace m with -3 and y with 0.

$y = -3x$ Simplify.

3. Write an equation in slope-intercept form for the graph shown.

The y-intercept is 4. From (0, 4), you move down 1 unit and right 2 units to another point on the line.

So, the slope is $-\frac{1}{2}$.

$y = mx + b$ Slope-intercept form

$y = -\frac{1}{2}x + 4$ Replace m with $-\frac{1}{2}$ and b with 4.

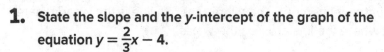

Got it? Do these problems to find out.

d. Write an equation in slope-intercept form for the graph shown.

e. Write an equation of a line in slope-intercept form with a slope of $\frac{3}{4}$ and a *y*-intercept of −3.

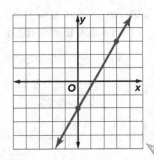

Show your work.

d. _____

e. _____

Interpret the *y*-Intercept

When an equation in slope-intercept form applies to a real-world situation, the slope represents the rate of change and the *y*-intercept represents the initial value.

Examples

Watch ▷   Tutor 💬

4. Student Council is selling T-shirts during spirit week. It costs $20 for the design and $5 to print each shirt. The cost *y* to print *x* shirts is given by $y = 5x + 20$. Graph $y = 5x + 20$ using the slope and *y*-intercept.

Step 1 Find the slope and *y*-intercept.
$y = 5x + 20$ slope = 5
   y-intercept = 20

Step 2 Graph the *y*-intercept (0, 20).

Step 3 Write the slope 5 as $\frac{5}{1}$. Use it to locate a second point on the line. Go up 5 units and right 1 unit. Then draw a line through the points.

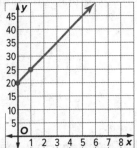

5. Interpret the slope and the *y*-intercept.

The slope 5 represents the cost in dollars per T-shirt. The *y*-intercept 20 is the one-time charge in dollars for the design.

Got it? Do these problems to find out.

A taxi fare y can be determined by the equation $y = 0.50x + 3.50$, where x is the number of miles traveled.

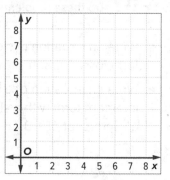

    f. Graph the equation.

    g. Interpret the slope and the y-intercept.

9. _____

Guided Practice

1. Liam is reading a 254-page book for school. He can read 40 pages in one hour. The equation for the number of pages he has left to read is $y = 254 - 40x$, where x is the number of hours he reads. (Examples 1, 4, and 5)

   a. State the slope and the y-intercept of the graph of

      the equation. _____

    b. Graph the equation.

   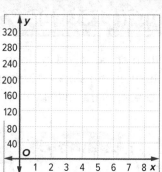

   c. Interpret what the slope and the y-intercept represent.

   _____

   _____

2. Write an equation in slope intercept form for the graph shown.

   (Examples 2 and 3) _____

   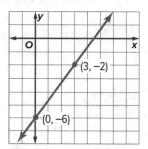

3. 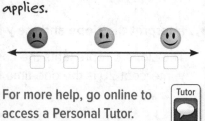 **Building on the Essential Question** How does the y-intercept appear in these three representations: table, equation, and graph? _____

   _____

   _____

   _____

   _____

Rate Yourself!

How confident are you about equations in slope-intercept form? Check the box that applies.

For more help, go online to access a Personal Tutor.

Name _____ My Homework _____

State the slope and the *y*-intercept for the graph of each equation.
(Example 1)

1. $y = 3x + 4$ _____

2. $y = -\dfrac{3}{7}x$ _____

3. $3x + y = -4$ _____

Show your work.

Write an equation of a line in slope-intercept form with the given slope and *y*-intercept. (Example 2)

4. slope: $-\dfrac{3}{4}$, *y*-intercept: 0 _____

 slope: $\dfrac{5}{6}$, *y*-intercept: 8 _____

Write an equation in slope-intercept form for each graph shown. (Example 3)

6. 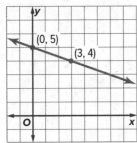 _____

7. 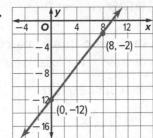 _____

8. Carson's grandma opens a savings account with $25 for Carson. Each week Carson adds $1 to the account. The amount *y* in Carson's savings account after *x* weeks is given by the equation $y = x + 25$. (Examples 4 and 5)

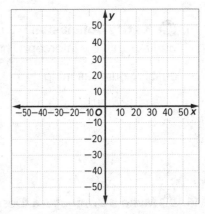

  a. Find the slope and the *y*-intercept. _____

  b. Graph the equation.

  c. Interpret the slope and *y*-intercept. _____

Copy and Solve. Graph each equation on a separate piece of grid paper.

9. $y = \dfrac{1}{3}x - 5$

10. $y = -x + \dfrac{3}{2}$

11 $y = -\dfrac{4}{3}x + 1$

12. **MP Model with Mathematics** Refer to the graphic novel frame below for Exercises a–b.

a. Write an equation in slope-intercept form for the total cost of any number of tickets at 7 tickets for $5. _____

b. Write an equation in slope-intercept form for the total cost of a wristband for all you can ride. _____

 ## H.O.T. Problems Higher Order Thinking

13. **MP Persevere with Problems** The x-intercept is the x-coordinate of the point where a graph crosses the x-axis. What is the slope of a line that has a y-intercept but no x-intercept? Explain. _____

14. **MP Reason Abstractly** Write an equation of a line that does not have a y-intercept. _____

15. **MP Justify Conclusions** Suppose the graph of a line has a negative slope and a positive y-intercept. Through which quadrants does the line pass? Justify your reasoning. _____

16. **MP Make a Conjecture** Describe what happens to the graph of $y = 3x + 4$ when the slope is changed to $\frac{1}{3}$. _____

Extra Practice

State the slope and the y-intercept for the graph of each equation.

17. $y = -5x + 2$ _-5; 2_

In the equation, $m = -5$ and $b = 2$ so the slope is -5 and the y-intercept is 2.

18. $y = \frac{1}{2}x$ _____

19. $y - 2x = 8$ _____

Write an equation of a line in slope-intercept form with the given slope and y-intercept.

20. slope: $-\frac{1}{4}$; y-intercept: 0

21. slope: -2; y-intercept: 3

22. slope: $-\frac{3}{5}$; y-intercept: $-\frac{1}{5}$

23. **MP Persevere with Problems** The equation $y = 15x + 37$ can be used to approximate the temperature y in degrees Fahrenheit based on the number of chirps x a cricket makes in 15 seconds. Graph the equation to estimate the number of chirps a cricket will make in 15 seconds if the temperature is 80°F.

_____

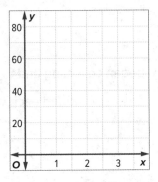

24. The Lakeside Marina charges a $35 rental fee for a boat in addition to charging $15 an hour for usage. The total cost y of renting a boat for x hours can be represented by the equation $y = 15x + 35$.

a. Graph the equation.

b. Interpret the slope and the y-intercept.

_____

_____

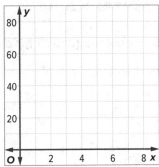

25. Write an equation in slope-intercept form for the table shown.

Number of Pizza Toppings	0	1	2	3	4
Cost ($)	9	10	11	12	13

_____

26. The table shows Mr. Blackwell's total earnings as a car salesman for different sale amounts.

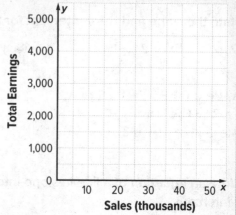

Sales (thousands), x	$10	$20	$30
Total Earnings, y	$1,750	$3,000	$4,250

Graph the points on the coordinate plane and connect them with a straight line.

Write an equation in slope-intercept form to represent the relationship.

27. Jaquie has 20 postcards in her collection. Each time she goes on vacation she buys 8 postcards to add to the collection. The total number of postcards y can be represented by the equation y = 8x + 20. Complete the following statements regarding the line.

The slope of the line is [ ] and the y-intercept is

[ ] .

The [ ] represents the number of postcards when she began collecting and the [ ] represents the number of postcards added each vacation.

Spiral Review

Solve each equation for d when c = 0.

28. 10c + 4d = 40

29. −5d = 2c + 10

30. −4c − 6d = 24

Determine whether each linear relationship is proportional. If so, state the constant of proportionality.

31.

Pictures, x	5	6	7	8
Profit, y	20	24	28	32

32.

Price, x	10	15	20	25
Tax, y	0.70	1.05	1.40	1.75

Inquiry HOW does graphing slope triangles on the coordinate plane help you analyze them?

Donte ordered the plans shown to build a skateboard ramp. Each unit represents one foot. He wants to keep the same slope of the ramp and extend the base of the triangle three feet. How tall will the ramp be?

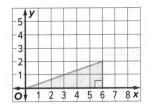

Hands-On Activity

Refer to the graph shown above. Triangle *ABC* is formed by the rise, run, and section of the line $y = \frac{1}{3}x$ between points *A* and *B*.

Step 1 Graph $y = \frac{1}{3}x$ on the grid paper.
Draw a right triangle using the points *A*(0, 0) and *B*(6, 2). Label the third point *C*.

What is the slope of $\overline{AB}$?

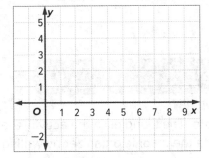

Step 2 Select any two different points on the line. Label them *D* and *E*. Draw another triangle from these two points.

Is the slope of $\overline{DE}$ the same as the slope of $\overline{AB}$? Explain.

_____

_____

Step 3 Donte wants to expand the base of the ramp 3 feet. Graph and give the coordinates of the point that will represent the extended base of the ramp. _____

Create a right triangle using the line and that point. What will be the height of the new ramp? _____

Investigate

Collaborate

Work with a partner. Draw two right triangles for each exercise using the rise, run, and portions of the line.

1. $y = -x + 2$

Show your work.

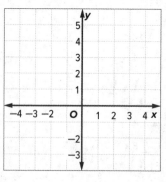

2. $y = x + 1$

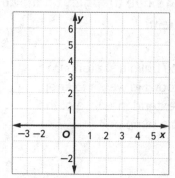

Analyze and Reflect

Collaborate

3. MP **Make a Conjecture** What do you notice about the shape and size of the pair of triangles in Exercises 1 and 2? _____

_____

Create

On Your Own

4. MP **Use Math Tools** The triangles in the activity are called *slope triangles*. Complete the graphic organizer by writing three observations about slope triangles.

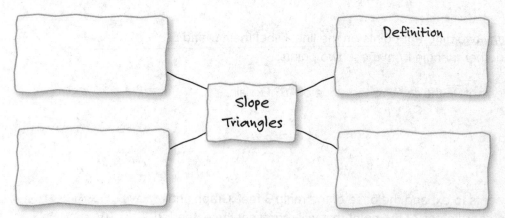

5. inquiry HOW does graphing slope triangles on the coordinate plane help you analyze them?

_____

_____

21ST CENTURY CAREER
in Veterinary Medicine

Veterinary Technician

If you love being around animals, enjoy working with your hands, and are good at analyzing problems, a challenging career in veterinary medicine might be a perfect fit for you. Veterinary technicians help veterinarians by helping to diagnose and treat medical conditions. They may work in private clinics, animal hospitals, zoos, aquariums, or wildlife rehabilitation centers.

College & Career
R E A D I N E S S

Is This the Career for You?

Are you interested in a career as a veterinary technician? Take some of the following courses in high school.

◆ Algebra
◆ Animal Science
◆ Biology
◆ Chemistry
◆ Veterinary Assisting

Find out how math relates to a career in Veterinary Medicine.

MP Vet Techs Don't Monkey Around

For each problem, use the information in the tables to write an equation. Then solve the equation.

1. The minimum tail length of an emperor tamarin is 1.6 inches greater than that of a golden lion tamarin. What is the minimum tail length of a golden lion tamarin?

2. The minimum body length of a golden lion tamarin is 5.3 inches less than the maximum body length. What is the maximum body length?

3. Tamarins live an average of 15 years. This is 13 years less than the years that one tamarin in captivity lived. How long did the tamarin in captivity live?

4. The maximum weight of a golden lion tamarin is about 1.97 times the maximum weight of an emperor tamarin. What is the maximum weight of an emperor tamarin? Round to the nearest tenth.

5. For an emperor tamarin, the maximum total length, including the body and tail, is 27 inches. What is the maximum body length of an emperor tamarin?

Golden Lion Tamarin Monkeys

Measure	Minimum	Maximum
Body length	7.9 in.	ℓ
Tail length	t	15.7 in.
Weight	12.7 oz	28 oz

Emperor Tamarin Monkeys

Measure	Minimum	Maximum
Body length	9.2 in.	b
Tail length	14 in.	16.6 in.
Weight	10.7 oz	w

MP Career Project

It's time to update your career portfolio! Go to the Occupational Outlook Handbook online and research a career as a veterinary technician. Include brief descriptions of the work environment, education and training requirements, and the job outlook.

Do you think you would enjoy a career as a veterinary technician? Why or why not?

-
-
-
-
-

Vocabulary Check

Unscramble each of the clue words.

TOW-SETP

☐☐☐☐ — ☐☐☐☐
7

PYORERPT

☐☐☐☐☐☐☐☐
       8

DODTIINA

☐☐☐☐☐☐☐☐
   6

NIIOSDIV

☐☐☐☐☐☐☐☐

LABVIERA

☐☐☐☐☐☐☐☐
     5

AILEYQUITN

☐☐☐☐☐☐☐☐☐☐
  2

BISTAUTORNC

☐☐☐☐☐☐☐☐☐☐☐
  3

ARNLEI

☐☐☐☐☐☐
1

TIULINTICPOLMA

☐☐☐☐☐☐☐☐☐☐☐☐☐☐
       4

Use the numbered letters to find another vocabulary term from this chapter.

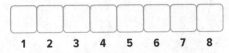

☐☐☐☐☐☐☐☐
1 2 3 4 5 6 7 8

Use Your FOLDABLES

Use your Foldable to help review the chapter.

Tape here

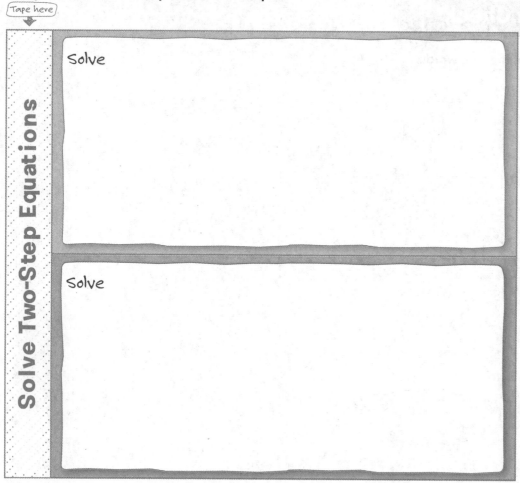

Solve Two-Step Equations

Solve

Solve

Got it?

Match each phrase with the correct term.

1. the value of a variable that makes an equation true

2. the numerical factor in a multiplication expression

3. equations that have the same solution

4. a sentence stating that two quantities are equal

a. equivalent equations

b. equation

c. Addition Property of Equality

d. coefficient

e. formula

f. solution

Fall Reading

Gordon's English teacher assigned a book to be read by October 31st. The students may select a book from the table, and Gordon chose *City Streets*.

Book	Number of Pages
City Streets	387
Life and Time	411
Myopia	435

Write your answers on another piece of paper. Show all of your work to receive full credit.

Part A

By October 19th, Gordon had read 35 pages. Starting on October 20th, he decides to read the same number of pages each day until he finishes the book on October 30th. Write and solve an equation to represent the situation. Let p represent the number of pages read per day. How many pages does Gordon read per day?

Part B

Gordon's friend, Kendrick, selected *Myopia*. He read eight pages in class on October 19th and begins reading again on October 23rd. He needs to read at least 350 pages by the end of the day on October 28th. Write and solve an inequality to represent this situation and graph the solution on a number line. Let p represent the number of pages read per day. How many pages must Kendrick read per day to accomplish his goal?

Reflect

 Answering the Essential Question

Use what you learned about equations and inequalities to complete the graphic organizer.

When do you use an equals sign?

Essential Question

WHAT does it mean to say two quantities are equal or that they have a linear relationship?

How do you know that two quantities have a linear relationship?

Answer the Essential Question. WHAT does it mean to say two quantities are equal or that they have a linear relationship?

Chapter 6
Measure Figures

Copyright © McGraw-Hill Education · Image Source/Getty Images

Essential Question

How do measurements help you describe real-world objects?

 Virginia Standards
7.4a, b; 7.5; 7.6a, b; 7.7

 ## Math in the Real World

Soccer is a sport that is played on a rectangular field. The dimensions of a regulation size soccer field are 100 yards long and 60 yards wide.

What is the area of the soccer field shown?

$A =$ _____ square yards

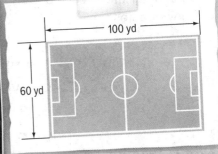

FOLDABLES
Study Organizer

1 Cut out the Foldable in the back of the book.

2 Place your Foldable on page 598.

3 Use the Foldable throughout this chapter to help you learn about measuring figures.

Vocabulary

composite figure	lateral area	surface area
composite solids	polyhedron	total surface area
cylinder	scale factor	volume
dilation	similar	
indirect measurement	similar polygons	

Study Skill: Studying Math

Power Notes *Power notes* are similar to lesson outlines, but they are simpler to organize. Power notes use the numbers 1, 2, 3, and so on. You can have more than one detail under each power. You can even add drawings or examples to your power notes.

Power 1: This is the main idea.

　　　Power 2: This provides details about the main idea.

　　　　　Power 3: This provides details about Power 2.

　　　　　　　and so on...

Complete the following sample of power notes for this chapter.

1: Circles

　2: Circumference

　　3: _____

　　3: _____

　2: Area

　　3: _____

What Do You Already Know?

Place a checkmark below the face that expresses how much you know about each concept. Then scan the chapter to find a definition or example of it.

😠 I have no clue.　😐 I've heard of it.　😊 I know it!

Integers				
Concept	😠	😐	😊	Definition or Example
area of composite figures				
indirect measurement				
scale factor				
similar polygons				
total surface area				
volume				

When Will You Use This?

Here are a few examples of how volume and surface area are used in the real world.

Activity 1 When wrapping a present, how do you determine how much paper to use? Describe a method that you could use to make sure that you cut the right size piece of wrapping paper.

_____

_____

Activity 2 Go online at **connectED.mcgraw-hill.com** to read the graphic novel **The Dunk Tank**. How many square feet of metal sheeting do they have to build the dunk tank?

_____

Caitlyn, Dario, and Hannah in

The Dunk Tank

The school carnival is coming up soon. It's our job to design a dunk tank.

Are You Ready?

Try the Quick Check below.
Or, take the Online Readiness Quiz.

Check ✓

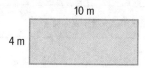
Quick Review

Example 1

Find the area of the rectangle.

10 m

4 m

$A = \ell w$ Area of a rectangle

$A = (10)(4)$ Replace ℓ with 10 and w with 4.

$A = 40$ Simplify.

The area of the rectangle is 40 square meters.

Example 2

Find the area of the triangle.

13 in.
5 in.
12 in.

$A = \frac{1}{2}bh$ Area of a triangle

$A = \frac{1}{2}(12)(5)$ Replace b with 12 and h with 5.

$A = \frac{1}{2}(60)$ Multiply.

$A = 30$ Simplify.

The area of the triangle is 30 square inches.

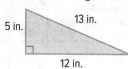
Quick Check

Area **Find the area of each figure.**

1.

14 m

3 m

Show your work.

$A =$ _____

2.

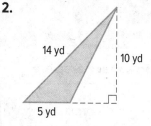

14 yd
10 yd
5 yd

$A =$ _____

3.

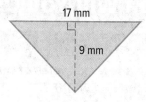

17 mm
9 mm

$A =$ _____

4. Anita's yard is in the shape of a triangle. It has a height of 35 feet and a base of 50 feet. What is the area of the yard?

_____

How Did You Do?

Which problems did you answer correctly in the Quick Check?
Shade those exercise numbers below.

① ② ③ ④

Area of Composite Figures

Real-World Link

Stained Glass Windows An image of a stained glass window is shown below.

1. Identify two of the shapes that make up the window.

   _____

   _____

2. How could you find the area of the entire window except for the shapes you identified in Exercise 1?

   _____

   _____

3. Draw a figure that is made up of a triangle and a rectangle on the grid below. Then find the area of your figure by counting square units.

   Area: _____ square units

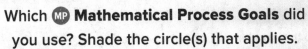

Which **MP** **Mathematical Process Goals** did you use? Shade the circle(s) that applies.

① Mathematical Problem Solving   ④ Mathematical Connections

② Mathematical Communication   ⑤ Mathematical Representations

③ Mathematical Reasoning

Find the Area of a Composite Figure

A **composite figure** is made up of two or more shapes.

To find the area of a composite figure, decompose the figure into shapes with areas you know. Then find the sum of these areas.

Shape	Words	Formula
Parallelogram	The area A of a parallelogram is the product of any base b and its height h.	$A = bh$
Triangle	The area A of a triangle is half the product of any base b and its height h.	$A = \frac{1}{2}bh$
Trapezoid	The area A of a trapezoid is half the product of the height h and the sum of the bases, b_1 and b_2.	$A = \frac{1}{2}h(b_1 + b_2)$
Circle	The area A of a circle is equal to π times the square of the radius r.	$A = \pi r^2$

parallelogram
half of a circle or semicircle
trapezoid

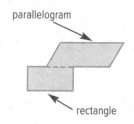

rectangle

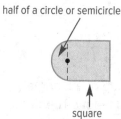

square

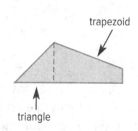

triangle

Example

Tutor

1. **Find the area of the composite figure.**

The figure can be separated into a semicircle and a triangle.

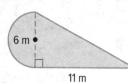

6 m

11 m

Area of semicircle

$A = \frac{1}{2}\pi r^2$

$A \approx \frac{1}{2} \cdot 3.14 \cdot 3^2$

$A \approx 14.1$

● 6 m

Area of triangle

$A = \frac{1}{2}bh$

$A = \frac{1}{2} \cdot 11 \cdot 6$

$A = 33$

6 m

11 m

The area of the figure is about $14.1 + 33$ or 47.1 square meters.

Got it? Do this problem to find out.

Show your work.

a. _____

a. Find the area of the figure. Round to the nearest tenth if necessary.

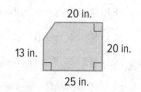

20 in.

13 in.   20 in.

25 in.

Example

2. A miniature golf hole is composed of a trapezoid and a parallelogram. How many square feet of turf does the hole cover?

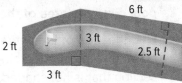

6 ft
2 ft
3 ft
2.5 ft
3 ft

Area of trapezoid

$A = \frac{1}{2}h(b_1 + b_2)$

$A = \frac{1}{2}(3)(2 + 3)$ 2 ft

$A = 7.5$

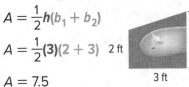

3 ft
3 ft

Area of parallelogram

$A = bh$

$A = 6 \cdot 2.5$

$A = 15$

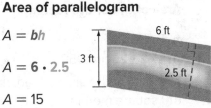

6 ft
3 ft
2.5 ft

So, 7.5 + 15 or 22.5 square feet of turf will be needed.

Got it? Do this problem to find out.

b. Pedro's father is building a shed. How many square feet of wood are needed to build the back of the shed shown at the right?

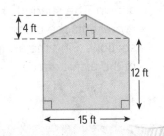

4 ft
12 ft
15 ft

Show your work.

b. _____

Find the Area of a Shaded Region

Use the areas you know to find the area of a shaded region.

Examples

Tutor

3. Find the area of the shaded region.

Find the area of the rectangle and subtract the area of the four congruent triangles.

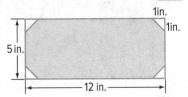

1 in.
1 in.
5 in.
12 in.

Congruent Triangles

Congruent triangles have corresponding sides and angles that are congruent.

Area of rectangle

$A = \ell w$

$A = 12 \cdot 5$ $\ell = 12, w = 5$

$A = 60$ Simplify.

Area of triangles

$A = 4 \cdot \left(\frac{1}{2}bh\right)$

$A = 4 \cdot \frac{1}{2} \cdot 1 \cdot 1$ $b = 1, h = 1$

$A = 2$ Simplify.

The area of the shaded region is 60 − 2 or 58 square inches.

4. The blueprint for a hotel swimming area is represented by the figure shown. The shaded area represents the pool. Find the area of the pool.

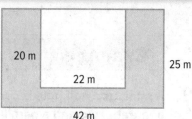

Find the area of the entire rectangle and subtract the section that is not shaded.

Area of the entire rectangle	**Area not shaded**
$A = \ell w$	$A = \ell w$
$A = 42 \cdot 25$ or 1,050	$A = 22 \cdot 20$ or 440

The area of the shaded region is $1,050 - 440$ or 610 square meters.

Got it? Do this problem to find out.

c. _____

c. A diagram for a park is shown. The shaded area represents the picnic sections. Find the area of the picnic sections.

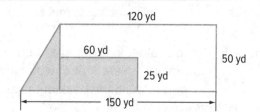

Guided Practice

1. Mike installed the window shown. How many square feet is the window? Round to the nearest tenth. Use 3.14 for π.

(Examples 1 and 2) _____

2. A triangle is cut from a rectangle. Find the area of the shaded region.

(Examples 3 and 4) _____

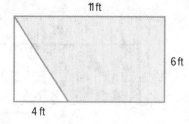

3. **Building on the Essential Question** Is your answer to Exercise 1 an exact or approximate answer? Explain.

_____

_____

_____

Independent Practice

Go online for Step-by-Step Solutions

Find the area of each figure. Round to the nearest tenth if necessary. (Example 1)

1.
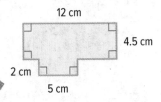
12 cm
4.5 cm
2 cm
5 cm

 Show your work.

2.
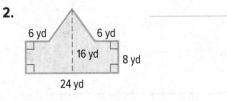
6 yd   6 yd
16 yd
8 yd
24 yd

3.
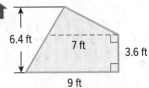
15 cm
8 cm

4.

7 m
15 m

5.
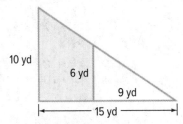
6.4 ft
7 ft
3.6 ft
9 ft

6.
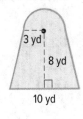
3 yd
8 yd
10 yd

7. Daniel is constructing a deck like the one shown. What is the area of the deck? (Example 2)

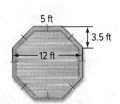
5 ft
3.5 ft
12 ft

Find the area of the shaded region. Round to the nearest tenth if necessary. (Examples 3 and 4)

8.
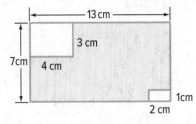
10 yd
6 yd
9 yd
15 yd

9.
13 cm
3 cm
7cm
4 cm
1cm
2 cm

10. **MP Persevere with Problems** Zoe's mom is carpeting her bedroom and needs to know the amount of floor space. How many square feet of carpeting are needed for the room? If she is also installing baseboards on the bottom of all the walls, how many feet of baseboards are needed? _____

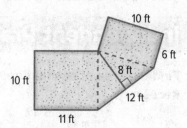

 H.O.T. Problems Higher Order Thinking

11. **MP Persevere with Problems** The composite figure shown is made from a rectangle and part of a circle. Find the approximate area and perimeter of the entire figure. Round to the nearest tenth.

_____

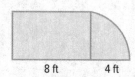

12. **MP Reason Abstractly** The side length of the square in the figure at the right is x units. Write expressions that represent the perimeter and area of the figure.

_____

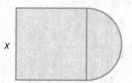

13. **MP Persevere with Problems** In the diagram shown at the right, a 2-foot-wide flower border surrounds the heart-shaped pond. What is the area of the border?

_____

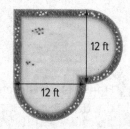

14. **MP Model with Mathematics** Find a real-world object that is a composite figure. Measure the dimensions of the figure. Draw a model of the figure with appropriate labels. Then find the area of the composite figure. _____

Extra Practice

Find the area of each figure. Round to the nearest tenth if necessary.

15. 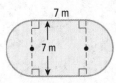 7 m 7 m $87.5\ m^2$

 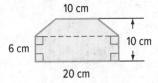

Area of circle   Area of square

$A = \pi r^2$ $A = lw$

$A = 3.14 \cdot 3.5^2$ or 38.5 $A = 7 \cdot 7$ or 49

$38.5 + 49 = 87.5$

16. 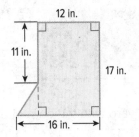 12 in. 11 in. 17 in. 16 in. _____

17. 10 cm 10 cm 6 cm 20 cm _____

18. 12 cm 12 cm 6 cm 18 cm _____

19. A necklace comes with a gold pendant. What is the area of the pendant in square centimeters? _____

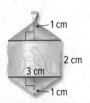 1 cm 2 cm 3 cm 1 cm

Find the area of the shaded region. Round to the nearest tenth if necessary.

20. 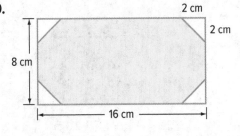 2 cm 2 cm 8 cm 16 cm _____

21. 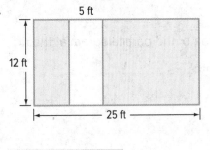 5 ft 12 ft 25 ft _____

22. The Patel's backyard has a rectangular vegetable garden and a triangular pet exercise area.

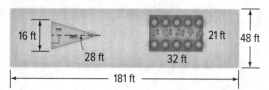

Match each part of the yard with the correct area.

Pet Exercise Area: [＿＿＿＿＿] ft²

Vegetable Garden Area: [＿＿＿＿＿] ft²

Total Backyard Area: [＿＿＿＿＿] ft²

106	672
224	1,092
458	7,520
544	8,688

How much of the backyard is not being used for the vegetable garden or pet exercise area?

[＿＿＿＿＿]

23. The figure is made up of a square and four semicircles. Fill in each box to complete each statement. Round to the nearest hundredth.

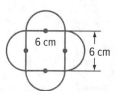

a. The area of the square is [＿＿＿＿＿] cm².

b. The area of each semicircle is about [＿＿＿＿＿] cm².

c. The total area of the figure is about [＿＿＿＿＿] cm².

Spiral Review

24. What is the area of a triangle with a base of 52 feet and a height of 38 feet? _____

25. Find the area of the parallelogram at the right. Round to the nearest tenth. _____

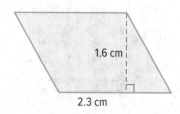

26. Find the height of a parallelogram with an area of 104 square yards and a base of 8 yards.

27. Find the base of a parallelogram with a height of 3.2 meters and an area of 15.04 square meters.

_____   _____

Volume of Prisms

Vocabulary Start-Up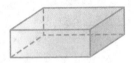

A three-dimensional figure with faces that are polygons is called a **polyhedron.** A prism is a polyhedron with two parallel, congruent bases. The bases of a *rectangular prism* are rectangles, and the bases of a *triangular prism* are triangles.

Write *rectangular prism* or *triangular prism* on the line below each figure.

_____   _____

 Essential Question

HOW do measurements help you describe real-world objects?

 Vocabulary

volume

 Virginia Standards
7.4a, b

Real-World Link

1. Suppose you observed the camping tent shown from directly above. What geometric figure would you see?

   _____

2. What formula would you use to find the area of the figure?

   _____

Which MP Mathematical Process Goals did you use? Shade the circle(s) that applies.

① Mathematical Problem Solving

② Mathematical Communication

③ Mathematical Reasoning

④ Mathematical Connections

⑤ Mathematical Representations

Volume of a Rectangular Prism

Words The volume V of a rectangular prism is the product of the length ℓ, the width w, and the height h. It is also the area of the base B times the height h.

Model

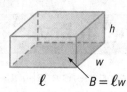

Symbols $V = \ell wh$ or $V = Bh$

The **volume** of a three-dimensional figure is the measure of space it occupies. It is measured in cubic units such as cubic centimeters (cm³) or cubic inches (in³).

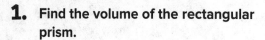

It takes 2 layers of 36 cubes to fill the box. So, the volume of the box is 72 cubic centimeters.

Work Zone

Decomposing Figures

Think of the volume of the prism as consisting of three congruent slices. Each slice contains the base area, 20 square centimeters, and a height of 1 centimeter.

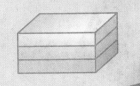

Example

Tutor

1. Find the volume of the rectangular prism.

$V = \ell wh$ Volume of a prism

$V = 5 \cdot 4 \cdot 3$ $\ell = 5$, $w = 4$, and $h = 3$

$V = 60$ Multiply.

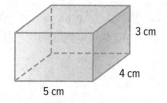

The volume is 60 cubic centimeters or 60 cm³.

Got it? Do this problem to find out.

Show your work.

a. _____

a. Find the volume of the rectangular prism shown below.

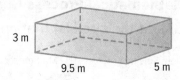

Volume of a Triangular Prism

Words	The volume V of a triangular prism is the area of the base B times the height h.	**Model**
Symbols	$V = Bh$, where B is the area of the base.	

The diagram below shows that the volume of a triangular prism is also the product of the area of the base B and the height h of the prism.

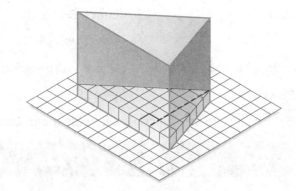

Example

 Tutor

2. Find the volume of the triangular prism shown.

The area of the triangle is $\frac{1}{2} \cdot 6 \cdot 8$, so replace B with $\frac{1}{2} \cdot 6 \cdot 8$.

$V = Bh$ Volume of a prism

$V = \left(\frac{1}{2} \cdot 6 \cdot 8\right)h$ Replace B with $\frac{1}{2} \cdot 6 \cdot 8$.

$V = \left(\frac{1}{2} \cdot 6 \cdot 8\right)9$ The height of the prism is 9.

$V = 216$ Multiply.

The volume is 216 cubic feet or 216 ft³.

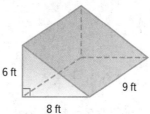

6 ft

9 ft

8 ft

Before finding the volume of a prism, identify the base. In Example 2, the base is a triangle, so you replace B with $\frac{1}{2}bh$.

Got it? Do this problem to find out.

b. Find the volume of the triangular prism.

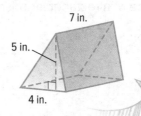

7 in.

5 in.

4 in.

Show your work.

b. _____

Example

3. Which lunch box holds more food?

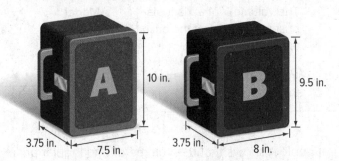

10 in.

9.5 in.

3.75 in.   7.5 in.

3.75 in.   8 in.

Find the volume of each lunch box. Then compare.

Lunch Box A

$V = \ell wh$

$V = 7.5 \cdot 3.75 \cdot 10$

$V = 281.25$ in^3

Lunch Box B

$V = \ell wh$

$V = 8 \cdot 3.75 \cdot 9.5$

$V = 285$ in^3

Since 285 in^3 > 281.25 in^3, Lunch Box B holds more food.

Guided Practice

Check ✓

Find the volume of each prism. Round to the nearest tenth if necessary.

(Examples 1–2)

1.

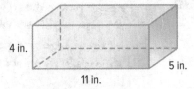

4 in.

5 in.

11 in.

2.

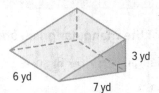

3 yd

6 yd

7 yd

Show your work.

3. One cabinet measures 3 feet by 2.5 feet by 5 feet. A second measures 4 feet by 3.5 feet by 4.5 feet. Which volume is greater? Explain. (Example 3)

_____

4. **Building on the Essential Question** Compare and contrast finding the volume of a rectangular prism and

a triangular prism. _____

_____

_____

FOLDABLES Time to update your Foldable!

Independent Practice

Go online for Step-by-Step Solutions

Find the volume of each prism. Round to the nearest tenth if necessary.
(Examples 1–2)

1
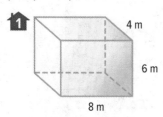
4 m
6 m
8 m

2.
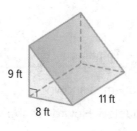
9 ft
8 ft
11 ft

3
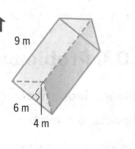
9 m
6 m
4 m

Show your work.

4. Which container holds more detergent? Justify your answer. (Example 3)

_____

_____

Soapy Suds
13 in.
12 in.
8 in.

CLEAN & BRIGHT
8 in.
9 in.
13 in.

5. **MP** **Model with Mathematics** Refer to the graphic novel frame below. The table shows possible dimensions for the dunk tank.

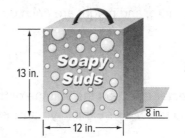

Length(ft)	Width(ft)	Height(ft)	Surface Area (ft²)
2	12	4	136
4	4	8	144
4	7	6	160
8	5	4	144
10	4	3	124

We only have 160 square feet of metal sheeting.

a. Find the volume of each given dunk tank.

_____

b. Which dimensions are reasonable for a dunk tank? Explain.

_____

_____

6. The diagram shows the dimensions of an office. It costs about $0.11 per year to air condition one cubic foot of space. On average, how much does it cost to air condition the office for one month? _____

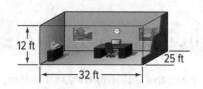

12 ft   25 ft

32 ft

 H.O.T. Problems Higher Order Thinking

7. (MP) **Reason Inductively** A rectangular prism is shown.

5 in.

4 in.

4 in.

a. Suppose the length of the prism is doubled. How does the volume change? Explain your reasoning. _____

_____

_____

b. Suppose the length, width, and height are each doubled. How does the volume change? _____

_____

c. Which will have a greater effect on the volume of the prism: doubling the height or doubling the width? Explain your reasoning.

_____

_____

_____

8. (MP) **Persevere with Problems** The prism shown has a base that is a trapezoid. Find the volume of the prism. _____

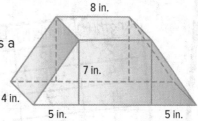

8 in.

7 in.

4 in.

5 in.   5 in.

9. (MP) **Model with Mathematics** Find the volume of a real-world object that is in the shape of a rectangular or triangular prism using appropriate units. Draw a model of the prism including the dimensions. _____

Show your work.

Extra Practice

Find the volume of each prism. Round to the nearest tenth if necessary.

10.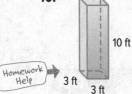

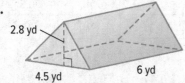

<u>90 ft³</u>

10 ft

3 ft

3 ft

$V = lwh$

$V = 3 \cdot 3 \cdot 10$

$V = 90$

11.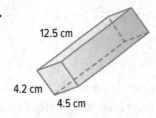

12.5 cm

4.2 cm

4.5 cm

12.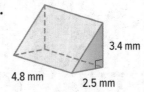

2.8 yd

4.5 yd

6 yd

13.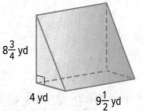

3.4 mm

4.8 mm

2.5 mm

14. A toy company makes rectangular sandboxes that measure 6 feet by 5 feet by 1.2 feet. A customer buys a sandbox and 40 cubic feet of sand. Did the customer buy too much or too little sand? Justify your answer.

_____

_____

15. The base of a rectangular prism has an area of 19.4 square meters and the prism has a volume of 306.52 cubic meters. Write an equation that can be used to find the height h of the prism. Then find the height of the prism.

_____

_____

Find the volume of each prism.

16.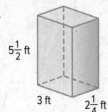

$5\frac{1}{2}$ ft

3 ft $2\frac{1}{4}$ ft

_____

17.

$8\frac{3}{4}$ yd

4 yd $9\frac{1}{2}$ yd

_____

18. **MP Reason Abstractly** Write a formula for finding the volume of a cube. Use an exponent and the variable s to represent the side lengths. Then use the formula to find the volume of a cube with side lengths of 7 inches.

_____

19. The volume of a paperclip box is 1.5 cubic inches. Which of the following are possible dimensions of the box? Select all that apply.

☐ 2 in. by 1.5 in. by 0.5 in.   ☐ 3 in. by 0.5 in. by 1.5 in.

☐ 2 in. by 1 in. by 1 in.   ☐ 3 in. by 1 in. by 0.5 in.

20. The table shows the dimensions of 4 mailing containers. Sort the containers from least to greatest volume.

Container	ℓ (ft)	w (ft)	h (ft)
A	2	2	2
B	1	3	3
C	3	4	0.5
D	3	2	0.5

	Container	Volume (ft³)
Least		
Greatest		

Which container has the greatest volume? ☐

Spiral Review

Find the perimeter of each figure.

21.

4.3 m
4.3 m   4.3 m
4.3 m   4.3 m
4.3 m

22.

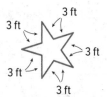

3 ft
3 ft   3 ft
3 ft
3 ft

23.

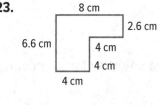

8 cm
2.6 cm
6.6 cm   4 cm
4 cm
4 cm

24. Write a formula for finding the perimeter of a square. Use your formula to find the perimeter of a square with side length of 0.5 inch.

Inquiry HOW are some three-dimensional figures related to circles?

Kenji is training his dog to run through an agility course. One of the activities in the course is the tunnel, an open tube through which the dog runs.

Hands-On Activity

There are three-dimensional figures that are *not* polyhedrons. Some examples of these figures are *cylinders*, *cones*, and *spheres*.

Step 1 For each figure, list three real-world items that represent the figure.

Cylinder	Cone	Sphere

Step 2 Just as a rectangular prism and a pyramid have bases, a cylinder and a cone have bases as well. What is the shape of the base of a cylinder?

_____ a cone? _____

Step 3 Interesting shapes can occur when you find the cross section of a figure that is not a polyhedron. Describe the shape of the figure resulting from a horizontal cross section of each of the following.

  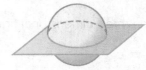

Work with a partner. Draw and describe the shape resulting from each cross section.

1.

Show your work.

2.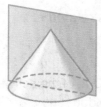

3.

4.

5.

6.

Create
On Your Own

7. **MP Use a Counterexample** *True* or *false*: The cross section of a cylinder, a cone, and a sphere will *always* be a circle or an oval. If false, provide a counterexample.

_____

_____

8. **Inquiry** HOW are some three-dimensional figures related to circles?

_____

_____

Volume of Cylinders

 Real-World Link

Jelly Beans Olivia's teacher filled a cylindrical jar with jelly beans. She is awarding a prize to the student who most accurately estimates the number of jelly beans in the jar. Olivia used a soup can to model the jar and centimeter cubes to model the jelly beans.

Essential Question

How do measurements help you describe real-world objects?

Vocabulary

volume
cylinder
composite solids

Virginia Standards
7.4a, b

 Work with a partner.

1. Set a soup can on a piece of grid paper. Trace the area around the base as shown.

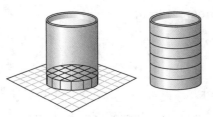

About how many centimeter cubes would fit at the bottom of the container? Remember to include partial cubes in your total. _____

2. Suppose each layer is 1 centimeter high. How many layers would it take to fill the cylinder? ▢

3. **Be Precise** Write a formula that allows you to find the volume of the container. _____

Which **Mathematical Process Goals** did you use? Shade the circle(s) that applies.

① Mathematical Problem Solving
② Mathematical Communication
③ Mathematical Reasoning
④ Mathematical Connections
⑤ Mathematical Representations

Volume of a Cylinder

Words	The volume V of a cylinder with radius r is the area of the base B times the height h.	**Model**
Symbols	$V = Bh$, where $B = \pi r^2$ or $V = \pi r^2 h$	

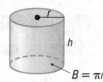

$B = \pi r^2$

STOP and Reflect

What formula do you use to find the area of the base of a cylinder?

Volume is the measure of the space occupied by a solid. Volume is measured in cubic units. A **cylinder** is a three-dimensional figure with two parallel congruent circular bases connected by a curved surface. The area of the base of a cylinder tells the number of cubic units in one layer. The height tells how many layers there are in the cylinder.

Examples

Watch ▶ Tutor 💬

1. Find the volume of the cylinder. Round to the nearest tenth.

5 cm

8.3 cm

$V = \pi r^2 h$ — Volume of a cylinder

$V = \pi (5)^2 (8.3)$ — Replace r with 5 and h with 8.3.

Use a calculator.

[2nd] [π] [×] 5 [x^2] [×] 8.3 [ENTER] 651.8804756

The volume is about 651.9 cubic centimeters.

Circles
Recall that the radius is half the diameter.

2. Find the volume of a cylinder with a diameter of 16 inches and a height of 20 inches. Round to the nearest tenth.

$V = \pi r^2 h$ — Volume of a cylinder

$V = \pi (8)^2 (20)$ — The diameter is 16 so the radius is 8. Replace h with 20.

$V \approx 4{,}021.2$ — Use a calculator.

The volume is about 4,021.2 cubic inches.

Got it? Do these problems to find out.

Show your work.

Find the volume of each cylinder. Round to the nearest tenth.

a.

3 in.

1.8 in.

b. diameter: 12 mm

height: 5 mm

a. _____

b. _____

Example

Tutor

3. A metal paperweight is in the shape of a cylinder. The paperweight has a height of 1.5 inches and a diameter of 2 inches. How much does the paperweight weigh if 1 cubic inch weighs 1.8 ounces? Round to the nearest tenth.

First find the volume of the paperweight.

$V = \pi r^2 h$ Volume of a cylinder

$V = \pi (1)^2 1.5$ Replace r with 1 and h with 1.5.

$V \approx 4.7$ Simplify.

To find the weight of the paperweight, multiply the volume by 1.8.

$4.7(1.8) = 8.46$

So, the weight of the paperweight is about 8.5 ounces.

Got it? Do this problem to find out.

c. The Roberts family uses a container shaped like a cylinder to recycle aluminum cans. It has a height of 4 feet and a diameter of 1.5 feet. The container is full. How much do the contents weigh if the average weight of aluminum cans is 37 ounces per cubic foot? Round to the nearest tenth.

Show your work.

c. _____

Volume of a Composite Solid

Objects made up of more than one type of solid are called **composite solids.** To find the volume of a composite solid, decompose the figure into solids whose volumes you know how to find.

Example

Tutor

4. Tanya uses cube-shaped beads to make jewelry. Each bead has a circular hole through the middle. Find the volume of each bead.

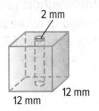

2 mm

12 mm

12 mm

The bead is made of one rectangular prism and one cylinder. Find the volume of each solid. Then subtract to find the volume of the bead.

Rectangular Prism	**Cylinder**
$V = Bh$	$V = Bh$
$V = (12 \cdot 12)12$ or 1,728	$V = (\pi \cdot 1^2)12$ or 37.7

The volume of the bead is $1,728 - 37.7$ or 1,690.3 cubic millimeters.

Got it? Do this problem to find out.

d. _____

d. The Service Club is building models of storage chests, like the one shown, to donate to a charity. Find the volume of the chest to the nearest tenth.

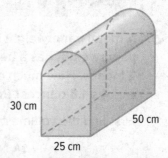

30 cm

50 cm

25 cm

Guided Practice

Check ✓

Find the volume of each cylinder. Round to the nearest tenth. (Examples 1 and 2)

1. _____

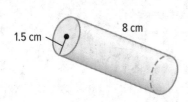

1.5 cm

8 cm

2. _____

diameter: 8 in.
height: 8 in.

3. A platform like the one shown was built to hold a sculpture for an art exhibit. What is the volume of the figure? (Example 4)

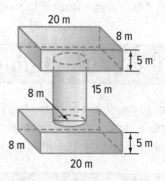

20 m

8 m

5 m

8 m

15 m

8 m

5 m

20 m

4. A scented candle is in the shape of a cylinder. The radius is 4 centimeters and the height is 12 centimeters. Find the mass of the wax needed to make the candle if 1 cubic centimeter of wax has a mass of 3.5 grams. Round to the nearest tenth. (Example 3)

5. e **Building on the Essential Question** How is the formula for the volume of a cylinder similar to the formula for the volume of a rectangular prism?

Rate Yourself!

How confident are you about volume of cylinders? Check the box that applies.

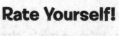

For more help, go online to access a Personal Tutor.

Tutor

FOLDABLES Time to update your Foldable!

Independent Practice

Go online for Step-by-Step Solutions

Find the volume of each cylinder. Round to the nearest tenth. (Examples 1 and 2)

 1. _____

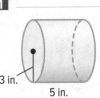

3 in.

5 in.

2. _____

diameter 4.5 m
height 6.5 m

3 Mia's parents have a cylindrical oak tree stump that has a diameter of 3 feet and a height of 2 feet. How much does the stump weigh if the average weight of oak is 59 pounds per cubic foot? Round to the nearest tenth. (Example 3) _____

4. An unused roll of paper towels is shown. What is the volume of the unused roll? (Example 4) _____

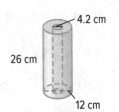

4.2 cm

26 cm

12 cm

5. **MP** **Model with Mathematics** Refer to the graphic novel frame below for Exercises a–c.

a. Find the volume of the bag and candle. Round to the nearest tenth.

_____

b. How much packing material is needed to fill the empty space in the bag after the candle is placed in the bag? _____

c. There are 70 teachers in the school. If each package of packing material contains 575 cubic inches of material, how many packages do they need to buy to fill all of the gift bags? _____

6. **MP Use Math Tools** Match each cylinder with its approximate volume.

radius = 4.1 ft, height = 5 ft	91 ft³
diameter = 8 ft, height = 2.2 ft	111 ft³
diameter = 6.2 ft, height = 3 ft	264 ft³

H.O.T. Problems Higher Order Thinking

7. **MP Persevere with Problems** Two equally-sized sheets of construction paper are rolled; one along the length and the other along the width, as shown. Which cylinder has the greater volume? Explain.

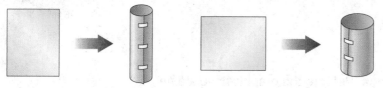

_____

_____

8. **MP Model with Mathematics** Draw and label a cylinder that has a larger radius but less volume than the cylinder shown below.

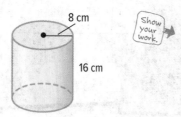

8 cm

Show your work.

16 cm

9. **MP Reason Abstractly** Find the ratios of the volume of cylinder A to cylinder B.

   a. Cylinder A has the same radius but twice the height of cylinder B.

   _____

   b. Cylinder A has the same height but twice the radius of cylinder B.

   _____

Extra Practice

Copy and Solve For Exercises 10–27, show your work and answers on a separate piece of paper.

Find the volume of each cylinder. Round to the nearest tenth.

10.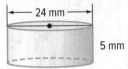
24 mm
5 mm

11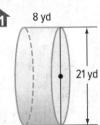
8 yd
21 yd

12.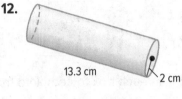
13.3 cm
2 cm

13. Kyle has a container of flour in the shape of a cylinder. The container has a diameter of 10 inches and a height of 8 inches. If the container is full, how much will the flour weigh if the average weight of flour is 0.13 ounces per cubic inch? Round to the nearest tenth.

14. Charlotte wants to make a mailbox like the one shown. What is the volume of the mailbox? Round to the nearest tenth.

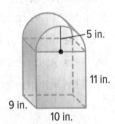
5 in.
11 in.
9 in.
10 in.

15. Cylinder A has a radius of 4 inches and a height of 2 inches. Cylinder B has a radius of 2 inches. What is the height of Cylinder B to the nearest inch if both cylinders have the same volume?

16. Which will hold more cake batter, the rectangular pan or two round pans? Explain your reasoning to a classmate.

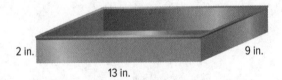
2 in.
9 in.
13 in.

8 in.
2 in.

17. **MP** **Multiple Representations** The dimensions for four cylinders are shown in the table.

a. **Symbols** Write an equation to find the volume of each cylinder.

b. **Words** Compare the dimensions of Cylinder A with the dimensions of Cylinders B, C, and D.

c. **Numbers** Complete the table.

d. **Words** Explain how changing the dimensions of a cylinder affects the cylinder's volume.

	Radius (cm)	Height (cm)	Volume (cm³)
Cylinder A	1	1	
Cylinder B	1	2	
Cylinder C	2	1	
Cylinder D	2	2	

18. Without doing any calculations, do you think Cylinder 1 and Cylinder 2 will have the same volume? Explain your reasoning.

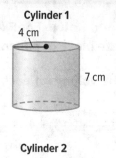

Cylinder 1

4 cm

7 cm

Fill in each box to complete the following statements.

To the nearest tenth, the volume of Cylinder 1 is [   ] .

To the nearest tenth, the volume of Cylinder 2 is [   ] .

Cylinder 2

7 cm

4 cm

19. The oatmeal container shown has a diameter of 3 inches and a height of 9 inches. Which of the following statements are true? Select all that apply.

☐ The area of each base is exactly 9π square inches.

☐ The volume of the container is exactly 20.25π cubic inches.

☐ The volume of the container to the nearest tenth is about 63.6 cubic inches.

3 in.

9 in.

Spiral Review

Find the area of each circle. Round to the nearest tenth.

20.

15 in.

21.
8 cm

22.
9 in.

23.
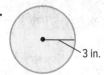
3 in.

24.
6.2 cm

25.

4 m

Find the volume of the prism.

26.

6 ft
2 ft   3 ft

Inquiry HOW can models and nets help you find the surface area of prisms?

Nets are used to design and manufacture items such as boxes and labels. Find the shapes that make up the net of a cereal box.

Hands-On Activity 1

Make a net from a rectangular prism.

Step 1 Use an empty cereal box. Cut off one of the two top flaps. The remaining top flap is the top face.

Step 2 Label the top and bottom faces using a green marker. Label the front and back faces using a blue marker. Label the left and right faces using a red marker.

Step 3 Carefully cut along the three edges of the top face. Then cut down each vertical edge.

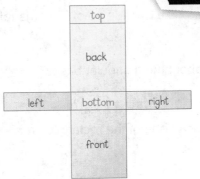

The net of a cereal box is made up of a total of ☐ rectangles.

What do you notice about the top and bottom faces, the left and right faces, and the front and back faces?

Make a triangular prism from a net.

Step 1 Draw a net on a piece of card stock with the dimensions shown below.

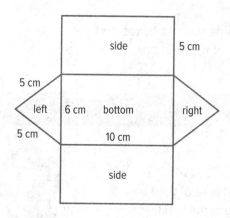

Step 2 Fold the net into a triangular prism. Tape together adjacent edges.

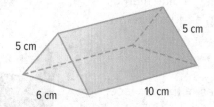

The triangular prism is made up of ☐ triangles and ☐ rectangles.

What is true about the triangular bases?

_____

How is the side of one of the rectangles related to the base of one of the triangles?

_____

Explain one way to find the total surface area of a triangular prism.

_____

_____

_____

Collaborate

Work with a partner to solve each problem.

1. A net of a rectangular prism that is 24 inches by 18 inches by 4 inches is shown. The net of the prism is labeled with *top*, *bottom*, *side*, and *end*. Fill in the boxes to find the total area of the rectangular prism.

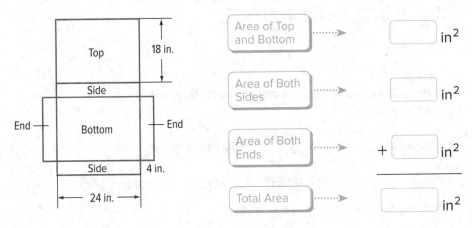

Area of Top and Bottom $\cdots\!\!\!\cdots\!\!\!\triangleright$ [ ] in^2

Area of Both Sides $\cdots\!\!\!\cdots\!\!\!\triangleright$ [ ] in^2

Area of Both Ends $\cdots\!\!\!\cdots\!\!\!\triangleright$ + [ ] in^2

Total Area $\cdots\!\!\!\cdots\!\!\!\triangleright$ [ ] in^2

2. Describe in words how you could find the total surface area of a rectangular prism.

_____

_____

3. A net of a triangular prism is shown. Fill in the boxes to find the total area of the triangular prism.

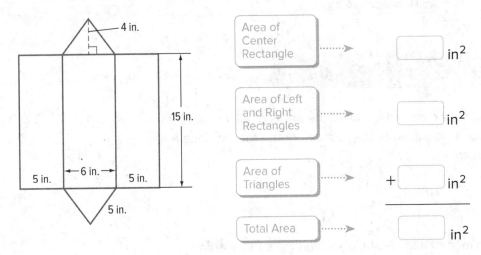

Area of Center Rectangle $\cdots\!\!\!\cdots\!\!\!\triangleright$ [ ] in^2

Area of Left and Right Rectangles $\cdots\!\!\!\cdots\!\!\!\triangleright$ [ ] in^2

Area of Triangles $\cdots\!\!\!\cdots\!\!\!\triangleright$ + [ ] in^2

Total Area $\cdots\!\!\!\cdots\!\!\!\triangleright$ [ ] in^2

4. Describe in words how you could find the total surface area of a triangular prism.

_____

_____

Work with a partner.

5. **MP Reason Inductively** Suppose Ladell wants to wrap a present in a container that is a rectangular prism. How can he determine the amount of wrapping paper that he will need? _____

_____

_____

Circle each correct surface area. Draw and label the net for each figure if needed. The first one is done for you.

Prism	Measures	Surface Area		
Rectangular	Length: 10 cm Width: 8 cm Height: 5 cm	170 cm^2	340 cm^2	400 cm^2
6. Rectangular	Length: 3 ft Width: 2 ft Height: 5 ft	30 ft^2	31 ft^2	62 ft^2
7. Rectangular	Length: 2 m Width: 1 m Height: 1.5 m	3 m^2	6.5 m^2	13 m^2
8. Triangular	Area of Top and Bottom Triangles: 3 mm^2 Area of Center Rectangle: 12 mm^2 Area of Left and Right Rectangles: 10 mm^2	25 mm^2	28 mm^2	38 mm^2
9. Triangular	Area of Top and Bottom Triangles: 6 in^2 Area of Center Rectangle: 50.4 in^2 Area of Left and Right Rectangles: 56 in^2	174.4 in^2	118.4 in^2	112.4 in^2

Create
On Your Own

10. **MP Be Precise** *Surface area* is the sum of the areas of all the surfaces of a three-dimensional figure. Write the formula for the total surface area of a rectangular prism.

_____

_____

11. **Inquiry** HOW can models and nets help you find the surface area

of prisms? _____

_____

_____

Surface Area of Prisms

Real-World Link

Message Board Members of a local recreation center are permitted to post messages on 8.5-inch by 11-inch paper on the board. Assume the signs are posted vertically and do not overlap, as shown below.

```
┌──────┬───────┬──────────────────────────┐
│ LOST │ Free  │                          │
│ DOG  │Kittens│                          │
│      │to a Good                          │
│      │ Home  │                          │
│      ├───────┤                          │
│Tutoring      │                          │
├──────┘       │                          │
│              │                          │
│              │                          │
└──────────────────────────────────────────┘
```

1. Suppose 6 messages fit across the board widthwise.

   What is the width of the board in inches? ☐ inches

2. Suppose 3 messages fit down the board lengthwise.

   What is the length of the board in inches? ☐ inches

3. What is the area in square inches of the message board?

   _____

4. Messages can also be posted on the other side of the board. What is the total area of the front and back of the board in square inches?

   _____

Vocabulary

surface area

 Virginia Standards
7.4a, b

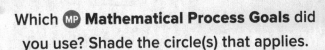

Which MP **Mathematical Process Goals did you use? Shade the circle(s) that applies.**

① Mathematical Problem Solving
② Mathematical Communication
③ Mathematical Reasoning
④ Mathematical Connections
⑤ Mathematical Representations

Surface Area of a Rectangular Prism

Words	The surface area *S.A.* of a rectangular prism with base ℓ, width *w*, and height *h* is the sum of the areas of its faces.	**Model**
Symbols	$S.A. = 2\ell h + 2\ell w + 2hw$	

The sum of the areas of all the surfaces, or faces, of a three-dimensional figure is the **surface area**. In the previous Inquiry Lab, you used a net to find the surface area of a rectangular prism. You can also use a formula to find surface area.

When you find the surface area of a three-dimensional figure, the units are square units, not cubic units.

Example

1. **Find the surface area of the rectangular prism shown at the right.**

   Replace ℓ with 9, *w* with 7, and *h* with 13.

   surface area $= 2\ell h + 2\ell w + 2hw$

   $= 2 \cdot 9 \cdot 13 + 2 \cdot 9 \cdot 7 + 2 \cdot 13 \cdot 7$

   $= 234 + 126 + 182$ Multiply first. Then add.

   $= 542$

   The surface area of the prism is 542 square inches.

Got it? Do these problems to find out.

Find the surface area of each rectangular prism.

a.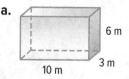

b.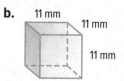

a. _____

b. _____

Example

 Tutor

2. Domingo built a toy box 60 inches long, 24 inches wide, and 36 inches high. He has 1 quart of paint that covers about 87 square feet of surface. Does he have enough to paint the outside of the toy box? Justify your answer.

Step 1 Find the surface area of the toy box.

Replace ℓ with 60, w with 24, and h with 36.

surface area $= 2\ell h + 2\ell w + 2hw$

$= 2 \cdot 60 \cdot 36 + 2 \cdot 60 \cdot 24 + 2 \cdot 36 \cdot 24$

$= 8{,}928 \text{ in}^2$

Step 2 Find the number of square inches the paint will cover.

$1 \text{ ft}^2 = 1 \text{ ft} \times 1 \text{ ft}$ *Replace 1 ft with 12 in.*

$= 12 \text{ in.} \times 12 \text{ in.}$ *Multiply.*

$= 144 \text{ in}^2$

So, 87 square feet is equal to 87×144 or 12,528 square inches.

Since $12{,}528 > 8{,}928$, Domingo has enough paint.

Got it? Do this problem to find out.

c. The largest corrugated cardboard box ever constructed measured about 23 feet long, 9 feet high, and 8 feet wide. Would 950 square feet of paper be enough to cover the box? Justify your answer.

Show your work.

c. _____

Surface Area of Triangular Prisms

To find the surface area of a triangular prism, it is more efficient to find the area of each face and calculate the sum of all of the faces rather than using a formula.

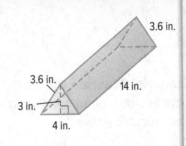

3.6 in.

3.6 in.

14 in.

3 in.

4 in.

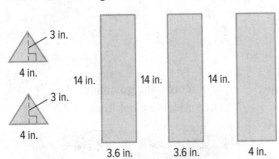

3 in.

4 in.

3 in.

4 in.

14 in.

14 in.

14 in.

3.6 in.

3.6 in.

4 in.

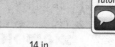

Example

3. Marty is mailing his aunt the package shown. How much cardboard is used to create the shipping container?

Find the area of each face and add.

The area of each triangle is $\frac{1}{2} \cdot 4 \cdot 3$ or 6.

The area of two of the rectangles is $14 \cdot 3.6$ or 50.4. The area of the third rectangle is $14 \cdot 4$ or 56.

The sum of the areas of the faces is $6 + 6 + 50.4 + 50.4 + 56$ or 168.8 square inches.

Got it? Do this problem to find out.

d._____

d. Find the surface area of the triangular prism.

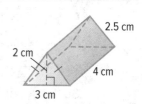

Guided Practice

 Check

Find the surface area of each prism. (Examples 1–3)

1.

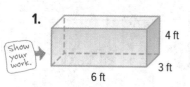

2.

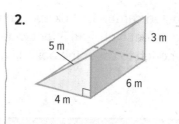

3. Building on the Essential Question Why is the surface area of a three-dimensional figure measured in square units rather than in cubic units?

_____

_____

Rate Yourself!

Are you ready to move on? Shade the section that applies.

YES   ?   NO

For more help, go online to access a Personal Tutor.

FOLDABLES Time to update your Foldable!

Independent Practice

Go online for Step-by-Step Solutions

Find the surface area of each rectangular prism. Round to the nearest tenth if necessary. (Example 1)

 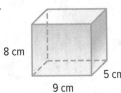

8 cm

9 cm

5 cm

Show your work.

2. 12 ft

1.7 ft

6.4 ft

_____

3 When making a book cover, Anwar adds an additional 20 square inches to the surface area to allow for overlap. How many square inches of paper will Anwar use to make a book cover for a book 11 inches long, 8 inches wide, and 1 inch high? (Example 2) _____

Find the surface area of each triangular prism. (Example 3)

4.

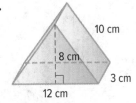

10 cm

8 cm

3 cm

12 cm

_____

5.

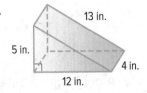

13 in.

5 in.

4 in.

12 in.

6. MP Model with Mathematics Refer to the graphic novel frame below. What whole number dimensions would allow the students to maximize the volume while keeping the surface area at most 160 square feet? Explain. _____

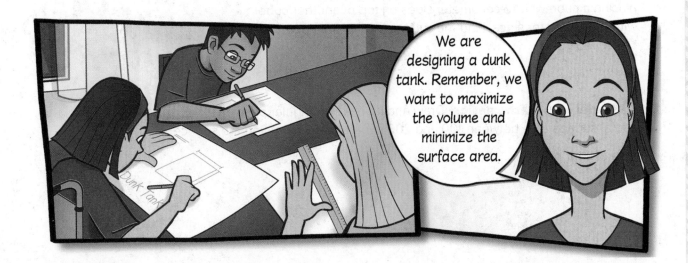

We are designing a dunk tank. Remember, we want to maximize the volume and minimize the surface area.

7. Write a formula for the surface area *S.A.* of a cube in which each side measures *x* units.

8. A company will make a cereal box with whole number dimensions and a volume of 100 cubic centimeters. If cardboard costs $0.05 per 100 square centimeters, what is the least cost to make 100 boxes?

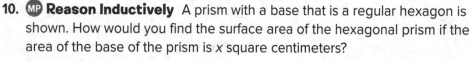

H.O.T. Problems Higher Order Thinking

9. **MP Reason Inductively** Determine if the following statement is *true* or *false*. Explain your reasoning.

> *If you double one of the dimensions of a rectangular prism, the surface area will double.*

10. **MP Reason Inductively** A prism with a base that is a regular hexagon is shown. How would you find the surface area of the hexagonal prism if the area of the base of the prism is *x* square centimeters?

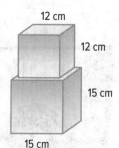

y cm

8 cm

11. **MP Persevere with Problems** The figure at the right is made by placing a cube with 12-centimeter sides on top of another cube with 15-centimeter sides. Find the surface area of the figure.

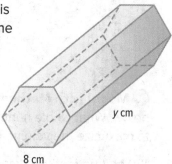

12 cm

12 cm

15 cm

15 cm

12. **MP Model with Mathematics** Draw and label a rectangular prism that has a total surface area between 100 and 200 square units. Then find the surface area of your prism.

Show your work.

Extra Practice

Find the surface area of each prism. Round to the nearest tenth if necessary.

13.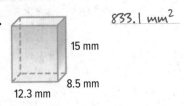

833.1 mm^2

15 mm
8.5 mm
12.3 mm

S.A. = 2lh + 2lw + 2hw

= 2 • 12.3 • 15 + 2 • 12.3 • 8.5 + 2 • 15 • 8.5

= 369 + 209.1 + 255

= 833.1

Homework Help

14.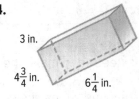

3 in.

$4\frac{3}{4}$ in. $6\frac{1}{4}$ in.

15.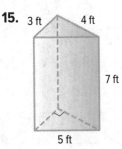

3 ft 4 ft

7 ft

5 ft

16.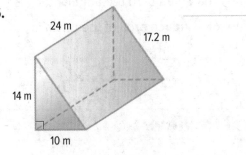

24 m

17.2 m

14 m

10 m

17. If one gallon of paint covers 350 square feet, will 8 gallons of paint be enough to paint the inside and outside of the fence shown once? Explain.

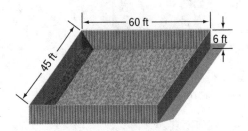

60 ft
45 ft
6 ft

_____

_____

_____

18. The attic shown is a triangular prism. Insulation will be placed inside all walls, not including the floor. Find the surface area that will be covered with insulation.

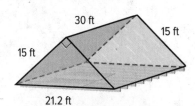

30 ft
15 ft
15 ft
21.2 ft

_____

19. **MP** **Be Precise** To the nearest tenth, find the approximate amount of plastic covering the outside of the CD case.

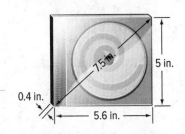

7.5 in.
5 in.
0.4 in.
5.6 in.

20. A cardboard box has the dimensions shown. Select the correct values to complete the formula to find the surface area of the box.

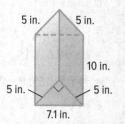

1.6
2
2.5

2 ft

1.6 ft

2.5 ft

$SA =$ ⬚ · ⬚ · ⬚ + ⬚ · ⬚ ·

⬚ + ⬚ · ⬚ · ⬚

How much cardboard is needed to make the box? ⬚

21. A triangular prism has the dimensions shown. Fill in each box to complete each statement.

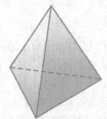

5 in.   5 in.

10 in.

5 in.   5 in.

7.1 in.

a. The area of each triangular base is ⬚ square inches.

b. The area of each of the two congruent rectangular faces is ⬚ square inches.

c. The area of the third rectangular face is ⬚ square inches.

d. The total surface area of the prism is ⬚ square inches.

Spiral Review

Describe the shape resulting from a vertical, horizontal, and angled cross section for each figure.

22.

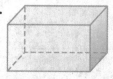

vertical: _____

horizontal: _____

angled: _____

23.

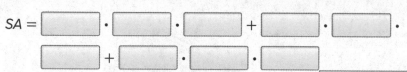

vertical: _____

horizontal: _____

angled: _____

24.

vertical: _____

horizontal: _____

angled: _____

25.

vertical: _____

horizontal: _____

angled: _____

HOW can the surface area of a cylinder be determined?

Nyombi used a clean frozen yogurt container for a school project. The container is shaped like a cylindrical tub that has a diameter of 20 centimeters and a height of 30 centimeters. She wants to know how much paper she will need to cover the entire container.

Hands-On Activity

Nets are two-dimensional patterns of three-dimensional figures. When you construct a net, you are decomposing the three-dimensional figure into separate shapes. You can use a net to find the area of each surface of a three-dimensional figure such as a cylinder.

Step 1 Use an empty cylinder shaped container that has a lid.

What is the height of the container? _____

Step 2 Take off the lid of the container and make 2 cuts as shown. Cut off the sides of the lid. Lay the lid, the curved side, and the bottom flat to form the net of the container. Sketch and label the parts of the net.

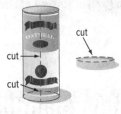

What are the shapes that make up the net of the

container? _____

Step 3 Make a mark on the top of the lid. Place the mark at the top edge of the flattened curved side as shown. Roll the lid along the edge of the side until it completes one rotation.

Where does the lid stop? _____

How does the length of the curved side compare to the distance

around the top? _____

Find the area of each shape.

Top _____ Bottom _____ Side _____

Find the sum of these areas. _____

Investigate

Work with a partner. Draw the net and label the parts of the cylinder and the measurements. Then complete the table to find the *total surface areas* for Exercises 1 and 2. Round to the nearest tenth.

1.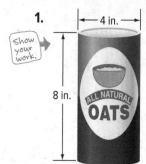

2.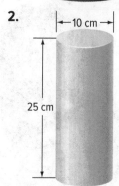

	Area of top (πr^2)	Area of bottom (πr^2)	Curved Area	Total Surface Area
3.				
4.				

Analyze and Reflect

5. What is the total surface area of the container described at the beginning

of the lesson? Round to the nearest tenth. _____

Create

6. **MP** **Reason Inductively** Describe how to find the area of the curved surface

of a cylinder. _____

_____

_____

7. **Inquiry** How can the surface area of a cylinder be determined?

_____

_____

Surface Area of Cylinders

 Real-World Link

Bakery The Shiny Bright bakery is making a cake for Maria's quinceañera. The cake will be in the shape of a cylinder with a height of 4 inches and a diameter of 14 inches.

1. What are the shapes that make up the net of the cake? Sketch the net in the space provided.

   _____

2. How is the length of the rectangle related to the circles that form the top and bottom of the cake?

   _____

   _____

3. Find the area of each part of the cake. Round to the nearest whole number.

   Top: ☐ in^2 Bottom: ☐ in^2 Side: ☐ in^2

4. Add the values from Exercise 3. What is the total surface area of the cake? ☐ in^2

 Essential Question

How do measurements help you describe real-world objects?

 Vocabulary

lateral area
total surface area

 Virginia Standards
7.4a, b

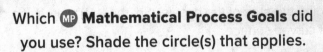

Which ⓜ Mathematical Process Goals did you use? Shade the circle(s) that applies.

① Mathematical Problem Solving
② Mathematical Communication
③ Mathematical Reasoning
④ Mathematical Connections
⑤ Mathematical Representations

Surface Area of a Cylinder

Lateral Area

Words The lateral area *L.A.* of a cylinder with height *h* and radius *r* is the circumference of the base times the height.

Symbols $L.A. = 2\pi r h$

Total Surface Area

Words The surface area *S.A.* of a cylinder with height *h* and radius *r* is the lateral area plus the area of the two circular bases.

Symbols $S.A. = L.A. + 2\pi r^2$ or $S.A. = 2\pi r h + 2\pi r^2$

Model

area of base $= \pi r^2$

You can find the surface area of a cylinder using a net.

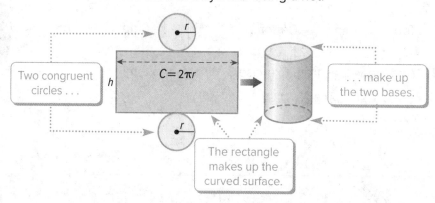

Two congruent circles . . .

$C = 2\pi r$

. . . make up the two bases.

The rectangle makes up the curved surface.

In the diagram above, the length of the rectangle is the same as the circumference of the circle, $2\pi r$. Also, the width of the rectangle is the same as the height of the cylinder.

The **lateral area** of a three-dimensional figure is the surface area of the figure, excluding the area of the base(s). So, the lateral area of a cylinder is the area of curved surface.

The **total surface area** of a three-dimensional figure is the sum of the areas of all its surfaces.

Example

Tutor

1. Find the surface area of the cylinder.
Round to the nearest tenth.

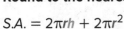

$S.A. = 2\pi rh + 2\pi r^2$ Surface area of a cylinder

$S.A. = 2\pi(2)(7) + 2\pi(2)^2$ Replace r with 2 and h with 7.

$S.A. \approx 113.1$ Simplify.

The surface area is about 113.1 square meters.

Got it? Do these problems to find out.

Find the surface area of each cylinder. Round to the nearest tenth.

a.   9 ft

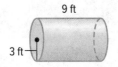

3 ft

b. |←14 cm→|

10 cm

Show your work.

a. _____

b. _____

 **Example**

Tutor

2. A circular fence that is 2 feet high is to be built around the outside of a carousel. The distance from the center of the carousel to the edge of the fence will be 35 feet. What is the area of the fencing material that is needed to make the fence around the carousel?

You need to find the lateral area. The radius of the circular fence is 35 feet. The height is 2 feet.

$L.A. = 2\pi rh$ Lateral area of a cylinder

$L.A. = 2\pi(35)(2)$ Replace r with 35 and h with 2.

$L.A. \approx 439.8$ Simplify.

So, about 439.8 square feet of material is needed to make the fence.

Got it? Do these problems to find out.

c. Find the area of the label of a can of tuna with a radius of 5.1 centimeters and a height of 2.9 centimeters. Round to the nearest tenth.

d. Find the total surface area of a cylindrical candle with a diameter of 4 inches and a height of 2.5 inches. Round to the nearest tenth.

c. _____

d. _____

Find the total surface area of each cylinder. Round to the nearest tenth. (Example 1)

1.

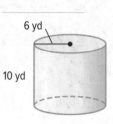

Show your work.

6 yd

10 yd

2.

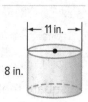

← 11 in. →

8 in.

3.

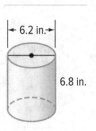

7.5 in.

6 in.

4.

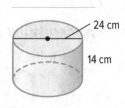

24 cm

14 cm

5. Find the total surface area of a water tank with a height of 10 meters and a diameter of 10 meters. Round to the nearest tenth. (Example 1) _____

Find the lateral area of each cylinder. Round to the nearest tenth. (Example 2)

6.

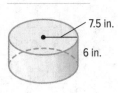

← 6.2 in. →

6.8 in.

7.

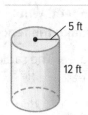

5 ft

12 ft

8. Find the area of the label of a cylindrical potato chip container with a radius of 3.1 inches and a height of 9.2 inches. Round to the nearest tenth. (Example 2)

_____

9. @ **Building on the Essential Question** How is a calculation affected if you round π to 3.14 or use the π key on your calculator? Explain.

_____

_____

_____

Rate Yourself!

Are you ready to move on?
Shade the section that applies.

I have a few questions.

I'm ready to move on.

I have a lot of questions.

For more help, go online to access a Personal Tutor.

Tutor

FOLDABLES Time to update your Foldable!

Independent Practice

Go online for Step-by-Step Solutions

Find the total surface area of each cylinder. Round to the nearest tenth.
(Example 1)

1. _____

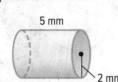

5 mm

2 mm

2. _____

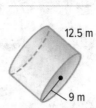

12.5 m

9 m

3. _____

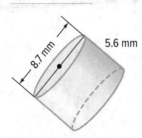

8.7 mm

5.6 mm

4. _____

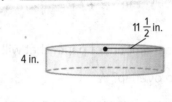

$11\frac{1}{2}$ in.

4 in.

5. A cylindrical candle has a diameter of 4 inches and a height of 7 inches. To the nearest tenth, what is the total surface area of the candle? (Example 1) _____

6. Find the total surface area of an unsharpened cylindrical pencil that has a radius of 0.5 centimeter and a height of 19 centimeters. Round to the nearest tenth. (Example 1) _____

Find the lateral area of each cylinder. Round to the nearest tenth. (Example 2)

7. _____

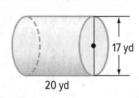

17 yd

20 yd

8. _____

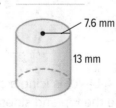

7.6 mm

13 mm

9. Find the lateral area of a cylindrical copper pipe that has a diameter of 6.4 inches and a height of 12 inches. Round to the nearest tenth.

(Example 2) _____

10. **MP Model with Mathematics** Refer to the graphic novel frame below.

a. What is the least amount of paper that will be needed to wrap one candle with no overlap? _____

b. How many square feet of wrapping paper will be needed to wrap all 70 candles? _____

 ## H.O.T. Problems Higher Order Thinking

11. **MP Persevere with Problems** If the height of a cylinder is doubled, will its surface area also double? Explain your reasoning.

_____

_____

12. **MP Reason Inductively** Which has a greater surface area: a cylinder with radius 6 centimeters and height 3 centimeters or a cylinder with radius 3 centimeters and height 6 centimeters? Explain your reasoning.

_____

_____

_____

13. **MP Reason Inductively** A baker is icing a cylindrical cake with radius r and height h. The baker will ice the top and sides of the cake. Write an equation giving the total area A that the baker will ice. Explain why your equation is not the same as the formula for the total surface area of a cylinder.

_____

_____

Extra Practice

Copy and Solve For Exercises 14–27, show your work and answers on a separate piece of paper.

Find the lateral area and the total surface area of each cylinder. Round to the nearest tenth.

14.
3 ft

18 ft

15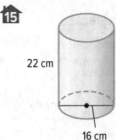
22 cm

16 cm

16.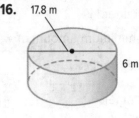
17.8 m

6 m

17. A lamp shade is in the shape of a cylinder with a height of 18 inches and a radius of $6\frac{3}{4}$ inches. Fabric will cover the lateral area of the lamp shade. Find the area of the fabric needed. Round to the nearest tenth.

MP Use Math Tools Estimate the surface area of each cylinder.

18.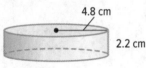
4.8 cm

2.2 cm

19.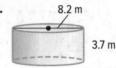
8.2 m

3.7 m

20.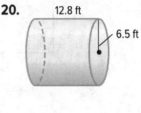
12.8 ft

6.5 ft

21. The mail tube shown is made of cardboard and has plastic end caps. Approximately what percent of the surface area of the mail tube is cardboard?

2.5 in.

15 in.

22. MP Persevere with Problems A hot cocoa canister is a cylinder with a height of 24.5 centimeters and a diameter of 13 centimeters.

   a. What is the lateral area of the hot cocoa canister to the nearest tenth?

   b. How does the lateral area change if the height is divided by 2?

13 cm

24.5 cm

Hot Cocoa Mix

23. Maria is comparing how much wrapping paper it would take to wrap the containers below.

Complete each statement with the correct answers. Round answers to the nearest square inch.

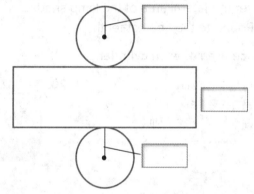

Container I   **Container II**

a. The minimum amount of wrapping paper needed for

Container I is [   ] square centimeters.

b. The minimum amount of wrapping paper needed for

Container II is [   ] square centimeters.

c. Container [   ] requires [   ] more square

centimeters of wrapping paper than Container [   ].

24. Stacey has a cylindrical paper clip holder with a diameter of 2 inches and a height of 1.5 inches. Label the net of the cylinder below with the correct dimensions.

To the nearest tenth, what is the surface area of the paper clip holder? [   ]

Spiral Review

Find the surface area of each prism.

25.

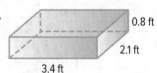

0.8 ft
2.1 ft
3.4 ft

26.

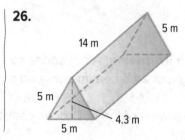

5 m
14 m
5 m
5 m
4.3 m

Case #1 Playgrounds

Liam is helping to mulch the play area at the community center. The diagram shows the dimensions of the play area.

What is the area of the play area to be mulched? Round to the nearest tenth if necessary.

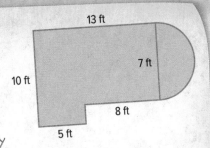

13 ft

7 ft

10 ft

8 ft

5 ft

Understand *What are the facts?*

You know the shape and dimensions of the play area.

Plan *What is your strategy to solve this problem?*

Find the area of the two rectangles and the semi-circle, and then add.

Solve *How can you apply the strategy?*

Area of Rectangle 1	Area of Rectangle 2	Area of Semi-Circle
$A = \ell w$	$A = \ell w$	$A = \dfrac{\pi r^2}{2}$
$A = 5 \cdot 10$	$A = 8 \cdot 7$	$A = \dfrac{3.14 \cdot (3.5)^2}{2}$
$A = \boxed{}$	$A = \boxed{}$	$A = \boxed{}$

The total area is $\boxed{}$ + $\boxed{}$ + $\boxed{}$ or $\boxed{}$ square feet.

Check *Does the answer make sense?*

The play area is about 13 · 10 or 130 square feet. So, an answer of $\boxed{}$ square feet is reasonable.

Analyze the Strategy   Tutor

MP Reason Inductively Why is breaking this problem into simpler parts a good strategy to solve it?

_____

_____

Case #2 Wallpaper

Dora is painting a wall in her house.

What is the area that will be painted?

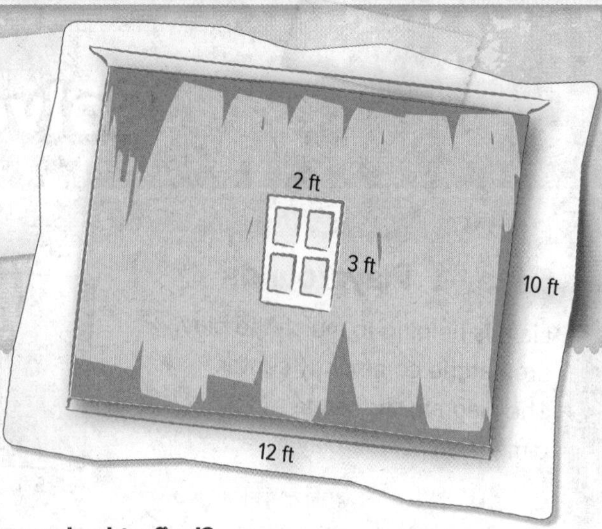

2 ft

3 ft

10 ft

12 ft

1 Understand

Read the problem. What are you being asked to find?

I need to find _____.

What information do you know?

The picture shows the wall is _____ long and _____ high.

There is a window that is _____ by _____.

2 Plan

Choose a problem-solving strategy.

I will use the _____ strategy.

3 Solve

Use your problem-solving strategy to solve the problem.

Find the area of the wall. Then subtract the area of the window.

The dimensions of the wall are [ ] feet by [ ] feet.

So, the area of the wall is [ ] × [ ] = [ ] ft².

The dimensions of the window are [ ] feet by [ ] feet.

So, the area of the window is [ ] × [ ] = [ ] ft².

[ ] − [ ] = [ ]

So, _____.

4 Check

Use information from the problem to check your answer.

Use estimation to check the reasonableness of your answer. The

area of the wall is approximately 10 × 12 = [ ] ft². The answer

is reasonable.

Work with a small group to solve the following cases.
Show your work on a separate piece of paper.

Case #3 Woodworking

Two workers can make two chairs in two days.

How many chairs can 8 workers working at the same rate make in 20 days?

_____

Case #4 Tips

Ebony wants to leave an 18% tip for a $19.82 restaurant bill. The tax is 6.25%, which is added to the bill before the tip.

How much money does Ebony spend at the restaurant? Explain.

_____

_____

_____

Case #5 Continents

The land area of Earth is 57,505,708 square miles.

To the nearest tenth, how much larger is the land area of Asia than North America? Explain.

_____

_____

_____

Continent	Percent of Earth's Land
Asia	30
Africa	20.2
North America	16.5

Use any strategy!

Case #6 Fountains

Mr. Flores has a circular fountain with a radius of 5 feet. He plans on installing a brick path around the fountain.

If each brick covers 2 square feet, how many bricks will he need to buy?.

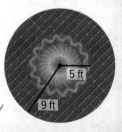

5 ft

9 ft

_____

Copyright © McGraw-Hill Education   Tim Abramowitz/E+/Getty Images

Vocabulary Check

1. Fill in the blank in the sentence below with the correct term.

   A _____ is made up of two or more shapes.

2. Define *cylinder*. What are the symbols used to find the volume of a cylinder?

   _____

   _____

   _____

Skills Check and Problem Solving

3. The dimensions of a cardboard box are shown in the figure at the right. What is the volume of the box?

   _____

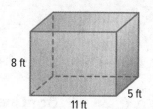

4. **MP Persevere with Problems** The figure at the right represents the design for a new hole for a miniature golf course. The new turf to cover the hole costs $1.50 per square foot. How much will it cost to cover the entire area?

   _____

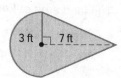

Find the volume of the prism.

5.

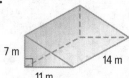

   _____

HOW can you find the volume and surface area of a composite figure?

A company made a model of a new office building. The building is composed of rectangular prisms. You can use centimeter cubes to find the volume of the building model.

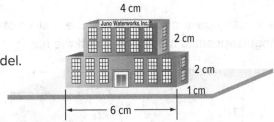

Hands-On Activity 1

The model is a *composite figure* because it is made from two rectangular prisms.

Step 1 Model the top and bottom rectangular prisms using cubes.

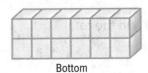
Bottom

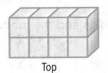
Top

Step 2 Count the cubes to find the dimensions. Write the dimensions in the table below. Then use the cube models to find the volume of both prisms. Write these measures in the table below step 3.

Step 3 Use the table to find the volume of the entire building model. Write these measures in the composite row of the table.

Model	Length (cm)	Width (cm)	Height (cm)	Volume (cm³)
Bottom	6	1		
Top				
Composite				

Mr. Wendell's class made a model of a house. The model was composed of a rectangular prism and a triangular prism. Determine the volume and surface area of the model house.

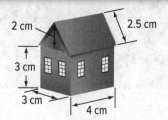

Hands-On Activity 2

Step 1   Use a rectangular prism to model the bottom of the house. Use a triangular prism to model the top of the house.

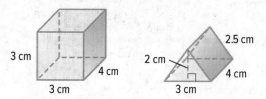

Step 2   Complete the tables below using the models from Step 1.

Prism	Length (cm)	Width (cm)	Height (cm)
Rectangular	4	3	

Prism	Length (cm)	Base (cm)	Height (cm)
Triangular	4	3	

Step 3   Use the information from the tables and the models to find the total volume of the model house.

☐ cm³   +   ☐ cm³   =   ☐ cm³

Volume of Rectangular Prism   Volume of Triangular Prism   Total Volume

Step 4   Use the information from the tables and the models to find the total surface area of the model house.

☐ cm² + ☐ cm² − ☐ cm² = ☐ cm²

Surface Area of Rectangular Prism   Surface Area of Triangular Prism   Areas where Prisms Connect   Total Surface Area

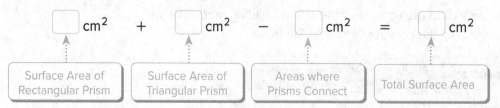

The total volume of the model house is ☐ cubic centimeters. The total surface area is ☐ square centimeters.

Investigate

Work with a partner.

1. **MP Model with Mathematics** Use the top, side, and front views to build a figure using centimeter cubes.

top · side · front

a. Make a sketch of the figure you built.

b. Find the volume and surface area of the figure.

Volume: _____   Surface Area: _____

Refer to the figure at the right for Exercises 2–4.

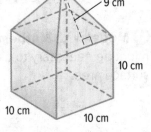

9 cm

10 cm

10 cm   10 cm

2. The figure is comprised of a _____ and a square _____.

3. Complete the following to find the volume of the figure.

a. The volume of the cube is [   ] cubic centimeters.

b. The volume of the square pyramid is 250 cubic centimeters.

c. So, the volume of the composite figure is [   ] cubic centimeters.

4. Complete the following to find the surface area of the figure.

a. The surface area of the cube is [   ] square centimeters.

b. The surface area of the square pyramid is [   ] square centimeters.

c. The area where the figures overlap is [   ] square centimeters.

d. The surface area of the composite figure is [   ] square centimeters.

Analyze and Reflect

MP Reason Inductively Work with a partner. Write each of the following statements in the correct location. One statement is done for you.

5. *measured in square units*

6. *measured in cubic units*

7. *involves adding measures of each figure*

8. *involves subtracting where figures overlap*

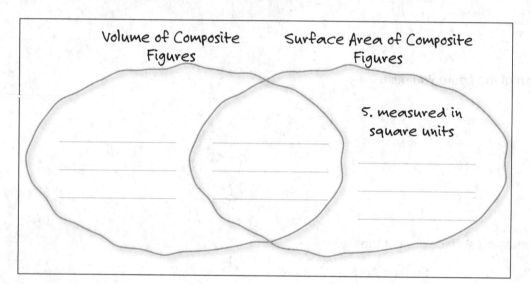

Volume of Composite Figures

Surface Area of Composite Figures

5. measured in square units

Create

On Your Own

9. **MP Model with Mathematics** Describe a real-world situation where it might be necessary to use a model or a drawing to find the volume or surface area.

10. **Inquiry** HOW can you find the volume and surface area of a composite figure?

Volume and Surface Area of Composite Figures

 Real-World Link

 Essential Question

HOW do measurements help you describe real-world objects?

Kaylee and Miles are making a bat house for their backyard like the one shown. They need to determine the surface area to find how much wood they will need.

1. Look at the largest bat house. What three-dimensional figures make up the bat house?

   _____

2. What method could you use to find the surface area of the bat house?

   _____

   _____

3. Suppose you wanted to find the volume of the bat house. What method could you use?

   _____

   _____

Which MP Mathematical Process Goals did you use? Shade the circle(s) that applies.

① Mathematical Problem Solving   ④ Mathematical Connections

② Mathematical Communication   ⑤ Mathematical Representations

③ Mathematical Reasoning

Volume of a Composite Figure

The volume of a composite figure can be found by decomposing the figure into solids whose volumes you know how to find.

Examples

1. Find the volume of the composite figure.

Find the volume of each prism.

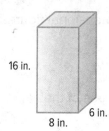

$V = \ell wh$

$V = 8 \cdot 6 \cdot 16$ or 768

$V = \ell wh$

$V = 8 \cdot 6 \cdot 8$ or 384

The volume is $768 + 384$ or 1,152 cubic inches.

---

2. Find the volume of the composite figure.

Find the volume of the cube and the pyramid. Round to the nearest tenth.

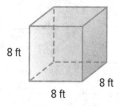

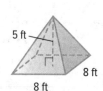

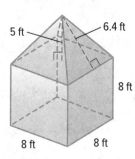

$V = \ell wh$

$V = 8 \cdot 8 \cdot 8$ or 512

$V = \dfrac{1}{3}Bh$

$V = \dfrac{1}{3}(8 \cdot 8)5$ or 106.7

The volume is $512 + 106.7$ or 618.7 cubic feet.

Got it? Do this problem to find out.

a. Find the volume of the composite figure.

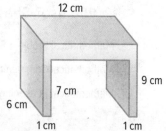

a. _____

Surface Area of a Composite Figure

You can also find the surface area of composite figures by finding the areas of the faces that make up the composite figure.

Examples

 Tutor

3. Find the surface area of the figure in Example 1.

The surface is made up of three different polygons.

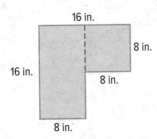

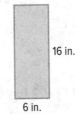

$A = \ell w + \ell w$

$A = (8 \cdot 16) + (8 \cdot 8)$

$A = 128 + 64$ or 192

$A = \ell w$

$A = 6 \cdot 16$

$A = 96$

$A = \ell w$

$A = 6 \cdot 8$

$A = 48$

The total surface area is $2(192) + 2(96) + 4(48)$ or 768 square inches.

- -

4. Find the surface area of the composite figure in Example 2.

The figure is made up of two different polygons.

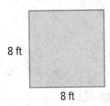

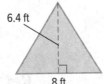

$A = \ell w$

$A = 8 \cdot 8$ or 64

$A = \frac{1}{2}bh$

$A = \frac{1}{2} \cdot 8 \cdot 6.4$ or 25.6

The total surface area is $5(64) + 4(25.6)$ or 422.4 square feet.

Surface Area
To make it easier to see each face, sketch the faces and label the dimensions of each.

Got it? Do this problem to find out.

b. Find the surface area of the steps that are represented by the composite figure shown.

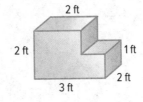

 Show your work.

b. _____

Find the volume of each composite figure. Round to the nearest tenth if necessary. (Examples 1 and 2)

1.

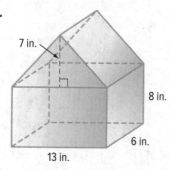

7 in.

8 in.

6 in.

13 in.

Show your work.

2.

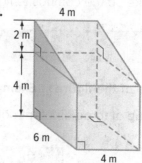

4 m

2 m

4 m

6 m

4 m

Find the surface area of each composite figure. Round to the nearest tenth if necessary. (Examples 3 and 4)

3.

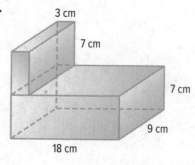

3 cm

7 cm

7 cm

9 cm

18 cm

4.

9 cm

2 cm

2 cm

2 cm   4 cm   2 cm   4 cm

5. 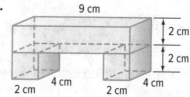 **Building on the Essential Question** How do the previous lessons in this chapter help you find the surface area and volume of a composite figure?

_____

_____

_____

Copyright © McGraw-Hill Education

Independent Practice

Go online for Step-by-Step Solutions

Find the volume of each composite figure. Round to the nearest tenth if necessary. (Examples 1 and 2)

1

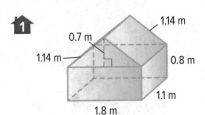

1.14 m

0.7 m

1.14 m

0.8 m

1.1 m

1.8 m

Show your work.

2.

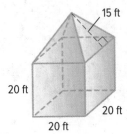

2.5 m

3 m

2 m

4 m

Find the surface area of each composite figure. Round to the nearest tenth if necessary. (Examples 3 and 4)

3.

15 ft

20 ft

20 ft

20 ft

4.

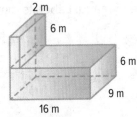

2 m

6 m

6 m

9 m

16 m

5 Find the volume of the figure at the right in cubic feet. Round to the nearest tenth. (Examples 1 and 2)

_____

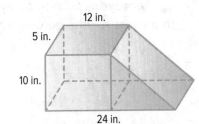

12 in.

5 in.

10 in.

24 in.

6. **MP Reason Inductively** The swimming pool at the right is being filled with water. Find the number of cubic feet that it will take to fill the swimming pool. (*Hint:* The area of a trapezoid is $A = \frac{1}{2}h(b_1 + b_2)$.) (Examples 1 and 2)

_____

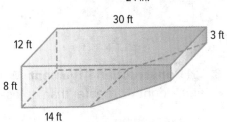

30 ft

3 ft

12 ft

8 ft

14 ft

Copy and Solve For Exercises 7–8, show your work on a separate piece of paper. Round to the nearest tenth. (Examples 1–4)

7. Find the surface area of the figure in Exercise 1.

8. Find the volume of the figure in Exercise 4.

9. A carryout container is shown. The bottom base is a 4-inch square and the top base is a 4-inch by 6-inch rectangle. The height of the container is 5 inches. Find the volume of food that it holds. _____

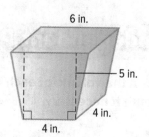

10. Refer to the house shown. Find the surface area and volume of the house. Do not include the bottom of the house when calculating the surface area. _____

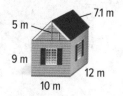

 H.O.T. Problems Higher Order Thinking

11. (MP) **Model with Mathematics** Draw a composite figure that is made up of a cube and a square pyramid. Label its dimensions and find the volume of the figure. _____

Show your work.

12. (MP) **Persevere with Problems** Draw an example of a composite figure that has a volume between 250 and 300 cubic units.

13. (MP) **Construct an Argument** Will the surface area of the figure at the right be greater than or less than 180 square inches? Explain your reasoning. _____

_____

_____

_____

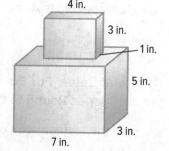

Extra Practice

Find the volume of each composite figure. Round to the nearest tenth if necessary.

14.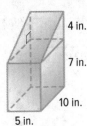

450 in^3

4 in.
7 in.
10 in.
5 in.

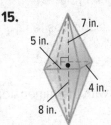

Rectangular Prism	Triangular Prism
$V = lwh$	$V = Bh$
$V = 5 \cdot 10 \cdot 7$	$V = \frac{1}{2} \cdot 10 \cdot 4 \cdot 5$
$V = 350$	$V = 100$

Total Volume = $350 + 100$ or 450 in^3

15.

7 in.
5 in.
4 in.
8 in.

Find the surface area of each composite figure. Round to the nearest tenth if necessary.

16.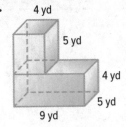

4 yd
5 yd
4 yd
5 yd
9 yd

17.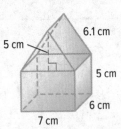

6.1 cm
5 cm
5 cm
6 cm
7 cm

18. **MP** **Find the Error** Seth is finding the surface area of the composite figure shown. Find his mistake and correct it.

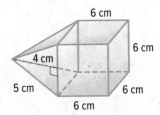

6 cm
6 cm
4 cm
5 cm
6 cm
6 cm

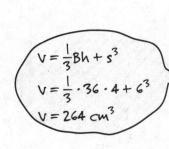

$V = \frac{1}{3}Bh + s^3$

$V = \frac{1}{3} \cdot 36 \cdot 4 + 6^3$

$V = 264 \text{ cm}^3$

GN-16A-891643

_____

_____

_____

19. Refer to the composite figure with the dimensions shown. Fill in the boxes to complete each statement.

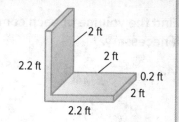

   a. The volume of the composite figure is [   ] .

   b. The total surface area of the composite figure is [   ] .

20. Refer to the composite figure with the dimensions shown.

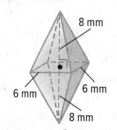

Select the correct values to complete the expression to find the volume of the figure.

$$V = \boxed{} \cdot \frac{1}{3} \cdot \boxed{} \cdot \boxed{} \cdot \boxed{}$$

What is the volume of the composite figure?

[   ]

2
3
4
6
8

Spiral Review

Draw a net for each figure.

21.

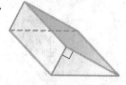
Show your work.

22.

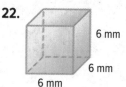

23.

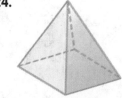

24.

WHAT are some rigid motions of the plane?

 Virginia Standards
7.7

Animated movies are created using frames. Each frame changes slightly from the previous one to create the impression of movement.

Hands-On Activity 1

In this Activity, you will make animation frames using index cards.

Step 1 Arrange ten index cards in a pile. On the top card, draw a circle at the top right hand corner.

Step 2 On the next card, draw the same circle slightly down and to the left.

Step 3 Repeat this for three or four more cards until your circle is at the bottom of the card. Use the remainder of the cards to draw the circle up and to the left.

Step 4 Place a rubber band around the stack, hold the stack at the rubber band, and flip the cards from front to back.

Describe what you see when you flip the cards from front to back.

_____

_____

Look at the circles on the first and second cards and then the second and third cards. How would you describe the change in the position of the circle from one card to the next?

_____

_____

Did the shape or size of the circle change when you moved it? If yes, describe the change. _____

Hands-On Activity 2

Step 1 Draw right angle *XYZ* on a piece of tracing paper. Place a dashed line on the paper as shown.

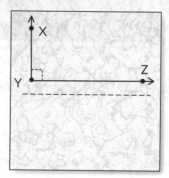

Step 2 Fold the paper along the dashed line. Trace the angle onto the folded portion of the paper. Unfold and label the angle *ABC* so that *A* matches up with *X*, *B* matches up with *Y*, and *C* matches up with *Z*. Tape the paper to your book.

Use a protractor to find the measure of ∠*XYZ* and ∠*ABC*. Did the

measure of the angle change after the flip? _____

Use a centimeter ruler to measure the shortest distance from *X* and *A* to the dashed line. Repeat for *Y* and *B* and for *Z* and *C*. What do you notice?

_____

_____

_____

Hands-On Activity 3

Step 1 Place a piece of tracing paper over the trapezoid shown. Copy the trapezoid. Draw points *A*, *B*, and *C*. Draw $\overrightarrow{AB}$.

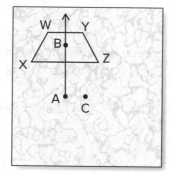

Step 2 Place the eraser end of your pencil on *A*. Turn the tracing paper until $\overrightarrow{AB}$ passes through *C*. Tape the paper to your book.

Did the shape of the trapezoid change when you moved it? If yes, describe

the change. _____

Did the size of the trapezoid change when you moved

it? If yes, describe the change. _____

Work with a partner. Use a ruler to draw the image when each figure is moved as directed.

1. $\frac{1}{2}$ inch down and 1 inch to the left.

2. 1 inch up and 1 inch to the right.

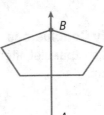

Draw the image when each figure is flipped over line ℓ.

3.

ℓ

4.

ℓ

Draw the image when each pentagon is turned until $\overrightarrow{AB}$ passes through C.

5.

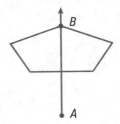

$\cdot$ C

6.

$\cdot$ C

7. Refer to Exercises 1–6.

   a. For which exercises, if any, did the size of the original figure change?

_____

   b. For which exercises, if any, did the shape of the original figure change?

_____

   c. For which exercises, if any, did the orientation of the original figure change?

_____

Analyze and Reflect

Collaborate

For each pair of figures, describe a movement or movements that will place the blue figure on top of the green figure.

8.

Figure	Movement(s)

9.

Figure	Movement(s)

10. Refer to Activity 1 and Exercises 1 and 2. Circle the word that best describes the movement of the figures: **flip** **slide** **turn**

11. Refer to Activity 2 and Exercises 3 and 4. Circle the word that best describes the movement of the figures: **flip** **slide** **turn**

12. Refer to Activity 3 and Exercises 5 and 6. Measure one side of the original figures. Then measure that same side after the turn. Did the length of the side change after you turned it? If yes, describe the change.

13. **MP Justify Conclusions** In Activity 3, $\overline{WY}$ and $\overline{XZ}$ are parallel. Were the segments still parallel after the turn? Would they still be parallel after a slide? flip? Explain.

Create

On Your Own

14. **MP Reason Inductively** Slides, flips, and turns are called *rigid motions of the plane*. Based on the Activities, describe two characteristics of a rigid motion of the plane.

15. **Inquiry** WHAT are some rigid motions of the plane?

Similarity and Transformations

Vocabulary Start-Up

Quadrilaterals and other polygons can be dilated by a scale factor. You can use the table below to explore the properties of quadrilaterals.

Properties of some quadrilaterals are listed across the top. Place check marks (✔) in the appropriate columns for properties of each quadrilateral.

Quadrilateral	All sides congruent	All angles congruent	Opposite sides congruent	Opposite angles congruent	Opposite sides parallel
Parallelogram			✔	✔	✔
Rectangle		✔	✔	✔	✔
Square	✔	✔	✔	✔	✔
Rhombus	✔		✔	✔	✔

1. Of the quadrilaterals listed in the table, which are parallelograms?

_____

2. What special property does a trapezoid have? _____

_____

 Essential Question

HOW do measurements help you describe real-world objects?

 Vocabulary

dilation
scale factor
similar

 Virginia Standards
7.5

Real-World Link

A *fractal* is a geometric image that can be divided into parts that are smaller copies of the whole. The photo at the right is an example of a fractal.

1. Circle two different size parts of the figure that are smaller copies of the whole.

Which MP Mathematical Process Goals did you use? Shade the circle(s) that applies.

① Mathematical Problem Solving
② Mathematical Communication
③ Mathematical Reasoning
④ Mathematical Connections
⑤ Mathematical Representations

Identify Similarity

Two figures are **similar** if the second can be obtained from the first by a sequence of transformations and dilations.

Examples

1. **Determine if the two triangles are similar by using transformations.**

    Since the orientation of the figures is the same, one of the transformations might be a translation.

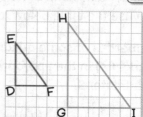

    Step 1 Translate △DEF down 2 units and 5 units to the right so D maps onto G.

    Step 2 Write ratios comparing the lengths of each side.

    $$\frac{HG}{ED} = \frac{8}{4} \text{ or } \frac{2}{1} \qquad \frac{GI}{DF} = \frac{6}{3} \text{ or } \frac{2}{1} \qquad \frac{IH}{FE} = \frac{10}{5} \text{ or } \frac{2}{1}$$

Since the ratios are equal, △HGI is the dilated image of △EDF. So, the two triangles are similar because a translation and a dilation maps △EDF onto △HGI.

STOP and Reflect

In Example 2, how are the properties of a rectangle affected by the transformation?

2. **Determine if the two rectangles are similar by using transformations.**

    The orientation of the figures is the same, so one of the transformations might be a rotation.

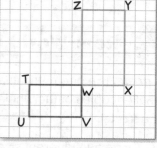

    Step 1 Rotate rectangle VWTU 90° clockwise about W so that it is oriented the same way as rectangle WXYZ.

    Step 2 Write ratios comparing the lengths of each side.

    $$\frac{WT}{XY} = \frac{5}{7} \qquad \frac{TU}{YZ} = \frac{3}{4}$$

    $$\frac{UV}{ZW} = \frac{5}{7} \qquad \frac{VW}{WX} = \frac{3}{4}$$

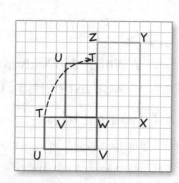

The ratios are not equal. So, the two rectangles are not similar since a dilation did not occur.

Got it? Do these problems to find out.

a.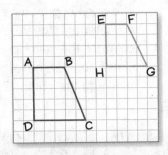

b.

Show your work.

a. _____

b. _____

Use the Scale Factor

Similar figures have the same shape, but may have different sizes. The scale factor is the ratio of the corresponding sides of two similar figures. The sizes of the two figures are related to the **scale factor** of the dilation.

If the scale factor of the dilation is ...	then the dilated figure is ...
between 0 and 1	smaller than the original
equal to 1	the same size as the original
greater than 1	larger than the original

Example

Tutor

3. Ken enlarges this photo by a scale factor of 2 for his webpage. He then enlarges the webpage photo by a scale factor of 1.5 to print. If the original is 2 inches by 3 inches, what are the dimensions of the print? Are the enlarged photos similar to the original?

Multiply each dimension of the original photo by 2 to find the dimensions of the webpage photo.

2 in. × 2 = 4 in.   3 in. × 2 = 6 in.

So, the webpage photo will be 4 inches by 6 inches. Multiply the dimensions of that photo by 1.5 to find the dimensions of the print.

4 in. × 1.5 = 6 in.   6 in. × 1.5 = 9 in.

The printed photo will be 6 inches by 9 inches. All three photos are similar since each enlargement was the result of a dilation.

STOP and Reflect

List below at least two topics in mathematics that use a scale factor.

Got it? Do this problem to find out.

c. _____

c. An art show offers different size prints of the same painting. The original print measures 24 centimeters by 30 centimeters. A printer enlarges the original by a scale factor of 1.5, and then enlarges the second image by a scale factor of 3. What are the dimensions of the largest print? Are both of the enlarged prints similar to the original?

Guided Practice

Check ✓

Determine if the two figures are similar by using transformations. Explain your reasoning. (Examples 1 and 2)

1.

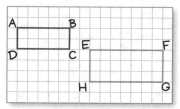

_____

_____

_____

2.

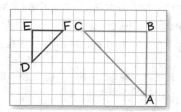

_____

_____

_____

3. A T-shirt iron-on measures 2 inches by 1 inch. It is enlarged by a scale factor of 3 for the back of the shirt. The second iron-on is enlarged by a scale factor of 2 for the front of the shirt. What are the dimensions of the largest iron-on? Are both of the enlarged iron-ons similar to the original? (Example 3) _____

4. **ℓ** **Building on the Essential Question** In a dilation of a parallelogram, how do the measures of sides and angles change?

_____

_____

_____

_____

Rate Yourself!

How confident are you about similar figures? Shade the ring on the target.

For more help, go online to access a Personal Tutor.

Tutor

FOLDABLES Time to update your Foldable!

Independent Practice

Go online for Step-by-Step Solutions

Determine if the two figures are similar by using transformations. Explain your reasoning. (Examples 1 and 2)

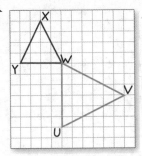

2.

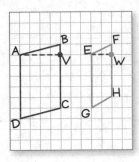

Show your work.

_____

_____

_____

_____

_____

_____

3 Felisa is creating a scrapbook of her family. A photo of her grandmother measures 3 inches by 5 inches. She enlarges it by a scale factor of 1.5 to place in the scrapbook. Then she enlarges the second photo by a scale factor of 1.5 to place on the cover of the scrapbook. What are the dimensions of the photo for the cover of

the scrapbook? Are all of the photos similar? (Example 3) _____

MP Persevere with Problems Each preimage and image are similar. Describe a sequence of transformations that maps the preimage onto the image.

4.

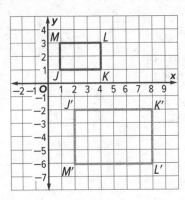

5.

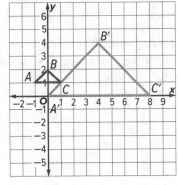

_____

_____

_____

_____

6. **MP Identify Structure** Use the graphic organizer to compare and contrast similar and congruent figures.

	Similar Figures	Congruent Figures
Side Measures		
Angle Measures		
Transformations Used		

H.O.T. Problems Higher Order Thinking

7. **MP Persevere with Problems** Using at least one dilation, describe a series of transformations where the image is congruent to the preimage.

_____

_____

_____

8. **MP Use Logical Reasoning** Use the properties of quadrilaterals to solve the following problems:

   a. The sum of the angles of any quadrilateral is 360°. One angle of a parallelogram is 65°. What are the measures of the other three angles?

   b. A rectangle that is 3 inches by 4 inches is rotated 90° and then dilated by a scale factor of 1.5. What is the perimeter of the image?

   _____

   _____

   _____

9. **MP Construct an Argument** *True* or *false*. If a dilation is in a composition of transformations, the order in which you perform the composition does not matter. Explain your reasoning.

   _____

   _____

   _____

10. **MP Model with Mathematics** Trapezoid *ABCD* is shown at the right. Perform a series of transformations on the trapezoid and draw the image on the coordinate plane. List the transformations used below.

    _____

    _____

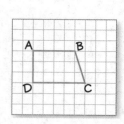

Extra Practice

Determine if the two figures are similar by using transformations. Explain your reasoning.

11.

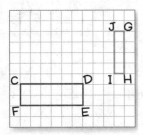

12.

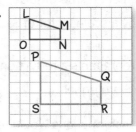

Homework Help

no; The ratios of the side lengths are not equal.

Find the ratios of the side lengths.
$\frac{CD}{GH} = \frac{6}{4}$ and $\frac{DE}{JG} = \frac{2}{1}$; $\frac{6}{4} \neq \frac{2}{1}$, so the two figures are not similar.

13. Shannon is making three different sizes of blankets from the same material. The first measures 2.5 feet by 2 feet. She wants to enlarge it by a scale factor of 2 to make the second blanket. Then she will enlarge the second one by a scale factor of 1.5 to make the third blanket. What are the dimensions of the third blanket? Are all of the blankets similar?

14. **MP Model with Mathematics** In the figure shown, trapezoid *RSTU* has vertices *R*(1, 3), *S*(4, 3), *T*(3, 1), and *U*(2, 1).

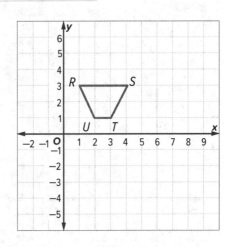

a. Draw the image of *RSTU* after a translation of 2 units down followed by a dilation with a scale factor of 2. Label the vertices *ABCD*.

b. Draw the image of *RSTU* after a dilation with a scale factor of 2, followed by a translation of 2 units down. Label the vertices *EFGH*.

c. Which figures are similar? Which figures are congruent?

_____

_____

d. Are *ABCD* and *EFGH* in the same location? If they are not, what transformation would map *ABCD* onto *EFGH*?

_____

_____

15. Triangle *DEF* is the image of triangle *ABC* after a sequence of transformations.

Determine if each statement is true or false.

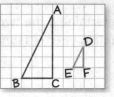

a. △*ABC* was dilated by a scale factor of 3 to create △*DEF*.　　☐ True　☐ False

b. The transformation represents a reduction.　　☐ True　☐ False

c. The ratios $\frac{AB}{DF}$ and $\frac{AC}{DE}$ are equal.　　☐ True　☐ False

16. Which sequences of transformations would result in similar figures that are enlargements or reductions? Select all that apply.

☐ translation, dilation, rotation, reflection

☐ reflection, translation, rotation

☐ translation, reflection, rotation, reflection

☐ rotation, translation, dilation

Spiral Review

Find the coordinates of the vertices of each figure after a dilation with the given scale factor *k*. Then graph the original image and the dilation.

17. *M*(0, 0), *N*(−1, 1), *O*(2, 3); *k* = 2

18. *A*(−3, 3), *B*(3, 3), *C*(3, −3); $k = \frac{2}{3}$

19. *G*(4, 4), *H*(2, −4), *I*(−4, −4), *J*(0, 2); $k = \frac{1}{2}$

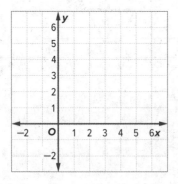

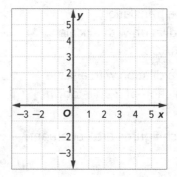

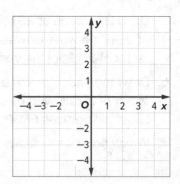

Need more practice? Download more Extra Practice at **connectED.mcgraw-hill.com.**

Properties of Similar Polygons

Real-World Link

Photos Elsa is printing pictures at a photo kiosk in the store. She can choose between 4 × 6 prints or 5 × 7 prints. Are the side lengths of the two prints proportional? Explain. _____

Follow the steps to discover how the triangles are related.

1. Using a centimeter ruler, measure the sides of the two triangles. Then, use a protractor to measure the angles. Write the results in the table.

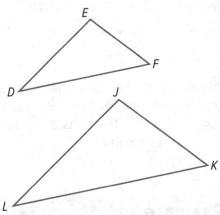

 Essential Question

HOW do measurements help you describe real-world objects?

 Vocabulary

similar polygons

Math Symbols
~ is similar to

Virginia Standards
7.5; 7.6a, b

Figure	Side Length (cm)			Angle Measure (°)		
△EFD	DE	EF	FD	∠D	∠E	∠F
△LJK	LJ	JK	KL	∠L	∠J	∠K

2. Are the side lengths proportional? Explain.

_____

3. What do you notice about the angles of the two triangles?

_____

Which MP Mathematical Process Goals did you use? Shade the circle(s) that applies.

① Mathematical Problem Solving
② Mathematical Communication
③ Mathematical Reasoning
④ Mathematical Connections
⑤ Mathematical Representations

Similar Polygons

Words If two polygons are similar, then
- their corresponding angles are congruent and
- the measures of their corresponding sides are proportional.

Model

$\triangle ABC \sim \triangle XYZ$

Symbols $\angle A \cong \angle X$, $\angle B \cong \angle Y$, $\angle C \cong \angle Z$, and $\dfrac{AB}{XY} = \dfrac{BC}{YZ} = \dfrac{AC}{XZ}$

Polygons that have the same shape are called **similar polygons**. In the Key Concept box, triangle *ABC* is similar to triangle *XYZ*. This is written as $\triangle ABC \sim \triangle XYZ$. The parts of similar figures that "match" are called corresponding parts.

Example

Watch ▶ Tutor 💬

1. Determine whether rectangle *HJKL* is similar to rectangle *MNPQ*. Explain.

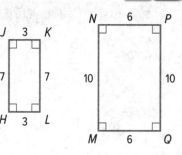

First, check to see if corresponding angles are congruent.

Since the two polygons are rectangles, all of their angles are right angles. Therefore, all corresponding angles are congruent.

Next, check to see if corresponding sides are proportional.

$$\frac{HJ}{MN} = \frac{7}{10} \qquad \frac{JK}{NP} = \frac{3}{6} \text{ or } \frac{1}{2} \qquad \frac{KL}{PQ} = \frac{7}{10} \qquad \frac{LH}{QM} = \frac{3}{6} \text{ or } \frac{1}{2}$$

Since $\frac{7}{10}$ and $\frac{1}{2}$ are not equivalent, the rectangles are *not* similar.

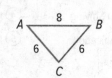

Common Error

Do not assume that two rectangles are similar just because their corresponding angles are congruent. Their corresponding sides must also be proportional.

Got it? Do this problem to find out.

a. _____

a. Determine whether $\triangle ABC$ is similar to $\triangle XYZ$. Explain.

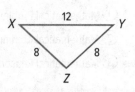

Find Missing Measures

You can use the scale factor of similar figures to find missing measures.

Example

2. Quadrilateral *WXYZ* is similar to quadrilateral *ABCD*.

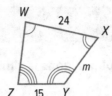

a. **Describe the transformations that map *WXYZ* onto *ABCD*.**

Since the figures are similar, they are not the same size. Choose two corresponding sides and determine what transformations will map one onto the other. A translation followed by a dilation will map $\overline{AB}$ onto $\overline{WX}$.

b. **Find the missing measure.**

Method 1

Find the scale factor from quadrilateral *ABCD* to quadrilateral *WXYZ*.

$$\text{scale factor: } \frac{YZ}{CD} = \frac{15}{10} \text{ or } \frac{3}{2}$$

So, a length on polygon *WXYZ* is $\frac{3}{2}$ times as long as the corresponding length on polygon *ABCD*. Let *m* represent the measure of $\overline{XY}$.

$m = \frac{3}{2}(12)$ Write the equation.

$m = 18$ Multiply.

Method 2

Set up a proportion to find the missing measure.

$\dfrac{XY}{BC} = \dfrac{YZ}{CD}$ Write the proportion.

$\dfrac{m}{12} = \dfrac{15}{10}$ $XY = m, BC = 12, YZ = 15, CD = 10$

$m \cdot 10 = 12 \cdot 15$ Find the cross products.

$10m = 180$ Simplify.

$m = 18$ Division Property of Equality

b. _____

c. _____

Got it? Do these problems to find out.

Find each missing measure.

b. *WZ*

c. *AB*

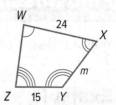

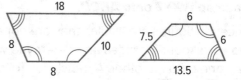

Guided Practice

Check ✓

Determine whether each pair of polygons is similar. Explain. (Example 1)

1.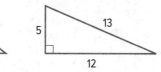

_____

_____

2.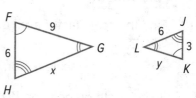

_____

_____

3. The two triangles are similar. (Example 2)

   a. Determine the transformations that map one figure onto the other.

   _____

   b. Find the missing side measures. _____

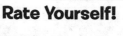

4. The two triangles are similar. (Example 2)

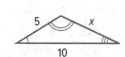

   a. Determine the transformations that map one figure onto the other.

   _____

   b. Find the missing side measure. _____

5. ℯ **Building on the Essential Question** How does the scale factor of a dilation relate to the ratio of two of the corresponding sides of the preimage and the image?

   _____

   _____

Rate Yourself!

Are you ready to move on?
Shade the section that applies.

For more help, go online to access a Personal Tutor.

Tutor

FOLDABLES Time to update your Foldable!

Independent Practice

Go online for Step-by-Step Solutions

Determine whether each pair of polygons is similar. Explain. (Example 1)

1.
3
4
7
8

 Show your work.

_____

_____

2.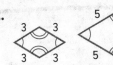
5 5
3 3
3 3
5 5

_____

_____

_____

Each pair of polygons is similar. Determine the transformations that map one figure onto the other. Then find the missing side measures. (Example 2)

3.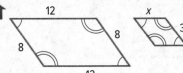
12
8
8
12
x
3

_____

_____

4.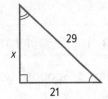
29
x
21

14.5
10
10.5

_____

_____

5. **MP** **Persevere with Problems** The figures at the right are similar.

a. Find the area of both figures.

_____

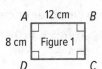
A   12 cm   B
8 cm   Figure 1
D   C

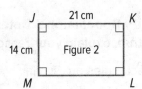
J   21 cm   K
14 cm   Figure 2
M   L

b. Compare the scale factor of the side lengths and the ratio of the areas.

_____

_____

_____

6. **STEM** The scale factor from the model of a human inner ear to the actual ear is 55:2. If one of the bones of the model is 8.25 centimeters

long, how long is the actual bone in a human ear? _____

7. **MP Model with Mathematics** Refer to the graphic novel frame below. The brochure says that the rope is 500 feet long. Use the properties of similar triangles to find the parasailer's height above the water. _____

H.O.T. Problems Higher Order Thinking

8. **MP Persevere with Problems** Suppose two rectangles are similar with a scale factor of 2. What is the ratio of their areas? Explain. _____

_____

_____

MP Justify Conclusions Determine whether each statement is *true* or *false*. If true, explain your reasoning. If false, provide a counterexample.

9. All rectangles are similar.

_____

_____

_____

10. All squares are similar.

_____

_____

_____

11. **MP Model with Mathematics** Draw two similar polygons in the space provided. Include the measures of the sides on your drawing, and identify the scale factor. _____

Extra Practice

Determine whether each pair of polygons is similar. Explain.

12.

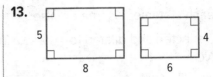

7.8 cm
3.25 cm
8.45 cm
13 cm
5 cm
12 cm

As indicated by the arc marks, corresponding angles are congruent. Check to see if the corresponding sides are proportional.

$$\frac{3.25}{5} = \frac{8.45}{13} = \frac{7.8}{12}$$

The sides are proportional so the triangles are similar.

13.

5
8
4
6

_____
_____

14. The two figures are similar. Determine the transformations that map one figure onto the other. Then find the missing side length.

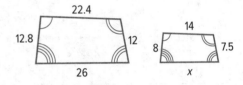

22.4
12.8   12
26
14
8   7.5
x

15. **MP Model with Mathematics**

Mrs. Henderson wants to build a fence around the rectangular garden in her backyard. In the scale drawing, the perimeter of the garden is 14 inches. If the actual length of $\overline{AB}$ is 20 feet, how many feet of fencing will she need?

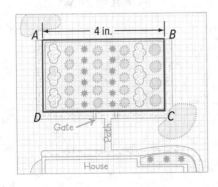

A ——— 4 in. ——— B
D   C
Gate → Path
House

16. Isaiah is making a mosaic using different pieces of tile. The tiles shown at the right are similar. If the perimeter of the larger tile is 23 centimeters, what is the perimeter of the smaller tile?

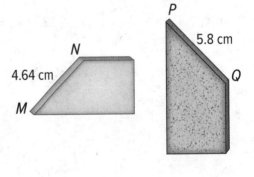

P
5.8 cm
N
Q
4.64 cm
M

17. Quadrilateral *FGHJ* was transformed to create similar quadrilateral *LMNO*.

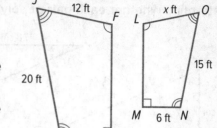

Determine if each statement is true or false.

a. *FGHJ* was reflected and dilated to create *LMNO*. ☐ True ☐ False

b. The scale factor of the dilation is $\frac{3}{4}$. ☐ True ☐ False

c. The value of *x* is 16. ☐ True ☐ False

18. Triangle *FGH* is similar to triangle *RST*. Select the correct values to label the missing side lengths of triangle *RST*.

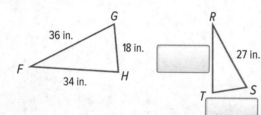

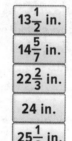

$13\frac{1}{2}$ in.

$14\frac{5}{7}$ in.

$22\frac{2}{3}$ in.

24 in.

$25\frac{1}{2}$ in.

Spiral Review

Find the scale factor for each scale drawing.

19. 6 in. = 12 ft _____

20. 20 cm = 10 m _____

21. 18 in. = 3 ft _____

22. 8 cm = 2.5 mm _____

23. 2 in. = 0.25 mi _____

24. 8 ft = 24 yd _____

Similar Triangles and Indirect Measurement

Vocabulary Start-Up

Indirect measurement allows you to use properties of similar polygons to find distances or lengths that are difficult to measure directly.

Complete the graphic organizer. List three real-world examples in the Venn diagram for each method of measurement.

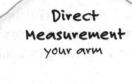

Direct
Measurement
your arm

Indirect
Measurement
Statue of
Liberty's arm

Write the name of an object that could be measured by either

method. _____

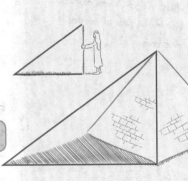

Real-World Link

Shadows Legend says that Thales, the first Greek mathematician, was the first to determine the height of the pyramids by examining the shadows made by the Sun.

1. What appears to be true about the corresponding

   angles in the two triangles? _____

2. If the corresponding sides are proportional, what could you

   conclude about the triangles? _____

Which 🅜🅟 Mathematical Process Goals did you use? Shade the circle(s) that applies.

① Mathematical Problem Solving

② Mathematical Communication

③ Mathematical Reasoning

④ Mathematical Connections

⑤ Mathematical Representations

Essential Question

HOW do measurements help you describe real-world objects?

Vocabulary

indirect measurement

Virginia Standards
7.5

Angle-Angle (AA) Similarity

Words If two angles of one triangle are congruent to two angles of another triangle, then the triangles are similar.

Symbols If $\angle A \cong \angle F$ and $\angle B \cong \angle G$, then $\triangle ABC \sim \triangle FGH$.

Model

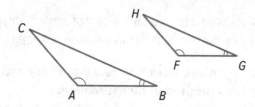

In the figure below, $\angle X \cong \angle P$ and $\angle Y \cong \angle Q$. If you extend the sides of each figure to form a triangle, you can see the two triangles are similar. So, triangle similarity can be proven by showing two pairs of corresponding angles are congruent.

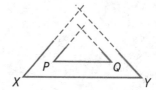

STOP and Reflect

What do you know about the third pair of angles in the triangle?

Example

1. **Determine whether the triangles are similar. If so, write a similarity statement.**

Angle A and $\angle E$ have the same measure, so they are congruent. Since $180 - 62 - 48 = 70$, $\angle G$ measures 70°. Two angles of $\triangle EFG$ are congruent to two angles of $\triangle ABC$, so $\triangle ABC \sim \triangle EFG$.

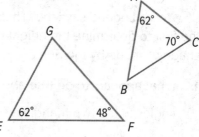

Got it? Do this problem to find out.

Show your work.

a. _____

a.

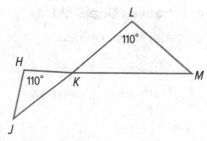

Use Indirect Measurement

One type of indirect measurement is *shadow reckoning*. Two objects and their shadows form two sides of right triangles. In shadow problems, you can assume that the angles formed by the Sun's rays with two objects at the same location are congruent. Since two pairs of corresponding angles are congruent, the two right triangles are similar. You can also use similar triangles that do not involve shadows to find missing measures.

Examples

Watch ▶ Tutor 💬

2. A fire hydrant 2.5 feet high casts a 5-foot shadow. How tall is a street light that casts a 26-foot shadow at the same time? Let *h* represent the height of the street light.

Shadow			Height
hydrant →			← hydrant
street light →	$\dfrac{5}{26} = \dfrac{2.5}{h}$		← street light

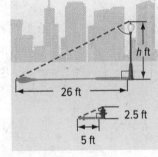
26 ft

2.5 ft

5 ft

$5h = 26 \cdot 2.5$ Find the cross products.

$5h = 65$ Multiply.

$\dfrac{5h}{5} = \dfrac{65}{5}$ Divide each side by 5.

$h = 13$

The street light is 13 feet tall.

3. In the figure at the right, triangle *DBA* is similar to triangle *ECA*. Ramon wants to know the distance across the lake.

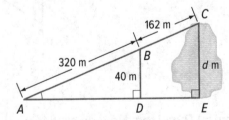
162 m
320 m
40 m
d m
A   *D*   *E*   *B*   *C*

$\dfrac{AB}{AC} = \dfrac{BD}{CE}$ $\overline{AB}$ corresponds to $\overline{AC}$ and $\overline{BD}$ corresponds to $\overline{CE}$.

$\dfrac{320}{482} = \dfrac{40}{d}$ Replace *AB* with 320, *AC* with 482, and *BD* with 40.

$320d = 482 \cdot 40$ Find the cross products.

$\dfrac{320d}{320} = \dfrac{19,280}{320}$ Multiply. Then divide each side by 320.

$d = 60.25$

The distance across the lake is 60.25 meters.

b. _____

b. At the same time a 2-meter street sign casts a 3-meter shadow, a nearby telephone pole casts a 12.3-meter shadow. How tall is the telephone pole?

Guided Practice

Check ✓

Determine whether the triangles are similar. If so, write a similarity statement. (Example 1)

1.

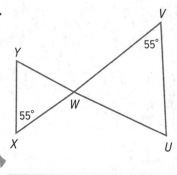

Show your work.

_____

_____

2.

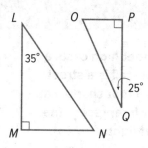

_____

_____

3. How tall is the tree? (Example 2) _____

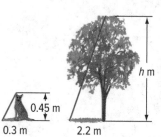

4. Find the distance from the house to the street light. (Example 3) _____

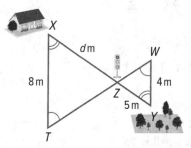

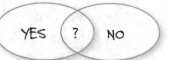

5. **Building on the Essential Question** How do similar triangles make it easier to measure very tall objects?

_____

_____

_____

_____

_____

Rate Yourself!

Are you ready to move on?
Shade the section that applies.

YES   ?   NO

For more help, go online to access a Personal Tutor.

Tutor

Independent Practice

Go online for Step-by-Step Solutions

Determine whether the triangles are similar. If so, write a similarity statement. (Example 1)

1.

Show your work.

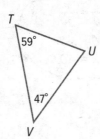

_____

_____

2.

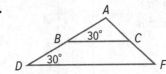

_____

_____

3. How tall is the building? (Example 2)

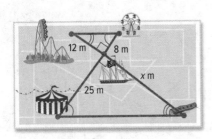

_h_ ft

50 ft

50 ft

12.5 ft

4. How tall is the taller flagpole? (Example 2)

_____

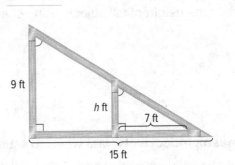

_h_ ft

7 ft

6 ft   2 ft

5 How far is it from the log ride to the pirate

ship? (Example 3) _____

12 m   8 m

_x_ m

25 m

6. Find the height of the brace. (Example 3)

_____

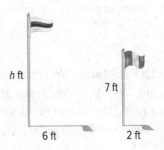

9 ft

_h_ ft   7 ft

15 ft

7 **MP Reason Abstractly** The Giant Wheel at Cedar Point in Ohio is one of the tallest Ferris wheels in the country at 136 feet tall. If the Giant Wheel casts a 34-foot shadow, write and solve a proportion to find the height of a nearby man who casts a $1\frac{1}{2}$-foot shadow.

_____

_____

H.O.T. Problems Higher Order Thinking

8. **MP** **Find the Error** Sara is finding the height of the lighthouse shown in the diagram. Find her mistake and correct it.

$$\frac{27}{60} = \frac{x}{90}$$
$$27 \cdot 90 = 60x$$
$$x = 40.5$$

x ft

27 ft

60 ft

90 ft

_____

_____

_____

_____

9. **MP** **Model with Mathematics** On a separate sheet of paper, draw two different triangles so that each one contains both of the angles shown. Then verify that they are similar by determining which transformation will map one onto the other.

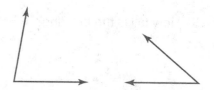

10. **MP** **Persevere with Problems** You cut a circular hole $\frac{1}{4}$-inch in diameter in a piece of cardboard. With the cardboard 30 inches from your face, the Moon fits exactly into the hole. The Moon is about 240,000 miles from Earth. Is the Moon's diameter more than 1,500 miles? Justify your reasoning.

_____

_____

11. **MP** **Identify Structure** What measures must be known in order to calculate the height of tall objects using shadow reckoning?

_____

_____

_____

12. **MP** **Reason Inductively** Mila wants to estimate the height of a statue in a local park. Mila's height and both shadow lengths are shown in the diagram. Is an estimate of 15 feet reasonable for the statue's height? Explain your reasoning.

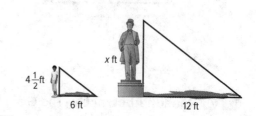

$4\frac{1}{2}$ ft

6 ft

x ft

12 ft

_____

_____

_____

Extra Practice

13. What is the height of the tree? _90 ft_

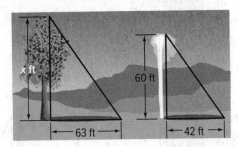

The triangles are similar. Write and solve a proportion.

$$\frac{63}{42} = \frac{x}{60}$$

$$63 \cdot 60 = 42x$$

$$90 = x$$

14. Find the distance across the river. _____

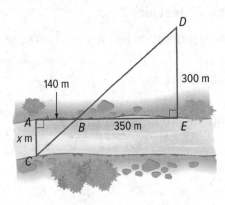

15. About how long is the log that goes across the creeks? _____

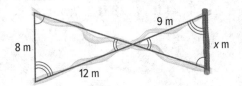

16. How deep is the water 62 meters from the shore?

_____

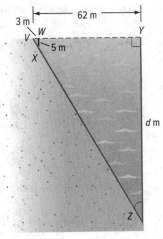

17. In the diagram shown at the right, $\triangle ABC \sim \triangle EDC$.

  a. Write a proportion that could be used to solve for the height h of the flag pole. _____

  b. What information would you need to know in order to solve this proportion?

_____

_____

_____

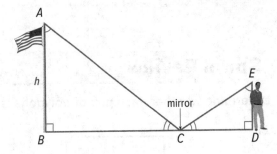

18. **MP** **Model with Mathematics** A 78-inch-tall man casts a shadow that is 54 inches long. At the same time, a nearby building casts a 48-foot-long shadow. Write and solve a proportion to find the height of the building.

_____

19. Horatio is 6 feet tall and casts a shadow 3 feet long. At the same time, a nearby tower casts a shadow that is 25 feet long.

Write a proportion Horatio can use to find the

height of the tower.

Using the proportion, the tower is [   ] feet tall.

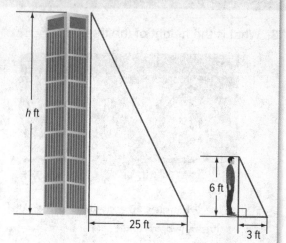

20. Lenno is 5 feet tall and is using similar triangles and a mirror to find the height of a telephone pole. The horizontal distance between Lenno and the telephone pole is 28 feet. He places the mirror on the ground 7 feet from himself so that he can see the top of the pole in the mirror's reflection as shown in the figure below.

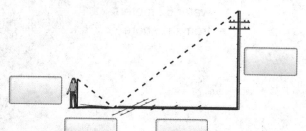

5 ft	7 ft	12 ft	14 ft
21 ft	28 ft	h ft	

Select values to label the diagram with the correct dimensions.

What is the height of the telephone pole? [   ]

Spiral Review

Determine whether each pair of polygons is similar. Explain.

21.

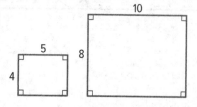

22.

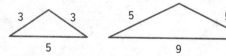

21ST CENTURY CAREER
in Landscape Architecture

Landscape Architect

Do you have an artistic side, and do you enjoy being outdoors? If so, a career in landscape design might be a perfect fit for you. Landscape architects design outside areas such as yards, parks, playgrounds, campuses, shopping centers, and golf courses. Their designed areas are not only meant to be beautiful, but also functional and compatible with the natural environment. A landscape architect must be proficient in mathematics, science, and the use of computer-aided design.

College & Career
READINESS

Is This the Career for You?

Are you interested in a career as a landscape architect? Take some of the following courses in high school.

◆ Algebra
◆ Botany
◆ Drafting/Illustrative Design Technology
◆ Geometry
◆ Architectural Design

Find out how math relates to a career in Landscape Architecture.

595

 Planting in Circles

For each problem, use the information in the designs.

1. In Design 2, what is the radius of the larger grassy area? _____

2. The small circular fountain in Design 1 is surrounded by a stone wall. Find the circumference of the wall. Use $\frac{22}{7}$ for π.

_____

3. Find the circumference of the smaller grassy area in Design 2. Use 3.14 for π.

_____

4. In Design 2, how much greater is the lawn area in the larger circle than in the smaller circle? Use 3.14 for π. _____

5. In Design 2, the smaller circle is surrounded by a path 1 meter wide. What is the outer circumference of the path? Use the π key on a calculator and round to the nearest tenth.

_____

6. In Design 1, the area of the large circular patio is about 201.1 square feet. What is the radius of the patio? Round to the nearest foot. _____

Design 1

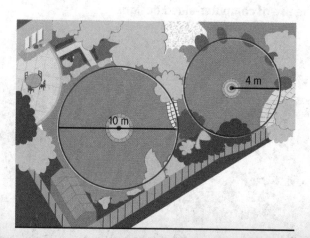

Design 2

Career Project

It's time to update your career portfolio! Download free landscaping software from the Internet and use it to create your own landscape design. Include a list of all the plants, materials, and hard elements used in your design. Also, provide an estimate of the total cost of the landscaping project.

_____

_____

_____

_____

What is something you really want to do in the next ten years?

- _____
- _____
- _____
- _____
- _____

Chapter Review ✓

Vocabulary Check

Complete each sentence using the vocabulary list at the beginning of the chapter. Then ⃝circle the word that completes the sentence in the word search.

1. Composite _____ are objects that are made up of more than one type of solid.

2. A _____ is a three-dimensional figure with two parallel congruent circular bases connected by a curved surface.

3. _____ measurement allows you to use properties of similar polygons to find distances or lengths that are difficult to measure directly.

4. The _____ area of a three-dimensional figure is the surface area of the figure, excluding the area of the base(s).

5. _____ factor is the ratio of the lengths of two corresponding sides o two similar polygons.

6. Two figures are similar if the second can be obtained from the first by a sequence of transformations and _____.

7. Polygons that have the same shape are called _____ polygons.

8. The _____ surface area of a three-dimensional figure is the sum of the areas of all its surfaces.

```
G U H M I R H X P E S F S S Q W C P A C O Q
P L B A E V O L U M E I V W Z A X S D I O C
P A J S O L I D S G E R M R Q A Q I E N I O
C T N C D E D Z M M L R L I I N A D P D I D
M E Z C K G H N L O C P I V L M C W Z I C Z
C R C I R C U M F E R E N C E A P M C R N P
X A O V G B L H V Z I B B T P T R S O E C N
S L V T D K L A B W C O E O T J L C V C D L
S P C T Y S U Z S I T R J T O R Y B L T Y Q
Y P V Y Z B E Z O C H N W A J C T T Q E H S
P R D B L T L D W T A N W L X Z S V J X L J
E K A J N I G W C M P L C D M K L M O S L P
A I Y D A Z N F Q F C X E Y M Y A W X F Z F
V X Y M I N H D I W D U Z L A T N Q L O Q J
Z U O Y M U U K E K L D I L A T I O N S U H
E C A F R U S G Z R X K W S T R X J X K I K
```

Use Your FOLDABLES

Use your Foldable to help review the chapter.

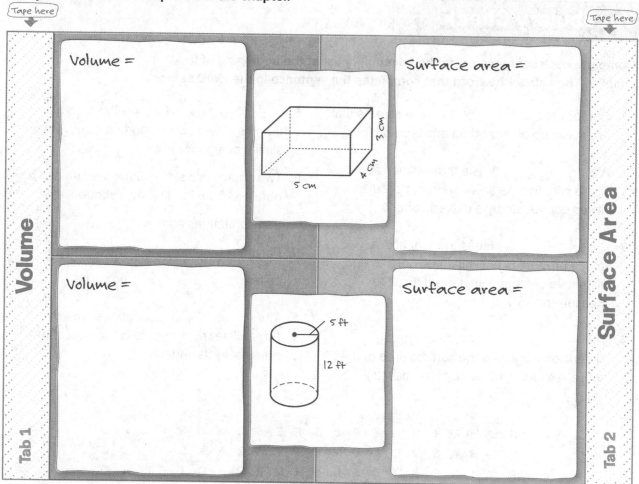

Tape here

Volume

Volume =

Surface area =

5 cm   4 cm   3 cm

Volume =

Surface area =

5 ft   12 ft

Surface Area

Tab 1   Tab 2

Tape here

Got it?

Circle the correct term or number to complete each sentence.

1. Polygons that have the same shape are called (similar polygons, rectangles).

2. (Direct, Indirect) measurement allows you to use properties of similar polygons to find distances or lengths that are difficult to measure directly.

3. The volume of a rectangular prism can be found by multiplying the area of the base times the (length, height).

4. To find the surface area of a triangular prism, find the area of each face and calculate the (sum, product) of all the faces.

Juice Box Packaging

Supreme Packaging Company manufactures juice boxes for juice companies. They are examining different ways to make the juice boxes using various lengths, widths, and heights. The measurements of one juice box are shown.

4 in.

1.5 in.   3 in.

Write your answers on another piece of paper. Show all of your to receive full credit.

Part A

What is the volume of the juice box shown? The company received an order to make a jumbo juice box that has twice the volume as the one shown. Could you double the current dimensions to make the jumbo juice box at the suggested volume? Explain.

Part B

Draw and label a net to find the surface area of the original juice box. It costs Supreme Packaging $0.02 per square inch to create one juice box. The company groups eight juice boxes together as one package. How much does it cost to create one package?

Part C

An artist created the picture of the citrus fruit on the label. The picture is a circle and has an area of 12.56 square inches. Will the artist's picture fit on the juice box label? Explain. Use 3.14 for π.

Answering the Essential Question

Use what you learned about measuring figures to complete the graphic organizer.

Volume

Surface Area

 Essential Question

HOW do measurements help you describe real-world objects?

Similar Polygons

Indirect Measurement

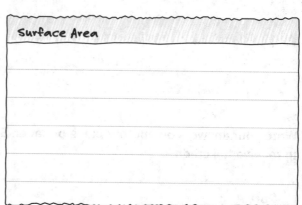 **Answer the Essential Question.** HOW do measurements help you describe real-world objects?

_____

_____

Chapter 7
Probability

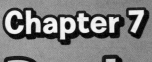

 Essential Question

HOW can you predict the outcome of future events?

 Virginia Standards
7.8a, b

 Math in the Real World

Probability is the likelihood or chance of an event occurring.

At the beginning of a football game, a coin is tossed to determine which team receives the ball first. Fill in the table below to indicate the number of times a team would expect to win the coin toss based on the number of games played.

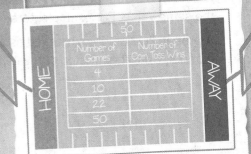

Number of Games	Number of Coin Toss Wins
4	
10	
22	
50	

FOLDABLES®
Study Organizer

 Cut out the Foldable in the back of the book.

2 Place your Foldable on page 670.

 Use the Foldable throughout this chapter to help you learn about probability.

Vocabulary

complementary events

compound event

experimental probability

Fundamental Counting Principle

outcome

permutation

probability

random

sample space

simple event

simulation

theoretical probability

tree diagram

uniform probability model

Review Vocabulary

Fractions, Decimals, and Percents Equivalent rational numbers are numbers that have the same value. For example, three-fourths is equivalent to 0.75 or 75%.

A probability can be expressed as a fraction, decimal, or percent. For each rational number, write the missing equivalent values. Write fractions in simplest form.

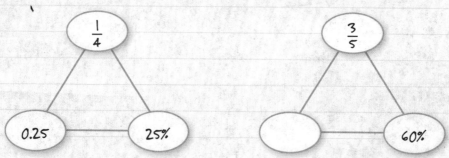

List three things you already know about probability in the first section. Then list three things you would like to learn about probability in the second section.

Probability	
What I know	**What I want to find out**

When Will You Use This?

Here are a few examples of how probability is used in the real world.

Activity 1 Have you ever read something like "The chances of winning are 75%." or "30% of the people surveyed said that they prefer vanilla ice cream."? Use the Internet to find an example like the ones given. Describe your example and what it means to you.

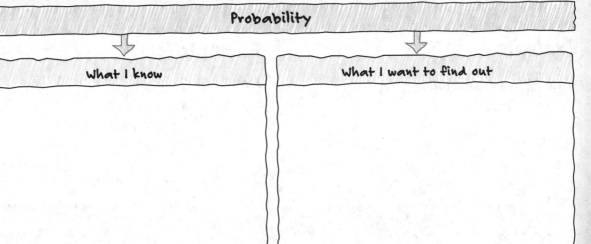

Jamar and Theresa in
Radio Surveys

Are you ready for our first task as radio station interns?

I'm ready! It's gonna be fun! What should we do first?

Activity 2 Go online at **connectED.mcgraw-hill.com** to read the graphic novel *Radio Surveys*. What type of information do Jamar and Theresa want to learn from their survey?

Are You Ready?

Try the Quick Check below.
Or, take the Online Readiness Quiz.

Check ✓

Quick Review

Example 1

Write $\frac{21}{28}$ in simplest form.

$$\frac{21}{28} = \frac{3}{4}$$

$\div 7$

$\div 7$

Divide the numerator and denominator by the GCF, 7.

Example 2

Find $7 \cdot 6 \cdot 5 \cdot 4$.

$$7 \cdot 6 \cdot 5 \cdot 4 = 42 \cdot 5 \cdot 4$$
$$= 210 \cdot 4$$
$$= 840$$

Multiply from left to right.

Quick Check

Fractions Write each fraction in simplest form.

Show your work.

1. $\frac{5}{15} =$ _____

2. $\frac{3}{18} =$ _____

3. $\frac{8}{12} =$ _____

4. $\frac{12}{20} =$ _____

Products Find each product.

5. $6 \cdot 5 =$ _____

6. $10 \cdot 9 \cdot 8 =$ _____

7. $4 \cdot 3 \cdot 2 \cdot 1 =$ _____

8. Suppose you listen to 9 songs each hour for 5 hours every day this week. How many songs will you have listened to this week?

How Did You Do?

Which problems did you answer correctly in the Quick Check?
Shade those exercise numbers below.

① ② ③ ④ ⑤ ⑥ ⑦ ⑧

Probability of Simple Events

Vocabulary Start-Up

Probability is the chance that some event will occur. A **simple event** is one outcome or a collection of outcomes. What is an **outcome**?

Math Definition		Real-World Definition
A possible result in a probability experiment.	Outcome	_____

Real-World Link

For a sledding trip, you randomly select one of the four hats shown. Complete the table to show the possible outcomes.

Hat Selection Outcomes			
Outcome 1	green hat	Outcome 3	
Outcome 2		Outcome 4	

1. Write a ratio that compares the number of blue hats to the total number of hats. _____

2. Describe a hat display in which you would have a better chance of selecting a red hat.

_____

_____

Essential Question

HOW can you predict the outcome of future events?

Vocabulary

probability
outcome
simple event
random
complementary events

Virginia Standards
7.8a

Which (MP) **Mathematical Process Goals** did you use? Shade the circle(s) that applies.

① Mathematical Problem Solving
② Mathematical Communication
③ Mathematical Reasoning
④ Mathematical Connections
⑤ Mathematical Representations

Probability

Words The probability of an event is a ratio that compares the number of favorable outcomes to the number of possible outcomes.

Symbols $P(event) = \dfrac{\text{number of favorable outcomes}}{\text{number of possible outcomes}}$

Work Zone

The probability of a chance event is a number between 0 and 1 that expresses the likelihood of the event occurring. Greater numbers indicate greater likelihood. A probability near 0 indicates an unlikely event, a probability around $\frac{1}{2}$ indicates an event that is neither unlikely nor likely, and a probability near 1 indicates a likely event.

Probability can be written as a fraction, decimal, or percent.

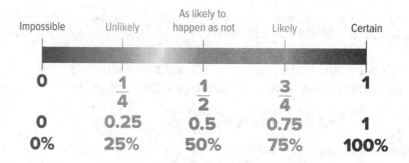

Impossible	Unlikely	As likely to happen as not	Likely	Certain
0	$\frac{1}{4}$	$\frac{1}{2}$	$\frac{3}{4}$	1
0	0.25	0.5	0.75	1
0%	25%	50%	75%	100%

Outcomes occur at **random** if each outcome is equally likely to occur.

Example

There are six equally likely outcomes if a number cube with sides labeled 1 through 6 is rolled.

1. **Find $P(6)$ or the probability of rolling a 6.**

There is only one 6 on the number cube.

$P(6) = \dfrac{\text{number of favorable outcomes}}{\text{number of possible outcomes}}$

$= \dfrac{1}{6}$

The probability of rolling a 6 is $\frac{1}{6}$, or about 17%, or about 0.17.

Show your work.

Got it? Do this problem to find out.

a. A coin is tossed. Find the probability of the coin landing on heads. Write your answer as a fraction, percent, and decimal.

a. _____

Example

2. Find the probability of rolling a 2, 3, or 4 on the number cube.

The word *or* indicates that the number of favorable outcomes needs to include the numbers 2, 3, and 4.

$$P(2, 3, \text{ or } 4) = \frac{\text{number of favorable outcomes}}{\text{number of possible outcomes}}$$

$$= \frac{3}{6} \text{ or } \frac{1}{2} \qquad \text{Simplify.}$$

The probability of rolling a 2, 3, or 4 is $\frac{1}{2}$, 50%, or 0.5.

Got it? Do these problems to find out.

The spinner at the right is spun once. Find the probability of each event. Write each answer as a fraction, percent, and decimal.

  b. $P(F)$ **c.** $P(D \text{ or } G)$ **d.** $P(\text{vowel})$

Show your work.

b. _____

c. _____

d. _____

Find Probability of the Complement

Complementary events are two events in which either one or the other must happen, but they cannot happen at the same time. For example, a coin can either land on heads or *not* land on heads. The sum of the probability of an event and its complement is 1 or 100%.

> **Complement**
> In everyday language complement means the quantity required to make something complete. This is similar to the math meaning.

Example

3. Find the probability of *not* rolling a 6 in Example 1.

The probability of *not* rolling a 6 and the probability of rolling a 6 are complementary. So, the sum of the probabilities is 1.

$$P(6) + P(not\ 6) = 1 \qquad P(6) \text{ and } P(not\ 6) \text{ are complements.}$$

$$\frac{1}{6} + P(not\ 6) = 1 \qquad \text{Replace } P(6) \text{ with } \frac{1}{6}.$$

$$\frac{1}{6} + \frac{5}{6} = 1 \qquad \text{THINK } \frac{1}{6} \text{ plus what number equals 1?}$$

The probability of *not* rolling a 6 is $\frac{5}{6}$, or about 83% or 0.83.

Got it? Do this problem to find out.

e. A bag contains 5 blue, 8 red, and 7 green marbles. A marble is selected at random. Find the probability the marble is *not* red.

e. _____

Example

4. Mr. Harada surveyed his class and discovered that 30% of his students have blue eyes. Identify the complement of this event. Then find its probability.

The complement of having blue eyes is *not* having blue eyes. The sum of the probabilities is 100%.

P(blue eyes) + P(*not* blue eyes) = 100% P(blue eyes) and P(*not* blue eyes) are complements.

30% + P(*not* blue eyes) = 100%   Replace P(blue eyes) with 30%.

30% + 70% = 100%   **THINK** 30% plus what number equals 100%?

So, the probability that a student does *not* have blue eyes is 70%, 0.7, or $\frac{7}{10}$.

Guided Practice

A letter tile is chosen randomly. Find the probability of each event. Write each answer as a fraction, percent, and decimal. (Examples 1–3)

1. P(D) _____

2. P(S, V, or L) _____

3. P(not D) _____

4. The probability of choosing a "Go Back 1 Space" card in a board game is 25%. Describe the complement of this event and find its probability. (Example 4) _____

_____

_____

_____

5. **Building on the Essential Question** Explain the relationship between the probability of an event and its complement. Give an example.

_____

_____

_____

_____

Rate Yourself!

How confident are you about finding the probability of simple events? Shade the ring on the target.

For more help, go online to access a Personal Tutor.

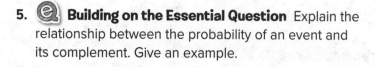

Time to update your Foldable!

Independent Practice

Go online for Step-by-Step Solutions

The spinner shown is spun once. Find the probability of each event. Write each answer as a fraction, percent, and decimal. (Examples 1–3)

1. *P*(blue)

_____

2. *P*(red or yellow)

_____

3 *P*(*not* brown)

4. *P*(*not* green)

_____

5 Refer to the table on air travel at selected airports. Suppose a flight that arrived at El Centro is selected at random. What is the probability that the flight did *not* arrive on time? Write the answer as a fraction, decimal, and percent. Explain your reasoning. (Example 4)

_____

_____

Air Travel	
Airport	**Arrivals (Percent on-time)**
El Centro (CA)	80
Baltimore (MD)	82

6. **MP** **Model with Mathematics** Refer to the graphic novel frame below. Jamar and Theresa decide to create a music mix and include an equal number of songs from each genre. What is the probability that any given song would be from the hip-hop genre? _____

Other surveys in cities like ours say there are five kinds of music that the kids like—country, classical, hip-hop, oldies, and alternative.

We gave surveys to 100 teens.

We want to make sure there are all five types on this mix CD for the school dance.

CD-R WRITING...

One jelly bean is picked, without looking, from the dish. Write a sentence that explains how likely it is for each event to happen.

7. black

_____

_____

_____

8. purple, red, or yellow

_____

_____

_____

H.O.T. Problems Higher Order Thinking

9. **MP** **Persevere with Problems** The probability of landing in a certain section on a spinner can be found by considering the size of the angle formed by that section. On spinner shown, the angle formed by the yellow section is one-fourth of the angle formed by the entire circle. So, $P(\text{yellow}) = \frac{1}{4}$, 0.25, or 25%.

a. Determine $P(\text{green})$ and $P(\text{orange})$ for the spinner. Write the probabilities as fractions, decimals, and percents.

_____

b. Determine $P(not \text{ yellow})$.

_____

10. **MP** **Persevere with Problems** A bag contains 6 red, 4 blue, and 8 green marbles. How many marbles of each color should be added so that the total number of marbles is 27, but the probability of randomly selecting

one marble of each color remains unchanged? _____

_____

_____

11. **MP** **Which One Doesn't Belong?** Circle the pair of probabilities that does not belong with the other three. Explain your reasoning.

| $0.625, \frac{3}{8}$ | $0.38, 62\%$ | $\frac{7}{8}, 0.125$ | $70\%, \frac{1}{3}$ |

_____

_____

_____

Extra Practice

Ten cards numbered 1 through 10 are mixed together and then one card is drawn. Find the probability of each event. Write each answer as a fraction, percent, and decimal.

12. $P(8)$

$\frac{1}{10}$, 10%, or 0.1

Only 1 card has an 8. So, $P(8)$ is $\frac{1}{10}$, 10%, or 0.1.

Homework Help

13. $P(7$ or $9)$

$\frac{1}{5}$, 20%, or 0.2

There is 1 card with a 7 and 1 card with a 9. So, $P(7$ or $9)$ is $\frac{1}{5}$, or 20%, or 0.2.

14. $P(\text{less than } 5)$

15. $P(\text{greater than } 3)$

16. $P(\text{odd})$

17. $P(\text{even})$

18. $P(not \text{ a multiple of } 4)$

19. $P(not \text{ 5, 6, 7, or 8})$

20. $P(\text{divisible by } 3)$

21. Of the students at Grant Middle School, 63% are girls. The school newspaper is randomly selecting a student to be interviewed. Describe the complement of selecting a girl and find the probability of the complement. Write the answer as a fraction, decimal, and percent.

_____

_____

22. The table shows the number of dogs and cats at a groomer. If a pet is selected at random to be groomed, find the probability that Patches the cat will be selected. Then find the probability that a cat will be selected.

Pets at the Groomer	
Cats	Dogs
12	16

_____

23. **MP Persevere with Problems** For a certain game, the probability of choosing a card with the number 13 is $\frac{8}{1,000}$. Find the probability of *not* choosing a card with the number 13. Then describe the likelihood of the event occurring.

_____

_____

24. The types of songs on Max's MP3 player are shown on the graph. Max will play one of the songs at random. Complete the model below to find *P*(country or R&B).

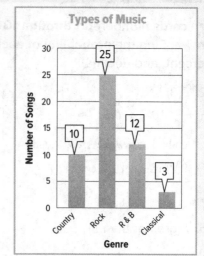

Types of Music

P(country or R&B) =

$$\frac{\boxed{} + \boxed{}}{\boxed{} + \boxed{} + \boxed{} + \boxed{}} = \boxed{}$$

25. Joel has a bowl containing the numbers of colored candies shown in the table. Which of the following probabilities are correct? Select all that apply.

☐ $P(\text{red}) = \frac{1}{4}$ ☐ $P(\text{orange}) = \frac{1}{5}$

☐ $P(\text{yellow}) = \frac{1}{10}$ ☐ $P(\text{green}) = \frac{2}{5}$

Color	Number
Red	5
Orange	3
Yellow	1
Green	6

Spiral Review

Compare each decimal using <, >, or =.

26. 0.2 ◯ 0.3

27. 0.75 ◯ 0.7

28. 5.89 ◯ 5.899

29. Dwayne misses 12% of his foul shots and Bryan misses 0.2 of his foul shots. Write 12% and 0.2 as fractions in simplest form. Then compare the fractions to determine who misses more foul shots.

Virginia Standards
7.8a

 Inquiry HOW is probability related to relative frequency?

In a board game, you get an extra turn if you roll doubles or two of the same number.

You can conduct an experiment to find the relative frequency of rolling doubles using two number cubes. **Relative frequency** is the ratio of the number of experimental successes to the number of experimental attempts.

Hands-On Activity

Tools

Step 1 Complete the table to show all of the possible outcomes for rolling two number cubes. Shade all of the possible outcomes that are doubles.

The probability of rolling

doubles is _____ .

(1, 1)	(2, 1)				
(1, 2)	(2, 2)				
(1, 3)	(2, 3)				
(1, 4)					
(1, 5)					
(1, 6)					

How many times would you expect doubles to be rolled if you roll the

number cubes 50 times? Explain. _____

_____

Step 2 Roll two number cubes and record the number of doubles in the table. Repeat the experiment 50 times.

Number of Rolls	50
Number of Doubles	

Step 3 Find the relative frequency of rolling doubles. Use the

ratio $\dfrac{\text{number of times doubles were rolled}}{\text{number of rolls}}$. _____

Compare the ratios in Steps 1 and 3. What do you notice? Explain.

_____

_____

Suppose the number cubes are rolled 100 times. Would you expect the results to be the same? Explain why or why not.

_____

_____

Work with a partner.

1. Place a paperclip around the tip of a pencil. Then place the tip on the center of the spinner. Spin the paperclip 40 times. Record the results in the table below.

Section	A	B	C	D
Frequency				
Relative Frequency				

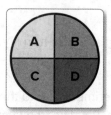

The spinner above is spun once. Find the probability of each event.

2. $P(A)$ _____

3. $P(B)$ _____

4. $P(C)$ _____

5. $P(D)$ _____

 Analyze and Reflect

Collaborate

6. Based on your results from the spinner experiment, are the outcomes of A, B, C, or D equally likely? _____

7. **MP Reason Inductively** What would you expect to happen to the long-run relative frequency of spinning an A as you increase the number of spins from 40 to 1,000? _____

_____

 Create

On Your Own

8. **MP Justify Conclusions** If you rolled a number cube 600 times, approximate the relative frequency of rolling a 3 or 6. Explain your reasoning to a classmate. _____

9. **Inquiry** HOW is probability related to relative frequency?

_____

_____

Theoretical and Experimental Probability

Real-World Link

Carnival Games The prize wheels for a carnival game are shown. You receive a less expensive prize if you spin and win on wheel A. You receive a more expensive prize if you spin and win on wheel B.

Wheel A

Wheel B

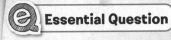 **Essential Question**

HOW can you predict the outcome of future events?

Vocabulary

uniform probability model
theoretical probability
experimental probability

Virginia Standards
7.8a, b

In a **uniform probability model**, each outcome has an equal probability of happening.

1. Which wheel has uniform probability? _____

2. Use a paperclip and the tip of your pencil to spin each wheel 4 times. Record your results.

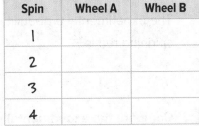

Spin	Wheel A	Wheel B
1		
2		
3		
4		

3. Why do you think winners on wheel A receive a less expensive prize than winners on wheel B?

_____

_____

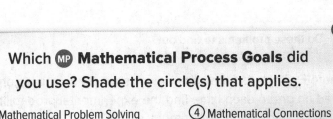

Which MP Mathematical Process Goals did you use? Shade the circle(s) that applies.

① Mathematical Problem Solving   ④ Mathematical Connections

② Mathematical Communication   ⑤ Mathematical Representations

③ Mathematical Reasoning

Experimental and Theoretical Probability

Theoretical probability is based on uniform probability — what *should* happen when conducting a probability experiment. **Experimental probability** is based on relative frequency — what *actually* occurrs during such an experiment.

The theoretical probability and the experimental probability of an event may or may not be the same. As the number of attempts increases, the theoretical probability and the experimental probability should become closer in value.

Trials

A trial is one experiment in a series of successive experiments.

 Examples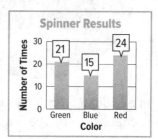

1. **The graph shows the results of an experiment in which a spinner with 3 equal sections is spun sixty times. Find the experimental probability of spinning red for this experiment.**

   The graph indicates that the spinner landed on red 24 times, blue 15 times, and green 21 times.

   $$P(\text{red}) = \frac{\text{number of times red occurs}}{\text{total number of spins}}$$
   $$= \frac{24}{60} \text{ or } \frac{2}{5}$$

   The experimental probability of spinning red is $\frac{2}{5}$.

   Spinner Results

   Number of Times — Color (Green, Blue, Red): Green 21, Blue 15, Red 24

2. **Compare the experimental probability you found in Example 1 to its theoretical probability.**

   The spinner has three equal sections: red, blue, and green. So, the theoretical probability of spinning red is $\frac{1}{3}$. Since $\frac{2}{5} \approx \frac{1}{3}$, the experimental probability is close to the theoretical probability.

Got it? Do these problems to find out.

a. Refer to Example 1. If the spinner was spun 3 more times and landed on green each time, find the experimental probability of spinning green for this experiment.

b. Compare the experimental probability you found in Exercise **a** to its theoretical probability.

a. _____

b. _____

Examples

Tutor

3. Two number cubes are rolled together 20 times. A sum of 9 is rolled 8 times. What is the experimental probability of rolling a sum of 9?

$$P(9) = \frac{\text{number of times a sum of 9 occurs}}{\text{total number of rolls}}$$

$$= \frac{8}{20} \text{ or } \frac{2}{5}$$

The experimental probability of rolling a sum of 9 is $\frac{2}{5}$.

- -

4. Compare the experimental probability you found in Example 3 to its theoretical probability. If the probabilities are not close, explain a possible reason for the discrepancy.

When rolling two number cubes, there are 36 possible outcomes.

The theoretical probability of rolling a sum of 9 is $\frac{4}{36}$ or $\frac{1}{9}$.

Rolls with Sum of 9	
First Cube	**Second Cube**
3	6
4	5
5	4
6	3

Since $\frac{1}{9}$ is not close to $\frac{2}{5}$, the experimental probability is *not* close to the theoretical probability. One possible explanation is that there were not enough trials.

Got it? Do these problems to find out.

c. In Example 3, what is the experimental probability of rolling a sum that is *not* 9?

d. Two coins are tossed 10 times. Both coins land on heads 6 times. Compare the experimental probability to the theoretical probability. If the probabilities are not close, explain a possible reason for the discrepancy.

e. Suppose three coins are tossed 10 times. All three coins land on heads 1 time. Compare the experimental probability to the theoretical probability. If the probabilities are not close, explain a possible reason for the discrepancy.

Show your work.

c. _____

d. _____

e. _____

Predict Future Events

Theoretical and experimental probability can be used to make predictions about future events.

 Example

5. Last year, a DVD store sold 670 action DVDs, 580 comedy DVDs, 450 drama DVDs, and 300 horror DVDs. A media buyer expects to sell 5,000 DVDs this year. Based on these results, how many comedy DVDs should she buy? Explain.

2,000 DVDs were sold and 580 were comedy. So, the probability is $\frac{580}{2,000}$ or $\frac{29}{100}$.

$$\frac{29}{100} = \frac{x}{5,000} \qquad \text{Write a proportion.}$$

$$29 \cdot 5,000 = 100 \cdot x \qquad \text{Find the cross products.}$$

$$145,000 = 100x \qquad \text{Multiply.}$$

$$1,450 = x \qquad \text{Divide each side by 100.}$$

She should buy about 1,450 comedy DVDs.

Solving Proportions

The cross products of any proportion are equal.

$\frac{29}{100} \bowtie \frac{x}{5,000}$

Guided Practice

1. A coin is tossed 50 times, and it lands on heads 28 times. Find the experimental probability and the theoretical probability of the coin landing on heads. Then, compare the experimental and theoretical probabilities. (Examples 1–4)

_____

_____

2. Yesterday, 50 bakery customers bought muffins and 11 of those customers bought banana muffins. If 100 customers buy muffins tomorrow, how many would you expect to buy a banana muffin? (Example 5)

_____

3. **Building on the Essential Question** How are experimental probability and theoretical probability alike?

_____

_____

Rate Yourself!

Are you ready to move on? Shade the section that applies.

I have a few questions. / I'm ready to move on. / I have a lot of questions.

For more help, go online to access a Personal Tutor.

FOLDABLES Time to update your Foldable!

Independent Practice

Go online for Step-by-Step Solutions

1 A number cube is rolled 20 times and lands on 1 two times and on 5 four times. Find each experimental probability. Then compare the experimental probability to the theoretical probability. (Examples 1–4)

a. landing on 5

_____

_____

b. *not* landing on 1

_____

_____

2. The spinner at the right is spun 12 times. It lands on blue 1 time.
   (Examples 1–4)

   a. What is the experimental probability of the spinner landing on blue?

   _____

   b. Compare the experimental and theoretical probabilities of the spinner landing on blue. If the probabilities are not close, explain a possible reason for the discrepancy.

   _____

   _____

3. The frequency table shows the results of a survey of 70 zoo visitors who were asked to name their favorite animal exhibit. (Example 5)

   a. Suppose 540 people visit the zoo. Predict how many people will choose the monkey exhibit as their favorite. _____

   b. Suppose 720 people visit the zoo. Predict how many people will choose the penguin exhibit as their favorite. _____

What is your Favorite Animal Exhibit?		
Exhibit	**Tally**	**Frequency**
Bears	ЖІ	6
Elephants	Ж Ж Ж ІІ	17
Monkeys	Ж Ж Ж Ж І	21
Penguins	Ж ЖІІІ	13
Snakes	Ж ЖІІІ	13

4. **MP Make a Conjecture** Cross out the part of the concept circle that does *not* belong. Then describe the relationship among the remaining parts.

_____

_____

_____

a coin landing on tails 8 out of 10 times | results based on an experiment

outcomes that should happen | rolling a sum of 9 twice in 5 trials

5 **MP** **Multiple Representations** A spinner with three equal-sized sections marked A, B, and C is spun 100 times.

a. **Numbers** What is the theoretical probability of landing on A?

_____

b. **Numbers** The results of the experiment are shown in the table. What is the experimental probability of landing on A? on C?

_____

c. **Models** Make a drawing of what the spinner might look like based on its experimental probabilities. Explain.

_____

_____

_____

_____

Section	Frequency
A	24
B	50
C	26

Show your work.

H.O.T. Problems Higher Order Thinking

6. **MP** **Persevere with Problems** The experimental probability of a coin landing on heads is $\frac{7}{12}$. If the coin landed on tails 30 times, find the number of tosses.

_____

7. **MP** **Reason Inductively** Twenty sharpened pencils are placed in a box containing an unknown number of unsharpened pencils. Suppose 15 pencils are removed at random and five of the removed pencils are sharpened. Based on this, is it reasonable to assume that the number

of unsharpened pencils was 40? Explain your reasoning. _____

_____

_____

8. **MP** **Reason Inductively** The results of spinning a spinner with six equal sections are shown. Determine the minimum number of additional spins needed and their frequency of landing on each color so that the experimental probabilities will be equal to the theoretical probabilities.

Explain your reasoning. _____

_____

_____

_____

_____

Color	Frequency
Blue	8
Green	6
Orange	12
Purple	10
Red	8
Yellow	4

Extra Practice

For Exercises 9 and 10, find each experimental probability. Then compare the experimental probability to its theoretical probability. If the probabilities are not close, explain a possible reason for the discrepancy.

9. A coin is tossed 20 times. It lands on heads 9 times.

Homework Help →

$P(heads) = \dfrac{\text{number of times heads occurs}}{\text{total number of coin tosses}} = \dfrac{9}{20}$

The experimental probability of $\dfrac{9}{20}$ is close to

the theoretical probability of $\dfrac{1}{2}$.

10. A heart is randomly chosen 7 out of 12 times from the cards shown.

_____

_____

_____

Solve.

11. Last month, customers at a gift shop bought 40 birthday cards, 19 congratulations cards, 20 holiday cards, and 21 thank you cards. Suppose 125 customers buy greeting cards next month. How many would you expect to buy a birthday card?

_____

12. Use the graph at the right.
   a. What is the probability that a mother received a gift of flowers or plants? Write the probability as a fraction in simplest form.

_____

   b. Suppose 400 mothers will receive a gift. Predict how many will receive flowers or plants.

_____

Most Popular Mother's Day Gifts

card 40%
flowers/plants 28%
dinner/brunch 8%
gardening items 8%
apparel 7%
jewelry 6%
home décor 3%

Percent

13. J.R. tossed a coin 100 times. Fill in the boxes to complete each statement.
Based on J.R.'s results, the [   ] probability

of tossing heads is [   ] %. This is [   ] than the
theoretical probability of tossing heads with a coin.

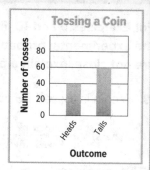

Tossing a Coin

14. Determine if each situation represents experimental or theoretical probability.

   a. Saul flips a coin 20 times and determines that the probability of flipping heads is 0.55.   ☐ experimental   ☐ theoretical

   b. Kelly has made 16 out of 25 free throws. The probability that she will make her next free throw is 64%.   ☐ experimental   ☐ theoretical

   c. There are 4 pennies, 2 nickels, 5 dimes, and 5 quarters in a jar. The probability that a randomly selected coin is a penny is $\frac{1}{4}$.   ☐ experimental   ☐ theoretical

Spiral Review

For Exercises 15 and 16, circle the greater probability.

15. The spinner at the right is spun.
   P(red) P(not red)

16. A number cube is rolled.
   P(multiple of 3) P(prime number)

17. A restaurant offers three flavors of ice cream on its dessert menu: vanilla, chocolate, and strawberry. Dessert options are sundaes or ice cream cones. List all of the possible desserts. Then determine if it is likely, unlikely, or equally likely of randomly choosing a sundae.

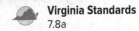

Virginia Standards
7.8a

 HOW can you determine if a game is fair?

In a counter-toss game, players toss three two-color counters. The winner of each game is determined by how many counters land with either the red or yellow side facing up. Find out if this game is fair or unfair.

Mathematically speaking, a two-player game is **fair** if each player has an equal chance of winning. A game is **unfair** if there is not such a chance.

Hands-On Activity 1

Work in pairs to play the game described above.

Step 1 Player 1 tosses the counters. If 2 or 3 counters land red-side up, Player 1 wins. If 2 or 3 counters land yellow-side up, Player 2 wins. Record the results in the table below. Place a check in the winner's column for each game.

Game	Player 1	Player 2	Game	Player 1	Player 2
1			6		
2			7		
3			8		
4			9		
5			10		

Step 2 Player 2 then tosses the counters and the results are recorded.

Step 3 Continue alternating turns until the counters have been tossed 10 times.

Based on your results, do you think the game is fair or unfair? Circle your response below.

Fair   Unfair

Investigate

Work with a partner.

1. Complete the organized list of all the possible outcomes resulting from one toss of the three counters described in Activity 1.

Counter 1	Counter 2	Counter 3	Outcome
red	red	red	red, red, red

2. In the outcome column of the table above, draw a circle around the outcomes that are a win for Player 1. Draw a box around the outcomes that are a win for Player 2.

3. Calculate the theoretical probability of each player winning. Write each probability as a fraction and as a percent. Is the game fair or unfair?

4. Use your results from Activity 1 to calculate the experimental probability of each player winning.

Analyze and Reflect

5. **MP Justify Conclusions** Compare the probabilities you found in Exercises 3 and 4. Explain any discrepancies.

6. **MP Reason Inductively** Predict the number of times Player 1 would win if the game were played 100 times. Explain your reasoning.

David and Lyn made up a game using a plastic cup. A cup is tossed. If it lands right-side up or open-end down, David wins. If it lands on its side, Lyn wins. Is this game fair?

Hands-On Activity 2

Work in pairs to play the game and determine if David and Lyn created a fair game.

Step 1 Player 1 tosses the cup. If it lands right-side up or open-end down, Player 1 gets a point. If the cup lands on its side, Player 2 gets a point. Record your results in the table below.

Toss	Player 1	Player 2	Toss	Player 1	Player 2
1			6		
2			7		
3			8		
4			9		
5			10		

Step 2 Player 2 then tosses the cup and the results are recorded.

Step 3 Continue alternating turns until there is a total of 10 tosses.

Based on your results, do you think the game David and Lyn created is fair or unfair? Circle your response below.

Fair   Unfair

There are three possible outcomes when tossing the cup and David wins if two of those outcomes happen. It may appear that David has a better chance of winning, however this is not necessarily true.

Explain why Lyn actually has a better chance at winning the game.

_____

_____

_____

What was the experimental probability for the cup landing right-side up or open-end down?

_____

Investigate

Work with a partner.

7. A game involves rolling two number cubes. Player 1 wins the game if the total of the numbers rolled is 5 or if a 5 is shown on one or both number cubes. Otherwise, Player 2 wins. Fill in the table for all of the possible outcomes of rolling two number cubes.

	1	2	3	4	5	6
1	1 + 1 = 2	1 + 2 = 3	1 + 3 = 4	1 + 4 = 5	1 + 5 = 6	1 + 6 = 7
2	2 + 1 = 3					
3						
4						
5						
6						

8. Shade in the cells of the table in which Player 1 is a winner.

Analyze and Reflect

9. For the number cube game, calculate the theoretical probability of each player winning. Write each probability as a fraction and as a percent.

_____

_____

10. **MP Justify Conclusions** Is the number cube game fair? Explain.

_____

_____

Create

11. **MP Model with Mathematics** Design and describe a game in which the outcome is not fair. Then explain how you could change the game to

make it fair. _____

12. **Inquiry** HOW can you determine if a game is fair? _____

_____

Probability of Compound Events

Real-World Link

Travel Aimee wants to pack enough items to create 6 different outfits. She packs 1 jacket, 3 shirts, and 2 pairs of jeans. Can Aimee create 6 different outfits from her clothing items?

1. Complete the table below.

Outfit	Clothing Items
1	jacket, shirt 1, jeans 1
2	jacket, shirt 1, jeans 2
3	jacket, shirt 2, jeans 1
4	jacket, shirt 2,
5	jacket, shirt 3,
6	jacket,

Essential Question

HOW can you predict the outcome of future events?

Vocabulary

sample space
tree diagram
compound event

2. The table is an example of an organized list. What is another way to show the different outfits that Aimee can create?

_____

3. Describe another situation for which you might want to list all of the possible outcomes.

_____

_____

_____

Which MP Mathematical Process Goals did you use? Shade the circle(s) that applies.

① Mathematical Problem Solving   ④ Mathematical Connections

② Mathematical Communication   ⑤ Mathematical Representations

③ Mathematical Reasoning

Find a Sample Space

The set of all of the possible outcomes in a probability experiment is called the **sample space**. Organized lists, tables, and **tree diagrams** can be used to represent the sample space.

Examples

1. **The three students chosen to represent Mr. Balderick's class in a school assembly are shown. All three of them need to sit in a row on the stage. Use a list to find the sample space for the different ways they can sit in a row.**

Students
Adrienne
Carlos
Greg

Use A for Adrienne, C for Carlos, and G for Greg. Use each letter exactly once.

ACG   AGC   CAG   CGA   GAC   GCA

So, the sample space consists of 6 outcomes.

2. **A car can be purchased in blue, silver, red, or purple. It also comes as a convertible or hardtop. Use a table or a tree diagram to find the sample space for the different styles in which the car can be purchased.**

Color	Top
blue	convertible
blue	hardtop
silver	convertible
silver	hardtop
red	convertible
red	hardtop
purple	convertible
purple	hardtop

Color	Top	Sample Space
Blue	Convertible	BC
	Hardtop	BH
Silver	Convertible	SC
	Hardtop	SH
Red	Convertible	RC
	Hardtop	RH
Purple	Convertible	PC
	Hardtop	PH

Using either method, the sample space consists of 8 outcomes.

Got it? Do this problem to find out.

Show your work.

a. The table shows the sandwich choices for a picnic. Find the sample space using a list, table, or tree diagram for a sandwich consisting one type of meat and one type of bread.

Meat	Bread
ham turkey	rye sourdough white

a. _____

Find Probability

A **compound event** consists of two or more simple events. The probability of a compound event, just as with simple events, is the fraction of outcomes in the sample space for which the compound event occurs.

Example

3. **Suppose you toss a quarter, a dime, and a nickel. Find the sample space. What is the probability of getting three tails?**

Make a tree diagram to show the sample space.

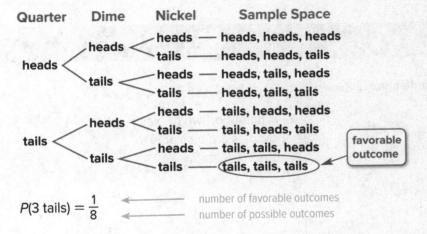

| Quarter | Dime | Nickel | Sample Space |

$$P(3 \text{ tails}) = \frac{1}{8}$$ ← number of favorable outcomes ← number of possible outcomes

So, the probability of getting three tails is $\frac{1}{8}$.

Got it? Do this problem to find out.

b. The animal shelter has both male and female Labrador Retrievers in yellow, brown, or black. There is an equal number of each kind. What is the probability of choosing a female yellow Labrador Retriever? Show your work in the space below.

> **Random**
> When choosing an outcome, assume that each outcome is chosen randomly.

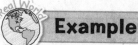

Example

4. To win a carnival prize, you need to choose one of 3 doors labeled 1 through 3. Then you need to choose a red, yellow, or blue box behind each door. What is the probability that the prize is in the blue or yellow box behind door 2?

The table shows that there are 9 total outcomes. Two of the outcomes are favorable.

So, the probability that the prize is in a blue or yellow box behind door 2 is $\frac{2}{9}$.

Outcomes	
door 1	red box
door 1	yellow box
door 1	blue box
door 2	red box
door 2	yellow box
door 2	blue box
door 3	red box
door 3	yellow box
door 3	blue box

Guided Practice

For each situation, find the sample space. (Examples 1–2)

1. A coin is tossed twice.

2. A pair of brown or black sandals are available in sizes 7, 8, or 9.

3. Gerardo spins a spinner with four equal sections, labeled A, B, C, and D, twice. If letter A is spun at least once, Gerardo wins. Otherwise, Odell wins. Use a list to find the sample space. Then find the probability that Odell wins. (Examples 3–4)

_____

_____

4. **Bulding on the Essential Question** How do tree diagrams, tables, and lists help you find the probability of a compound event? _____

_____

_____

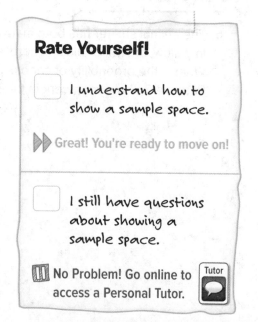

Rate Yourself!

☐ I understand how to show a sample space.

▶▶ Great! You're ready to move on!

☐ I still have questions about showing a sample space.

▐▌ No Problem! Go online to access a Personal Tutor.

Independent Practice

Go online for Step-by-Step Solutions

For each situation, find the sample space. (Examples 1–2)

1. tossing a coin and spinning the spinner at the right

2. picking a number from 1 to 5 and choosing the color red, white, or blue

3 choosing a purple, green, black, or silver bike having 10, 18, 21, or 24 speeds

4. choosing a letter from the word SPACE and choosing a consonant from the word MATH

For each game, find the sample space. Then find the indicated probability. (Examples 3–4)

5. Alana tosses 2 number cubes. She wins if she rolls double sixes.

   Find *P*(Alana wins). _____

6. Ming rolls a number cube, tosses a coin, and chooses a card from two cards marked A and B. If an even number and heads appears, Ming wins, no matter which card is chosen. Otherwise Lashonda wins.

   Find *P*(Ming wins). _____

7 **Persevere with Problems** The following is a game for two players.

- Three counters are labeled according to the table at the right.
- Toss the three counters.
- If exactly 2 counters match, Player 1 scores a point. Otherwise, Player 2 scores a point.

Counters	Side 1	Side 2
Counter 1	red	blue
Counter 2	red	yellow
Counter 3	blue	yellow

Find the probability that each player scores a point.

_____

_____

_____

H.O.T. Problems Higher Order Thinking

8. **MP** **Persevere with Problems** Refer to Exercise 7. Do the two players both have an equal chance of winning? Explain.

_____

_____

9. **MP** **Find the Error** Caitlyn wants to determine the probability of guessing correctly on two true-false questions on her history test. She draws the tree diagram below using C for correct and I for incorrect. Find her mistake and correct it.

_____

_____

_____

Question 1	Question 2	Sample Space

10. **MP** **Model with Mathematics** Write a real-world problem in which the probability of a compound event occurring is 0.25.

_____

_____

_____

Extra Practice

11. Three-course dinners can be made from the menu shown. Find the sample space for a dinner consisting of an appetizer, entrée, and dessert.

Appetizers	Entrees	Desserts
Soup	Steak	Carrot cake
Salad	Chicken	Apple pie

Homework Help ➡

Appetizer	Entree	Dessert	Sample Space

```
                                    C ————— SSC
                            S <
                          /       A ————— SSA
                    S <
                          \ C <   C ————— SCC
                                  A ————— SCA

                            S <   C ————— SaSC
                          /       A ————— SaSA
                    Sa <
                          \ C <   C ————— SaCC
                                  A ————— SaCA
```

12. Mr. and Mrs. Romero are expecting triplets. Suppose the chance of each child being a boy is 50% and of being a girl is 50%. Find the probability of each event.

   a. P(all three children will be boys) _____

   b. P(at least one boy and one girl) _____

   c. P(two boys and one girl) _____

   d. P(at least two girls) _____

Copy and Solve For Exercises 13 and 14, show your work on a separate piece of paper.

13. The University of Oregon's football team has many different uniforms. The coach can choose from four colors of jerseys and pants: green, yellow, white, and black. There are three helmet options: green, white, and yellow. Also, there are the same four colors of socks and two colors of shoes, black and yellow.

   a. How many jersey/pant combinations are there?
   b. If the coach picks a jersey/pant combination at random, what is the probability he will pick a yellow jersey with green pants?
   c. Use a tree diagram to find all of the possible shoe and sock combinations.

14. **MP** **Use Math Tools** Use the Internet or another source to find the top five best-selling animated movies. Then create a list of the possibilities for choosing a movie and choosing a wide-screen or full-screen version.

15. Mr. Skeels will choose one student from each of the two groups to present their history report to the class. Which of the following represent possible outcomes? Select all that apply.

Group 1	Group 2
Ava	Mario
Antoine	Brooke
Greg	

☐ (Ava, Brooke)   ☐ (Greg, Brooke)

☐ (Antoine, Greg)   ☐ (Antoine, Mario)

16. Campers choose one activity from each of the morning, afternoon, and evening activities shown below.

Morning	Afternoon	Evening
Hiking (H)	Archery (A)	Horseback Riding (R)
Canoeing (C)	Bird Watching (B)	Campfire Building (F)
		Navigating (N)

Make a list to show the sample space for the possible morning, afternoon, and evening activities.

[ ]

What is the probability that a randomly selected camper will be horseback riding in the evening?

[ ]

Spiral Review

Eight cards numbered 1–8 are shuffled together. A card is drawn at random. Find the probability of each event.

17. $P(8)$ _____

18. $P(\text{greater than } 5)$ _____

19. $P(\text{even})$ _____

20. $P(3 \text{ or } 7)$ _____

21. What is the probability of rolling a number greater than 4 on a number cube? Explain.

_____

_____

Simulations

 Real-World Link

Music Downloads A new electronics store is opening at the mall. One out of six new customers will receive a free music download. The winners are chosen at random. On Monday, the store had 50 customers. You can act out or *simulate* 50 random customers by using the random number generator on a graphing calculator.

Type in the following keystrokes to set 1 as the lower bound and 6 as the upper bound for 50 trials.

Keystrokes: MATH ◀ 5 1 6 50) ENTER

The screen should look similar to the screen shown below.

A set of 50 numbers ranging from 1 to 6 appears. Use the right arrow key to see the next number in the set.

1. Let the number 3 represent a customer who wins a free download. Write the experimental probability of winning a download.

2. Compare the experimental probabilities found in Exercise 1 to the theoretical probability of winning a download.

 Essential Question

HOW can you predict the outcome of future events?

 Vocabulary

simulation

Which **MP Mathematical Process Goals** did you use? Shade the circle(s) that applies.

① Mathematical Problem Solving
② Mathematical Communication
③ Mathematical Reasoning
④ Mathematical Connections
⑤ Mathematical Representations

Model Equally Likely Outcomes

A **simulation** is an experiment that is designed to model the action in a given situation. For example, you used a random number generator to simulate rolling a number cube. Simulations often use models to act out an event that would be impractical to perform.

 Real World

Example

 Tutor

1. **A cereal company is placing one of eight different trading cards in its boxes of cereal. If each card is equally likely to appear in a box of cereal, describe a model that could be used to simulate the cards you would find in 15 boxes of cereal.**

Choose a method that has 8 possible outcomes, such as tossing 3 coins. Let each outcome represent a different card.

For example, the outcome of all three coins landing heads up could simulate finding card 1.

Toss 3 coins to simulate the cards that might be in 15 boxes of cereal. Repeat 15 times.

Coin Toss Simulation			
Outcome	Card	Outcome	Card
HHH	1	TTT	5
HHT	2	TTH	6
HTH	3	THT	7
HTT	4	THH	8

 Show your work.

Got it? Do this problem to find out.

a. A restaurant is giving away 1 of 5 different toys with its children's meals. If the toys are given out randomly, describe a model that could be used to simulate which toys would be given with 6 children's meals.

a. _____

Example

2. Every student who volunteers at the concession stand during basketball games will receive a free school T-shirt. The T-shirts come in 3 different designs.

Design a simulation that could be used to model this situation. Use your simulation to find how many times a student must volunteer in order to get all 3 T-shirts.

Use a spinner divided into 3 equal sections. Assign each section one of the T-shirts. Spin the spinner until you land on each section.

first spin

second spin

third spin

fourth spin

Based on this simulation, a student should volunteer 4 times in order to get all 3 T-shirts.

Got it? Do this problem to find out.

b. Mr. Chen must wear a dress shirt and a tie to work. Each day he picks one of his 6 ties at random. Design a simulation that could be used to model this situation. Use your simulation to find how many days Mr. Chen must work in order to wear all of his ties.

Show your work.

b. _____

Model Unequally Likely Outcomes

Simulations can also be used to model events in which the outcomes are not equally likely.

Show your work.

c. _____

Example

3. There is a 60% chance of rain for each of the next two days. Describe a method you could use to find the experimental probability of having rain on both of the next two days.

Place 3 red and 2 blue marbles in a bag. Let 60% or $\frac{3}{5}$ of them represent rain. Let 40% or $\frac{2}{5}$ of them represent no rain.

Randomly pick one marble to simulate the first day. Replace the marble and pick again to simulate the second day. Find the probability of rain on both days.

Got it? Do this problem to find out.

c. During the regular season, Jason made 80% of his free throws. Describe an experiment to find the experimental probability of Jason making his next two free throws.

Guided Practice

1. An ice cream store offers waffle cones or sugar cones. Each is equally likely to be chosen. Describe a model that could be used to simulate this situation. Based on your simulation, how many people must order an ice cream cone in order to sell all possible combinations? (Examples 1 and 2)

_____

_____

2. An electronics store has determined that 45% of its customers buy a wide-screen television. Describe a model that you could use to find the experimental probability that the next three television-buying customers will buy a wide-screen television. (Example 3)

_____

_____

_____

3. **Building on the Essential Question** Explain how using a simulation is related to experimental probability.

_____

_____

Independent Practice

Go online for Step-by-Step Solutions

1 The questions on a multiple-choice test each have 4 answer choices. Describe a model that you could use to simulate the outcome of guessing the correct answers to a 50-question test. (Example 1)

_____

_____

_____

2. A game requires drawing balls numbered 0 through 9 for each of four digits to determine the winning number. Describe a model that could be used to simulate the selection of the number. (Example 1)

_____

_____

_____

MP **Model with Mathematics** Describe a model you could use to simulate each event.

3 A jar of cookies contains 18 different types of cookies. Each type is equally likely to be chosen. Based on your simulation, how many times must a cookie be chosen in order to get each type? (Example 2)

_____

_____

_____

4. A cooler contains 5 bottles of lemonade, 4 bottles of water, and 3 bottles of juice. Each type is equally likely to be chosen. Based on your simulation, how many times must a drink be chosen in order to get each type? (Example 3)

_____

_____

_____

5. Players at a carnival game win about 30% of the time. Based on your simulation, what is the experimental probability that the next four players will win. (Example 3)

_____

_____

_____

6. **MP Model with Mathematics** Suppose a mouse is placed in the maze at the right. If each decision about direction is made at random, create a simulation to determine the probability that the mouse will find its way out before coming to a dead end or going out the In opening.

_____

_____

_____

_____

🔥 H.O.T. Problems Higher Order Thinking

7. **MP Model with Mathematics** Describe a situation that could be represented by a simulation. What objects could be used in your simulation?

_____

_____

_____

8. **MP Persevere with Problems** A simulation uses cards numbered 0 through 9 to generate five 2-digit numbers. A card is selected for the tens digit and not replaced. Then a card for the ones digit is drawn and not replaced. The process is repeated until all the cards are used. If the simulation is performed 10 times, about how many times could you expect a 2-digit number to begin with a 5? Explain.

_____

_____

9. **MP Justify Conclusions** Determine whether the following statement is *sometimes*, *always*, or *never* true. Justify your answer.
   A spinner can be used to model equally likely outcomes.

_____

_____

10. **MP Justify Conclusions** Barton believes that the coin his teacher uses for an experiment gives an advantage to one team of students. His teacher has students toss the coin 50 times each and record their results. Based on the results in the table, do you think the coin is fair? Explain.

Student	Heads	Tails
1	17	33
2	22	28
3	28	22
4	21	29
5	13	37
6	20	30

_____

Extra Practice

11. A store employee randomly gives scratch-off discount cards to the first 50 customers. The cards offer discounts of 10%, 20%, 25%, 30%, or 40%. There is an equal chance of receiving any of the 5 cards. Describe a model that could be used to simulate the discount received by 4 customers.

> **Homework Help** ➡
>
> Use a spinner with 5 equal sections to represent the 5 different discounts. Spin 4 times to simulate 4 customers receiving cards.

12. On average, 75% of the days in Henderson county are sunny, with little or no cloud cover. Describe a model that you could use to find the experimental probability of sunny days each day for a week in Henderson county.

_____

_____

_____

_____

MP **Model with Mathematics** Describe a model you could use to simulate each event.

13. Every student who participated in field day activities received a water bottle. The water bottles came in 2 different colors. Based on your simulation, how many students had to receive a water bottle in order to distribute water bottles in both colors?

_____

_____

_____

14. A field hockey team wins 80% of its games. Based on your simulation, what is the experimental probability of the team winning its next 3 games?

_____

_____

_____

15. There are 4 different magazines on Hannah's nightstand. Each evening, she randomly selects one magazine to read. Based on your simulation, how many days must she select a magazine in order to read all 4 magazines?

_____

_____

16. The table shows the chance of rain this weekend. Select values to fill in the boxes in the model below to describe a method you could use to find the experimental probability of having rain on both days.

Day	Saturday	Sunday
Chance of Rain	30%	30%

Place 3 red and [ ] blue marbles in a bag. Let the [ ] marbles represent rain since [ ] % of the marbles are this color. Let the

[ ] marbles represent no rain since [ ] % of the marbles are this color.

2	4	6	7	red
10	30	60	70	blue

Randomly pick one marble to simulate the first day. Replace the marble and pick again to simulate the second day. Find the experimental probability of rain on both days. Do you think it matters how many trials of the simulation you conduct? Will conducting more trials result in a better prediction? Explain your reasoning.

17. At a restaurant, 1 out of every 6 kids' meals wins a prize. Determine which probability models could be used to simulate winning a prize. Select all that apply.

☐ Toss a coin. Let tossing heads represent winning a prize and let tossing tails represent not winning a prize.

☐ Spin a spinner with equal size spaces labeled A, B, C, D, E, and F. Let spinning A represent winning a prize and let spinning other letters represent not winning a prize.

☐ Roll a number cube. Let rolling a 1 represent winning a prize and let rolling a 2, 3, 4, 5, or 6 represent not winning a prize.

Spiral Review

18. A local video store has advertised that one out of every four customers will receive a free box of popcorn with their video rental. So far, 15 out of 75 customers have received popcorn. Compare the experimental and theoretical probabilities of receiving popcorn.

_____

_____

Inquiry HOW do simulations help you understand the probability of events happening?

A local shop randomly gives coupons to 3 out of every 8 customers. Use a spinner to determine the probability that a customer will receive a coupon two days in a row.

Hands-On Activity 1

 Tools

Step 1 A spinner with eight equal sections can be used to simulate the situation. Label three of the sections with the letter C to represent the people that receive a coupon. Label five of the sections with the letter D to represent the people that do not receive a coupon.

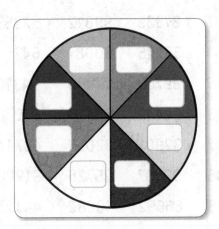

Step 2 Every two spins of the spinner represents one trial. Use a paperclip and the tip of your pencil to spin the spinner twice and record the results in the table. Perform a total of 15 trials.

Trial	Spin 1	Spin 2	Trial	Spin 1	Spin 2	Trial	Spin 1	Spin 2
1			6			11		
2			7			12		
3			8			13		
4			9			14		
5			10			15		

Based on your results, what is the experimental probability that a customer will receive a coupon two days in a row?

_____

You can also use a random number table to simulate a compound event.

There is a 10% chance of rain for a city on Sunday and a 20% chance of rain on Monday. Use a random number table to find the probability that it will rain on both days.

Hands-On Activity 2

Step 1 A random number table has random digits in rows that can be grouped in different combinations as needed. These digits are arranged in groups of 5, but the grouping often does not matter. Since the situation we want to represent involves two days, continue drawing lines to separate the numbers into two-digit numbers.

48587	49460	89640	30270
19507	87835	99812	52353
11364	35645	90087	64254
87045	39769	77995	14316
69913	93449	68497	31270
81827	32901	82033	43714
33386	99637	25725	31900
41575	86692	40882	44123
77351	12790	62795	77307

Step 2 Using the digits 0 through 9, assign one digit in the tens place for rain on Sunday and assign two different digits in the ones place for rain on Monday. For example, the digit 1 in the tens place can represent rain occurring on Sunday and the digits 1 and 2 in the ones place can represent rain occurring on Monday.

Step 3 Find the numbers in the table that have a 1 in the tens place and either a 1 or 2 in the ones place. Those numbers are 11 and 12. Circle those numbers in the table.

Step 4 Find the probability using the numbers found in Step 3.

There were ☐ instances of the random numbers 11 and 12 occurring out of 90 random numbers.

So, the probability that it will rain on both days is $\dfrac{\square}{90}$ or $3\dfrac{1}{3}\%$.

Investigate

Work with a partner.

1. Luke plays goalie on his soccer team. He usually stops 2 out of every 6 penalty kicks. Label the sections of the spinner at the right. Then use the spinner to determine the experimental probability that Luke stops 2 penalty kicks in a row.

Trial	Spin 1	Spin 2	Trial	Spin 1	Spin 2	Trial	Spin 1	Spin 2
1			6			11		
2			7			12		
3			8			13		
4			9			14		
5			10			15		

The experimental probability is _____ .

2. Suppose 40% of customers who enter a pet store own a cat. What is the probability that it will take at least 4 customers before a cat owner enters the store? Use a random number table to simulate this compound event.

In the table below, separate the numbers into groups of 4. Then use the digits 0, 1, 2, and 3 to represent people who own cats. You are looking for groups of 4 numbers that do *not* contain a 0, 1, 2, or 3. Circle those groups.

18771	47374	36541	83454
97907	40978	34947	78482
26071	12644	94567	35467
02459	78467	06161	85897
44480	71716	13166	44096
72769	18974	24186	50866
35842	78478	45468	15441
58438	37487	16187	89892
83711	54631	19846	08483

In this case, the probability is $\dfrac{\boxed{}}{45}$ or 15.6%.

So, the experimental probability that it takes at least 4 customers before a cat owner enters the store is 15.6%.

Analyze and Reflect

3. In Exercise 1, what does spinning a Stop on your first spin, and spinning a Goal on your second spin represent in this situation?

_____

_____

_____

4. **MP Justify Conclusions** Explain how your results might change for Exercise 1 if you simulated 100 penalty kicks.

_____

_____

5. In Exercise 2, why were the numbers from the random number table separated into groups of four?

_____

_____

6. In Exercise 2, you could have used any 4 numbers to represent cat owners. Complete the simulation four more times using the numbers in the table to represent the cat owners.

Numbers that Represent Cat Owners	Experimental Probability
4, 5, 6, 7	▢ / 45
0, 1, 8, 9	▢ / 45
3, 4, 5, 6	▢ / 45

Create

7. **MP Model with Mathematics** Design a simulation that could be used to predict the probability of taking a four question multiple-choice test with four answer choices and getting all four questions correct by guessing. Conduct 50 trials of the experiment. Then calculate the experimental probability of getting all four questions correct by guessing.

8. **inquiry** HOW do simulations help you understand the probability of events happening?

_____

_____

_____

Case #1 Winning Serves

Edie has been practicing her volleyball serve every day after school. She hits a good serve an average of 3 out of 4 times.

What is the probability that Edie will hit two good serves in a row?

Understand *What are the facts?*

You know that Edie hits a good serve an average of 3 out of 4 times. Act it out with a spinner.

Plan *What is your strategy?*

Spin a spinner, numbered 1 to 4, two times. If the spinner lands on 1, 2, or 3, she hits a good serve. If the spinner lands on 4, she doesn't. Repeat the experiment 10 times.

Solve *How can you apply the strategy?*

Here are some possible results. Circle the columns that show two good serves. The first two are done for you.

Trials	1	2	3	4	5	6	7	8	9	10
First Spin	4	1	4	3	1	2	2	1	3	2
Second Spin	2	3	3	2	1	4	1	4	3	3

The circled columns show that six out of 10 trials resulted in two good serves

in a row. So, the probability is ☐ %.

Check *Does the answer make sense?*

Repeat the experiment several times to see whether the results agree.

Analyze the Strategy

MP Reason Inductively Describe an advantage of using the *act it out* strategy?

Case #2 Tests

James uses a spinner with four equal sections to answer a five-question multiple-choice quiz. Each question has choices A, B, C, and D.

Is this a good way to answer the quiz questions?

Understand

- **Read the problem. What are you being asked to find?**

  I need to find _____

  _____

- **What information do you know?**

  The spinner has 4 equal parts. There are 5 multiple-choice questions.

  The answer choices are A, B, C, and D.

Plan

- **Choose a problem-solving strategy.**

  I will use the _____ strategy.

Solve

Use your problem-solving strategy to solve the problem.
Spin a spinner with four equal parts labeled A, B, C, and D five times.
Repeat the experiment two times. Make a table of the results.

Question	1	2	3	4	5
Trial 1					
Trial 2					

With each spin there is an equal chance of landing on any section. Since the

probability of an answer being A, B, C, or D is _____ likely, any answer
choice is possible.

Is using a spinner to answer a multiple-choice question a good idea? _____

Check

Use information from the problem to check your answer.
Repeat the experiment several times to see if the results agree.

Work with a small group to solve the following cases.
Show your work on a separate piece of paper.

Case #3 Chess

A chess tournament will be held and 32 students will participate.
If a player loses one match, he or she will be eliminated.

How many total games will be played in the
tournament?

_____

Case #4 Running

Six runners are entered in a race. Assume there are no ties.

In how many ways can first and second places be awarded?

_____

Case #5 Fair Games

Karla and Jason are playing a game with number cubes. Each number cube is
numbered 1 to 6. They roll both number cubes. If the product is a multiple of 3,
Jason wins. If the product is a multiple of 4, Karla wins.

Is this game fair or unfair? Justify your response.

_____

_____

_____

Use any
strategy!

Case #6 Algebra

The figure shown at the right is
known as Pascal's Triangle.

Make a conjecture for the
numbers in the 6th and
7th rows.

_____

Mid-Chapter Check

1. Define *probability*. Give an example of the probability of a simple event.

_____

_____

2. Fill in the blank in the sentence below with the correct term.

A(n) _____ is an experiment that is designed to act out a given situation.

Skills Check and Problem Solving

The table shows the number of science fiction, action, and comedy movies Jason has in his collection. Suppose one movie is selected at random. Find each probability. Write as a fraction in simplest form.

Type of Movie	
Science Fiction	10
Action	7
Comedy	3

3. *P*(science fiction) _____

4. *P*(*not* action) _____

5. A coin is tossed 20 times. It lands heads 4 times. Compare the experimental probability to its theoretical probability. If the probabilities are not close, explain a possible reason for the discrepancy.

_____

_____

6. A weather forecaster predicts a 30% chance of rain for each of the next three days. Describe a way to simulate the chance that it will rain the next three days. _____

_____

_____

7. **MP** **Persevere with Problems** Without looking, Santiago took a handful of multi-colored candies from a bag and found that 20% of the candies were yellow and 15% were green. Suppose there were 480 candies in the bag. Based on Santiago's results, how many more yellow candies would you

expect there to be than green candies? _____

Fundamental Counting Principle

Real-World Link

Classes Tyler wants to take a class at the community center. The table shows the class options he is considering. All of the classes are offered only on Monday and Tuesday.

Class	Day
Drawing Martial Arts Dance	Monday Tuesday

Essential Question

HOW can you predict the outcome of future events?

Vocabulary

Fundamental Counting Principle

1. According to the table, how many classes is he considering? _____

2. How many days are the classes offered?

_____

3. Complete the tree diagram to find the number of different class and day outcomes.

Class	Day	Sample Space
Drawing	Monday	Drawing, Monday
	Tuesday	Drawing, Tuesday
Martial Arts	_____	Martial Arts, Monday
	_____	_____
_____	_____	_____
	_____	_____

4. Find the product of the two numbers you found in Exercises 1 and 2. How does the number of outcomes compare to the product?

_____

Which MP Mathematical Process Goals did you use? Shade the circle(s) that applies.

① Mathematical Problem Solving
② Mathematical Communication
③ Mathematical Reasoning
④ Mathematical Connections
⑤ Mathematical Representations

Fundamental Counting Principle

If event *M* has *m* possible outcomes and event *N* has *n* possible outcomes, then event *M* followed by event *N* has $m \times n$ possible outcomes.

You can use multiplication instead of making a tree diagram to find the number of possible outcomes in a sample space. This is called the **Fundamental Counting Principle**.

Example

1. Find the total number of outcomes when a coin is tossed and a number cube is rolled.

A coin has 2 possible outcomes. A number cube has 6 possible outcomes. Multiply the possible outcomes of each event.

coin	number cube	total

$$2 \cdot 6 = 12 \quad \text{Fundamental Counting Principle}$$

There are 12 different outcomes.

Check   Draw a tree diagram to show the sample space.

Coin	Number Cube	Sample Space
heads	1	heads, 1
	2	heads, 2
	3	heads, 3
	4	heads, 4
	5	heads, 5
	6	heads, 6
tails	1	tails, 1
	2	tails, 2
	3	tails, 3
	4	tails, 4
	5	tails, 5
	6	tails, 6

The tree diagram also shows that there are 12 outcomes. ✓

 Show your work.

Got it? Do this problem to find out.

a. _____

a. Find the total number of outcomes when choosing from bike helmets that come in three colors and two styles.

Find Probability

You can use the Fundamental Counting Principle to help find the probability of events.

 Real World

Examples Tutor

2. **Find the total number of outcomes from rolling a number cube with sides labeled 1–6 and choosing a letter from the word NUMBERS. Then find the probability of rolling a 6 and choosing an M.**

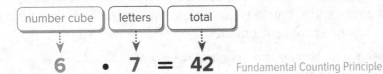

| number cube | letters | total |

$$6 \cdot 7 = 42 \quad \text{Fundamental Counting Principle}$$

There are 42 different outcomes.

There is only one favorable outcome. So, the probability of rolling a 6 and choosing an M is $\frac{1}{42}$ or about 2%.

3. **Find the number of different jeans available at The Jeans Shop. Then find the probability of randomly selecting a size 32 × 34 slim fit. Is it likely or unlikely that the jeans would be chosen?**

The Jeans Shop		
Waist Size	**Length (in.)**	**Style**
30	30	slim fit
32	32	bootcut
34	34	loose fit
36		
38		

> **Jean Size**
> In men's jeans, the size is labeled waist × length. So, a 32 × 34 is a 32-inch waist with a 34-inch length.

| size | length | style | total |

$$5 \cdot 3 \cdot 3 = 45 \quad \text{Fundamental Counting Principle}$$

There are 45 different types of jeans to choose. Out of the 45 possible outcomes, only one is favorable. So, the probability of randomly selecting a 32 × 34 slim fit is $\frac{1}{45}$ or about 2%.

It is very unlikely that the size would be chosen at random.

Got it? Do this problem to find out.

b. Two number cubes are rolled. What is the probability that the sum of the numbers on the cubes is 12? How likely is it that the sum would be 12?

 Show your work.

 b. _____

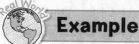

Example

4. A box of toy cars contains blue, orange, yellow, red, and black cars. A separate box contains a male and a female action figure. What is the probability of randomly choosing an orange car and a female action figure? Is it likely or unlikely that this combination is chosen?

First, find the number of possible outcomes.

There are 5 choices for the car and 2 choices for the action figure.

$5 \cdot 2 = 10$ Fundamental Counting Principal

There are 10 possible outcomes. There is one way to choose an orange car and a female action figure. It is very unlikely that this combination is chosen at random.

$P(\text{orange car, female action figure}) = \frac{1}{10}$ or 10%.

Guided Practice

1. Use the Fundamental Counting Principle to find the number of outcomes from tossing a quarter, a dime, and a nickel. (Example 1)

2. How many outcomes are possible when rolling a number cube and picking a cube from 4 different colored cubes? (Example 1)

3. Find the number of different outfits that can be made from 3 sweaters, 4 blouses, and 6 skirts. Then find the probability of randomly selecting a particular sweater-blouse-skirt outfit. Is the probability of this event likely or unlikely? (Examples 2–4)

4. **Building on the Essential Question** Compare and contrast tree diagrams and the Fundamental Counting Principle.

Rate Yourself!

How confident are you about using the Fundamental Counting Principle? Shade the ring on the target.

For more help, go online to access a Personal Tutor.

Name _____ My Homework _____

Independent Practice

Go online for Step-by-Step Solutions

Use the Fundamental Counting Principle to find the total number of outcomes for each situation. (Example 1)

1 choosing a bagel with one type of cream cheese from the list shown in the table

Bagels	Cream Cheese
Plain	Plain
Blueberry	Chive
Cinnamon raisin	Sun-dried tomato
Garlic	

2. choosing a sandwich and a side from the list shown in the table

Sandwiches	Sides
Ham	Pasta Salad
Turkey	Fruit Cup
Roast Beef	Potato Chips
Tuna Salad	Side Salad
Vegetarian	

3. picking a month of the year and a day of the week _____

4. choosing from a comedy, horror, or action movie each shown in four different theaters

5. Find the number of possible routes from Eastland to Johnstown that pass through Harping. Then find the probability that State and Fairview will be used if a route is selected at random. State the probability as a fraction and percent. (Examples 2–3)

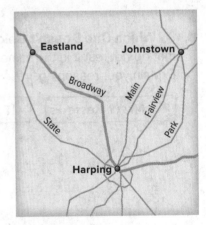

6. Find the number of possible choices for a 2-digit number that is greater than 19. Then find the number of possible choices for a 4-digit Personal Identification Number (PIN) if the digits cannot be repeated. (Example 1)

7. An electronics company makes educational apps for 5 subjects, including math. The app has 10 versions, with a different avatar in each version. One version has an avatar that looks similar to a lion. The company is randomly giving free apps to its customers. Find the probability of randomly receiving a math app with a lion avatar. How likely is the probability of receiving this app at random? (Examples 2–4)

Copyright © McGraw-Hill Education

Lesson 5 Fundamental Counting Principle **655**

8. A sandwich shop offers 4 different meats and 2 different cheeses. Suppose the sandwich shop offers 24 different meat-cheese sandwiches. How many different breads does the sandwich shop use?

_____

9 (MP) **Justify Conclusions** A store offers 32 different T-shirt designs and 11 choices of color. Is the store's advertisement true? Explain.

_____

_____

A
T-shirt for
Every Day of the
Year!

32 designs!   **11** colors!

🔥 H.O.T. Problems Higher Order Thinking

10. (MP) **Persevere with Problems** Determine the number of possible outcomes when tossing one coin, two coins, and three coins. Then determine the number of possible outcomes for tossing *n* coins. Describe the strategy you used.

_____

_____

_____

11. (MP) **Which One Doesn't Belong?** Identify the choices for events *M* and *N* that do not result in the same number of outcomes as the other two. Explain your reasoning.

| 9 drinks, 8 desserts | 18 shirts, 4 pants | 10 groups, 8 activities |

_____

_____

12. (MP) **Justify Conclusions** Marcus has a choice of a white, gray, or black shirt to wear with a choice of tan, black, brown, or denim pants. Without calculating the number of possible outcomes, how many more outfits can he make if he buys a green shirt? Explain your reasoning to a classmate.

_____

_____

13. (MP) **Persevere with Problems** Write an algebraic expression to find the number of outcomes if a number cube is rolled *x* times.

_____

Extra Practice

Use the Fundamental Counting Principle to find the total number of outcomes for each situation.

14. rolling a number cube and spinning a spinner with eight equal sections _48_

$$6 \cdot 8 = 48$$

Homework Help

15. tossing a coin and selecting one letter from the word MATH _____

16. selecting one sweatshirt from a choice of five sweatshirts and one pair of pants from a choice of four pairs of pants _____

17. selecting one entrée from a choice of nine entrées and one dessert from a choice of three desserts _____

18. rolling a number cube and tossing two coins _____

19. choosing tea in regular, raspberry, lemon, or peach; sweetened or unsweetened; and in a glass or bottle _____

20. A cafeteria offers oranges, apples, or bananas as its fruit option. It offers peas, green beans, or carrots as the vegetable option. Find the number of fruit and vegetable options. If the fruit and the vegetable are chosen at random, what is the probability of getting an orange and carrots? Is it likely or unlikely that a customer would get an orange and carrots?

_____

21. **MP Justify Conclusions** The table shows cell phone options offered by a wireless phone company. If a phone with one payment plan and one accessory is given away at random, predict the probability that it will be Brand B and have a headset. Explain your reasoning.

Phone Brands	Payment Plans	Accessories
Brand A	Individual	Leather case
Brand B	Family	Car mount
Brand C	Business	Headset
	Government	Travel charger

_____

_____

_____

_____

22. A restaurant has 24 different lunch combinations. Which of the following could describe the lunch options? Select all that apply.

☐ 3 drink sizes, 4 main dishes, 2 side dishes

☐ 2 appetizers, 6 main dishes, 3 desserts

☐ 3 kinds of bread, 8 kinds of sandwiches

☐ 2 drink sizes, 7 appetizers, 2 main dishes

23. Hat Shack sells 9 different styles of hats in several different colors for 2 different sports teams. The company makes 108 kinds of hats in all. Select the correct values to complete the formula below to find the number of different color hats the Hat Shack makes.

Hat Shack		
Styles	**Colors**	**Teams**
9	?	2

	=		×		×	

2
9
108
c

How many different colors does the company use for hats?

Spiral Review

Find each probability.

24. A coin is tossed and a spinner with 4 equal sections labeled W–Z is spun. Find *P*(heads and Z).

_____

25. A pizza shop offers a single item pizza with choice of pepperoni, green peppers, pineapple, sausage, or mushroom toppings. The pizza can be thick crust or thin crust. Find *P*(thick crust).

_____

Describe a model that could be used to simulate each situation.

26. There is a fifty percent chance of rain on Monday.

_____

27. A restaurant randomly gives away 1 of 6 toys. Determine the number of times a child needs to visit the restaurant to receive all 6 toys.

_____

_____

Essential Question

HOW can you predict the outcome of future events?

 Vocab **Vocabulary**

permutation

Real-World Link

Scheduling Colt is planning his Saturday. He wants to mow the grass, go swimming, and do his homework. How many different ways are there to arrange what he wants to do?

Fill in the blanks of the organized list below to find all of the possible arrangements of the activities.

1: Mowing	2: Swimming	3: Homework
1: Mowing	2: Homework	3: _____
1: Swimming	2: Mowing	3: Homework
1: Swimming	2: Homework	3: _____
1: Homework	2: _____	3: _____
1: _____	2: _____	3: _____

1. How many choices does Colt have for his first activity?

   _____

2. Once the first activity is selected, how many choices does Colt have for the second activity?

   _____

3. Once the first and second activities are selected, how many choices does Colt have for the third activity?

   _____

Which MP Mathematical Process Goals did you use? Shade the circle(s) that applies.

① Mathematical Problem Solving
② Mathematical Communication
③ Mathematical Reasoning
④ Mathematical Connections
⑤ Mathematical Representations

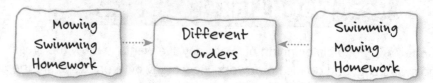

Find a Permutation

A **permutation** is an arrangement, or listing, of objects in which order is important.

Mowing
Swimming
Homework
········> Different Orders <········ Swimming
Mowing
Homework

You can use the Fundamental Counting Principle to find the number of permutations.

Examples

1. Julia is scheduling her first three classes. Her choices are math, science, and language arts. Use the Fundamental Counting Principle to find the number of different ways Julia can schedule her first three classes.

There are **3** choices for the first class.

There are **2** choices that remain for the second class.

There is **1** choice that remains for the third class.

3 • 2 • 1 = 6 ◄──── the number of permutations of 3 classes

There are 6 possible arrangements, or permutations, of the 3 classes.

2. An ice cream shop has 31 flavors. Carlos wants to buy a three-scoop cone with three different flavors. How many cones could he buy if the order of the flavors is important?

There are 31 choices for the first scoop, 30 choices for the second scoop, and 29 choices for the third scoop.

Use the Fundamental Counting Principle.

$31 \cdot 30 \cdot 29 = 26,970$

Carlos could buy 26,970 different cones.

Show your work.

Got it? Do these problems to find out.

a. In how many ways can the starting six players of a volleyball team stand in a row for a picture?

b. In a race with 7 runners, in how many ways can the runners end up in first, second, and third place?

a. _____

b. _____

The symbol $P(31, 3)$ represents the number of permutations of 31 things taken 3 at a time.

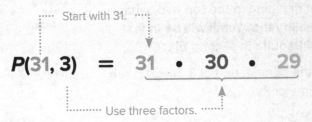

Start with 31.

$$P(31, 3) = 31 \cdot 30 \cdot 29$$

Use three factors.

Example

 Tutor

3. Find $P(8, 3)$.

$P(8, 3) = 8 \cdot 7 \cdot 6$ or 336   8 things taken 3 at a time

Got it? Do these problems to find out.

   c. $P(12, 2)$ **d.** $P(4, 4)$ **e.** $P(10, 5)$

c. _____

d. _____

Show your work

e. _____

Find ProbabilILty

Permutations can be used when finding probabilities of real-world situations.

Examples

 Tutor

4. Ashley's MP3 player has a setting that allows the songs to play in a random order. She has a playlist that contains 10 songs. What is the probability that the MP3 player will randomly play the first three songs in order?

First find the permutation of ten things taken three at a time or $P(10, 3)$.

10 songs ·······→ ·······→ Choose 3

$$P(10, 3) = 10 \cdot 9 \cdot 8$$
$$= 720$$

←······ 10 choices for the 1st song
9 choices for the 2nd song
8 choices for the 3rd song

So, there are 720 different ways to play the first 3 songs. Since you want the first three songs in order, there is only 1 out of the 720 ways to do this.

So, the probability that the first 3 songs will play in order is $\frac{1}{720}$.

Notation

In Example 4, the notation $P(10, 3)$ indicates a permutation while the notation P(playing the first three songs in order) indicates probability.

5. A swimming event features 8 swimmers. If each swimmer has an equally likely chance of finishing in the top two, what is the probability that Yumii will be in first place and Paquita in second place?

Swimmers	
Octavia	Eden
Natasha	Paquita
Calista	Samantha
Yumii	Lorena

First find the permutation of 8 things taken two at a time or $P(8, 2)$.

$$P(8, 2) = 8 \cdot 7$$
$$= 56$$

There are 56 possible arrangements, or permutations, of the two places. Since there is only one way of having Yumii come in first and Paquita second, the probability of this event is $\frac{1}{56}$.

Reasonable Answers
A possible probability of $\frac{1}{56}$ indicates that it is very unlikely that Yumii will finish first and Paquita will finish second.

Show your work.

Got it? Do this problem to find out.

f. Two different letters are randomly selected from the letters in the word *math*. What is the probability that the first letter selected is *m* and the second letter is *h*?

f. _____

Guided Practice

1. In how many ways can a president, vice president, and secretary be randomly selected from a class of 25 students? (Examples 1 and 2)

2. Find the value of $P(5, 3)$. (Example 3)

3. Adrianne, Julián, and two of their friends will sit in a row at a baseball game. If each friend is equally likely to sit in any seat, what is the probability that Adrianne will sit in the first seat and Julián will sit in the second seat? (Examples 4 and 5)

4. **ⓔ Building on the Essential Question** HOW can you find the number of permutations of a set of objects?

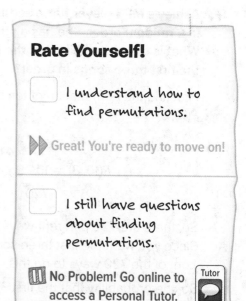

Rate Yourself!

☐ I understand how to find permutations.

▶▶ Great! You're ready to move on!

☐ I still have questions about finding permutations.

📖 No Problem! Go online to access a Personal Tutor.

Independent Practice

Go online for Step-by-Step Solutions

1 In the Battle of the Bands contest, in how many ways can the four participating bands perform? (Examples 1 and 2)

_____

2. A garage door code has 5 digits. If no digit is repeated, how many codes are possible?

_____

Find each value. Use a calculator if needed. (Example 3)

3. $P(7, 4)$ _____

4. $P(12, 5)$ _____

5. $P(8, 8)$ _____

6. You have five seasons of your favorite TV show on DVD. If you randomly select two of them from a shelf, what is the probability that you will select season one first and season two second? (Examples 4 and 5)

_____

7. **MP Model with Mathematics** The graphic novel frame below explains how the survey has students rank their favorite kinds of music. In how

many ways can the survey be answered? _____

8. A certain number of friends are waiting in line to board a new roller coaster. They can board the ride in 5,040 different ways. How many friends are in line?

_____

 9 The Coughlin family discovered they can stand in a row for their family portrait in 720 different ways. How many members are in the Coughlin family? _____

10. Howland Middle School assigns a four-digit identification number to each student. The number is made from the digits 1, 2, 3, and 4, and no digit is repeated. If assigned randomly, what is the probability that an ID number will end with a 3? _____

H.O.T. Problems Higher Order Thinking

11. **MP** **Model with Mathematics** Describe a real-world situation that has 6 permutations.

_____

_____

12. **MP** **Persevere with Problems** There are 1,320 ways for three students to win first, second, and third place during a debate match. How many students are there on the debate team? Explain your reasoning.

_____

_____

13. **MP** **Persevere with Problems** A *combination* is an arrangement where order is *not* important. You can find the number of combinations of items by dividing the number of permutations by the number of ways the smaller set can be arranged. The combination at the right shows the number of combinations if you choose 2 flavors of ice cream out of 5 flavors. Use this method to find each value.

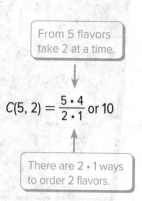

From 5 flavors take 2 at a time.

$$C(5, 2) = \frac{5 \cdot 4}{2 \cdot 1} \text{ or } 10$$

There are $2 \cdot 1$ ways to order 2 flavors.

    a. $C(6, 4)$ _____   **b.** $C(10, 3)$ _____

    c. $C(5, 3)$ _____   **d.** $C(8, 6)$ _____

Extra Practice

14. How many permutations are possible of the letters in the word FRIEND? _720_

 $6 \cdot 5 \cdot 4 \cdot 3 \cdot 2 \cdot 1 = 720$

15. How many different 3-digit numbers can be formed using the digits 9, 3, 4, 7, and 6? Assume no number can be used more than once. _____

Find each value. Use a calculator if needed.

16. $P(9, 2)$ _____

17. $P(5, 5)$ _____

18. $P(7, 7)$ _____

19. The members of the Evergreen Junior High Quiz Bowl team are listed in the table. If a captain and an assistant captain are chosen at random, what is the probability that Walter is selected as captain and Mi-Ling as co-captain? _____

Evergreen Junior High Quiz Bowl Team	
Jamil	Luanda
Savannah	Mi-Ling
Tucker	Booker
Ferdinand	Nina
Walter	Meghan

20. Alex, Aiden, Dexter, and Dion are playing a video game. If they each have an equally likely chance of getting the highest score, what is the probability that Dion will get the highest score and Alex the second highest? _____

21. A child has wooden blocks with the letters shown. Find the probability that the child randomly arranges the letters in the order TIGER. _____

22. The schools listed in the table are finalists in a science competition. First through third places will win a prize. Each school is equally likely to win the competition. Select values to complete the model below to find the probability that Lincoln wins first place, River Valley wins second place, and Glenwood wins third place.

Finalists
Chester Middle School
Glenwood Middle School
Lincoln Middle School
River Valley Middle School
South Middle School

Find the number of ways the schools can finish in first, second, and third place:

$P\left(\boxed{} , \boxed{}\right) = \boxed{}$

The number of ways that Lincoln can finish first, River Valley second, and Glenwood third is equal to $\boxed{}$.

1	2	3	4	5
10	20	30	60	90

$P(\text{Lincoln first, River Valley second, Glenwood third}) = \dfrac{\boxed{}}{\boxed{}}$

23. The five finalists in a writing contest are Cesar, Teresa, Sean, Nikita, and Alfonso. There will be a first place award and a second place award. Each finalist is equally likely to win an award. Determine if each statement is true or false.

a. There are 10 permutations of 5 finalists taken 2 at a time. ☐ True ☐ False

b. There is only 1 way that Teresa can earn first place and Sean can earn second place. ☐ True ☐ False

c. The probability that Teresa earns first place and Sean earns second place is 0.05. ☐ True ☐ False

Spiral Review

A card is pulled from a stack of 30 cards labeled 1–30. Find each probability. Write as a fraction in simplest form.

24. $P(\text{greater than 5})$ _____

25. $P(not\ 1)$ _____

26. $P(\text{an even number})$ _____

27. A cross country athlete has a white, a red, and a gray sweatshirt. She has black and gray running pants. Make a list to show the possible combinations of training outfits. _____

21ST CENTURY CAREER
in Medicine

Pediatricians

Do you have compassion, a sense of humor, and the ability to analyze data? You might want to consider a career in medicine. Pediatricians care for the health of infants, children, and teenagers. They diagnose illnesses, interpret diagnostic tests, and prescribe and administer treatment.

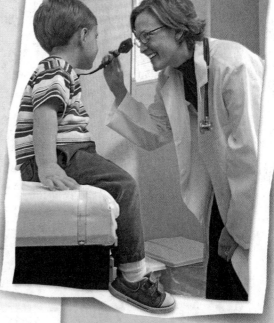

College & Career
READINESS

Is This the Career for You?

Are you interested in a career as a pediatrician? Take some of the following courses in high school.

- ◆ Algebra
- ◆ Biology
- ◆ Calculus
- ◆ Chemistry
- ◆ Psychology

Find out how math relates to a career in Medicine.

ⓂⓅ On Call for Kids

Use the information in the table below to solve each problem. Write each answer as a percent rounded to the nearest whole number.

1. What is the probability that one of the patients tested has strep throat? _____

2. If a patient has strep throat, what is the probability that they have a positive test?

   _____

3. What is the probability that a patient with the disease has a negative test? _____

4. If a patient does not have the disease, what is the probability that they have a positive test? _____

5. What is the probability that a patient that does *not* have strep throat tested negative for the disease? _____

6. The *positive predictive value*, or *PPV*, is the probability that a patient with a positive test result will have the disease. What is the PPV? _____

7. The *negative predictive value*, or *NPV*, is the probability that a patient with a negative test result will not have the disease. What is the NPV? _____

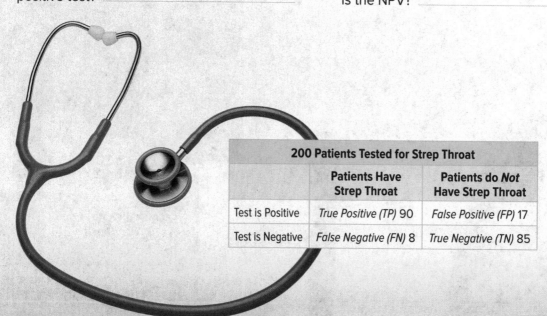

200 Patients Tested for Strep Throat		
	Patients Have Strep Throat	**Patients do *Not* Have Strep Throat**
Test is Positive	True Positive (TP) 90	False Positive (FP) 17
Test is Negative	False Negative (FN) 8	True Negative (TN) 85

ⓂⓅ Career Project

It's time to update your career portfolio! Interview your pediatrician. Be sure to ask what he or she enjoys most about being a pediatrician and what is most challenging. Include all the interview questions and answers in your portfolio.

_____

_____

_____

_____

What are some short term goals you need to achieve to become a pediatrician?

- _____
- _____
- _____
- _____
- _____

Vocabulary Check

Unscramble each of the clue words. After unscrambling all of the terms, use the numbered letters to find a sentence associated with probability.

HELATCORTEI

          8   5

PORTUNMETAI

          2   9

LEAPMS ECPAS

4   3   6

COAPELMERTMYN

  7   1

1 2 3 4   5   6 7 8 9

Complete each sentence using one of the unscrambled words above.

1. The _____ is the set of all of the possible outcomes of a probability experiment.

2. A _____ is an arrangement, or listing, of objects in which order is important.

3. The _____ probability is based on what should happen when conducting a probability experiment.

4. Two events in which one or the other must happen, but they cannot happen at the same time are _____.

Use Your FOLDABLES

Use your Foldable to help review the chapter.

Tape here

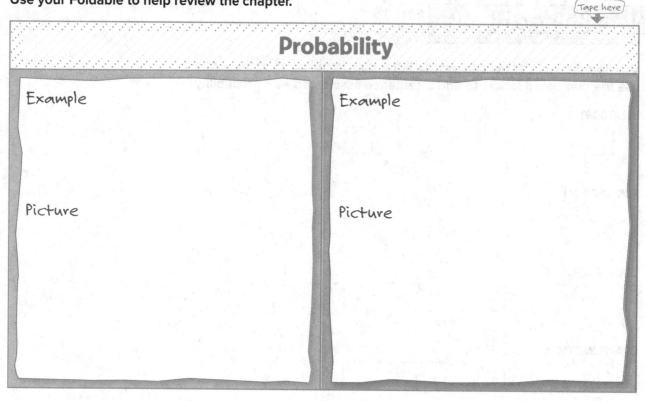

Probability

Example

Picture

Example

Picture

Got it?

Match each term or phrase on the left with the words on the right.

1. Based on what actually occurred in a probability experiment

2. A listing of objects in which order is important

3. Consists of two or more simple events

4. Can be used to find the sample space

a. compound event

b. experimental probability

c. Fundamental Counting Principle

d. permutation

e. tree diagrams

f. organized lists

Power Up! Performance Task

Carnival Prizes

Kelli is in charge of a game booth at the school carnival. The game has two simple rules.

- Randomly pick one blue card and one red card.
- If the product of the two numbers is greater than or equal to 45, you win a prize.

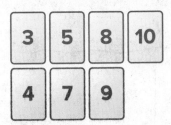

Write your answers on another piece of paper. Show all of your work to receive full credit.

Part A
Create a sample space and find the product of each combination. What is the probability that a person wins the game? Express your answer as a fraction in lowest terms and as a percent rounded to the nearest whole number.

Part B
The sponsor of the booth determines that they are giving away too many prizes. Recommend a minimum winning number that lowers the chance of winning to 25%. Explain your reasoning.

Part C
Participants achieving a winning score of 70 or higher in four consecutive attempts will receive a large stuffed animal. What is the probability of this occurring?

Part D
After changing the game rules, patrons and onlookers are disappointed when the first five games yield products of 12, 21, 32, 35, and 12. Recommend a statement that the sponsor can use to reassure customers that the game is fair.

Reflect

 Answering the Essential Question

Use what you learned about probability to complete the graphic organizer.

Theoretical Probability

Experimental Probability

Essential Question

HOW can you predict the outcome
of future events?

Sample Space

Simulation

Answer the Essential Question. HOW can you predict the outcome of
future events?

Chapter 8
Statistics

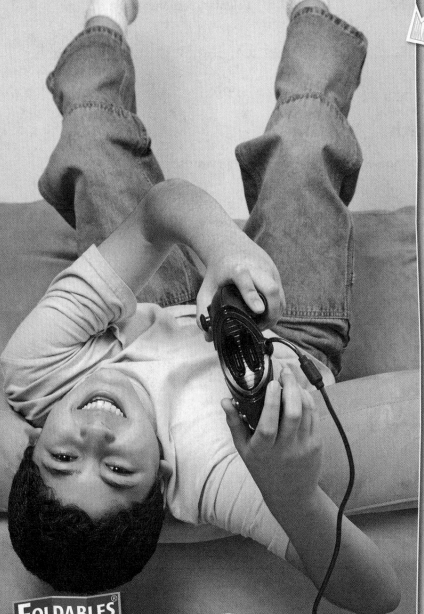

 Essential Question

HOW do you know which type of graph to use when displaying data?

 Virginia Standards
7.9a, b, c

 Math in the Real World

Surveys are used to collect information. Survey results can be shown in graphs.

The results of a survey of 50 middle school students are shown in the table. On the circle graph, write the percent of students who preferred each activity.

Activity	Number of Students
Gaming	22
Social Networking	18
Viewing Movies	6
Other	4

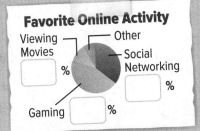

Favorite Online Activity

Viewing Movies [ ] % · Other · Social Networking [ ] %
Gaming [ ] %

 FOLDABLES
Study Organizer

1. Cut out the Foldable in the back of the book.

2. Place your Foldable on page 730.

3. Use the Foldable throughout this chapter to help you learn about statistics.

Vocabulary

biased sample	population	survey
convenience sample	sample	systematic random sample
frequency distribution	simple random sample	unbiased sample
histogram	statistics	voluntary response sample

Study Skill: Writing Math

Describe Data When you *describe* something, you represent it in words.

The table shows the prices for takeout orders at Lombardo's Restaurant.

Use the table to complete the following statements.

Takeout	Price ($)
Main Dish	8.00
Side Dish	2.50
Dessert	4.00

1. The price of a dessert is _____ .

2. The price of a main dish is twice the price of

   _____ .

3. A _____ is the least expensive item.

Write two other statements that describe the data.

4. _____

   _____

   _____

5. _____

   _____

   _____

Read each statement. Decide whether you agree (A) or disagree (D). Place a checkmark in the appropriate column and then justify your reasoning.

Statistics			
Statement	A	D	Why?
Statistics deal with collecting, organizing, and interpreting data.			
A sample is the same thing as the entire population.			
A biased sample accurately represents the entire population.			
Graphs are sometimes made to influence conclusions by misrepresenting the data.			
Any type of display can be used to represent data.			

When Will You Use This?

Here are a few examples of how statistics are used in the real world.

Activity 1 Find the average monthly high and low temperatures for the city where you live. Then find the average monthly high and low temperatures for another city. How do these temperatures compare to the temperatures for your city?

_____

_____

Activity 2 Go online at **connectED.mcgraw-hill.com** to read the graphic novel **Record Highs**. Blake, Hannah, and Jamar need to compare the record high temperatures for two different cities.

What cities do they use? _____

Blake, Hannah, and Jamar in

Record Highs

For our report we decided to compare record temperatures for 2 of the hottest places in the U.S.

Let's find the U.S. city that is closest to the equator.

Are You Ready?

Try the Quick Check below.
Or, take the Online Readiness Quiz.

Check ✓

Quick Review

Example 1

Which players averaged more than 10 points per game?

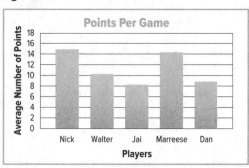

Nick, Walter, and Marreese averaged more than 10 points per game.

Example 2

Use the circle graph. Suppose 300 people were surveyed. How many people have two accounts?

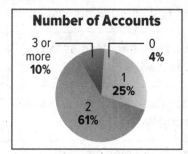

Find 61% of 300.

61% of 300 = 61% × 300
= 0.61 × 300 or 183

So, 183 people have two accounts.

Quick Check

Graphs The bar graph at the right shows the number of items each student obtained during a scavenger hunt.

1. Who obtained the most items?

_____

2. Who obtained the least items?

_____

3. Refer to the circle graph in Example 2. Suppose 300 people were surveyed. How many people have 1 account?

_____

How Did You Do?

Which problems did you answer correctly in the Quick Check?
Shade those exercise numbers below.

Make Predictions

Vocabulary Start-Up

Statistics deal with collecting, organizing, and interpreting data. A **survey** is a method of collecting information. The group being studied is the **population**. Sometimes the population is very large. To save time and money, part of the group, called a **sample**, is surveyed.

For each survey topic, determine which set represents the population and which represents a sample of the population. Write *population* or *sample*.

	Survey Topic	Set A	Set B
1.	dress code changes	the students in a middle school	the seventh graders in the middle school
2.	favorite flavors of ice cream	the customers at an ice cream shop in the town	the residents of a town

 Essential Question

HOW do you know which type of graph to use when displaying data?

Vocabulary

statistics
survey
population
sample

Real-World Link

Logan wants to survey students in his school about their favorite and least favorite zoo exhibit. Describe a possible sample Logan could survey instead of surveying the entire school.

_____

_____

Which **MP** **Mathematical Process Goals** did you use? Shade the circle(s) that applies.

① Mathematical Problem Solving   ④ Mathematical Connections

② Mathematical Communication   ⑤ Mathematical Representations

③ Mathematical Reasoning

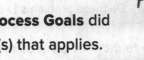

Copyright © McGraw-Hill Education   ©Digital Vision Ltd.

Make Predictions Using Ratios

You can use the results of a survey or past actions to predict the actions of a larger group. Since the ratios of the responses of a good sample are often the same as the ratios of the responses of the population.

 Examples

The students in Mr. Blackwell's class brought photos from their summer break. The table shows how many students brought each type of photo.

Summer Break Photos	
Location	**Students**
beach	6
campground	4
home	7
theme park	11

1. What is the probability that a student brought a photo taken at a theme park?

$$P(\text{theme park}) = \frac{\text{number of theme park photos}}{\text{number of students with a photo}} = \frac{11}{28}$$

So, the probability of a theme park photo is $\frac{11}{28}$.

2. There are 560 students at the school where Mr. Blackwell teaches. Predict how many students would bring in a photo taken at a theme park.

Let s represent the number of theme park photos.

$\frac{11}{28} = \frac{s}{560}$ Write an equivalent ratio.

$\frac{11}{28} = \frac{s}{560}$ Since 28 × 20 = 560, multiply 11 by 20 to find s.   ×20

$\frac{11}{28} = \frac{220}{560}$ s = 220

Of the 560 students, you can expect about 220 to bring a photo from a theme park.

Got it? Do these problems to find out.

A survey found that 6 out of every 10 students have a blog.

   a. What is the probability that a student at the school has a blog?

   b. Suppose there are about 250 students at the school. About how many have a blog?

a. _____

b. _____

Make Predictions Using Equations

You can also use the percent equation to make predictions.

Examples

3. A survey found that 85% of people use emoticons on their instant messengers. Predict how many of the 2,450 students at Washington Middle School use emoticons.

Words	What number of students is 85% of 2,450 students?
Variable	Let n represent the number of students.
Equation	$n = 0.85 \cdot 2,450$

$n = 0.85 \cdot 2,450$ Write the percent equation.

$n = 2,082.5$ Multiply.

About 2,083 of the students use emoticons.

- -

4. The circle graph shows the results of a survey in which children ages 8 to 12 were asked whether they have a television in their bedroom. Predict how many out of 1,725 students would not have a television in their bedroom.

You can use the percent equation and the survey results to predict what part p of the 1,725 students have no TV in their bedroom.

TV's in the Bedroom

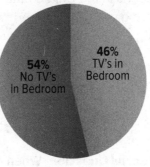

54% No TV's in Bedroom

46% TV's in Bedroom

part = percent · whole

$p = 0.54 \cdot 1,725$ Survey results: 54%

$p = 931.5$ Multiply.

About 932 students do not have a television in their bedroom.

> **Got it?** Do this problem to find out.

c. Refer to Example 4. Predict how many out of 1,370 students have a television in their bedroom.

STOP and Reflect

What proportion could you use to solve Example 4? Write your answer below.

Show your work.

c. _____

The table shows the results of a survey of Hamilton Middle School seventh graders. Use the table to find the following probabilities. (Examples 1 and 2)

Career Field	Students
Entertainment	17
Education	14
Medicine	11
Public service	6
Sports	2

1. the probability of choosing a career in public service

_____

2. the probability of choosing a career in education

_____

3. the probability of choosing a career in sports

_____

4. Predict how many students out of 400 will enter the education field.

_____

5. Predict how many students out of 500 will enter the medical field.

_____

6. Use the circle graph that shows the results of a poll to which 60,000 teens responded. Predict how many of the approximately 28 million teens in the United States would buy a music CD if they were given $20. (Examples 3 and 4)

_____

How Would You Spend a Gift of $20?

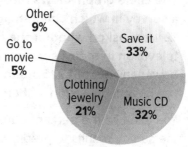

Other 9%
Go to movie 5%
Save it 33%
Clothing/jewelry 21%
Music CD 32%

7.  **Building on the Essential Question** When can statistics be used to gain information about a population from a sample?

_____

_____

_____

Rate Yourself!

How confident are you about making predictions? Check the box that applies.

For more help, go online to access a Personal Tutor.

Independent Practice

Go online for Step-by-Step Solutions eHelp

The table shows the results of a survey of 150 students. Use the table to find the probability of a student participating in each sport. (Example 1)

Sport	Students
Baseball/softball	36
Basketball	30
Football	45
Gymnastics	12
Tennis	18
Volleyball	9

1. football

_____

2. tennis

_____

3. gymnastics

_____

4. volleyball

_____

5. Three out of every 10 students ages 6–14 have a magazine subscription. Suppose there are 30 students in Annabelle's class. About how many will have a magazine subscription? (Example 2)

_____

6. Use the graph that shows the percent of cat owners who train their cats in each category. (Examples 3 and 4)

   a. Out of 255 cat owners, predict how many owners trained their cat not to climb on furniture.

   _____

   b. Out of 316 cat owners, predict how many cat owners trained their cat not to claw on furniture.

   _____

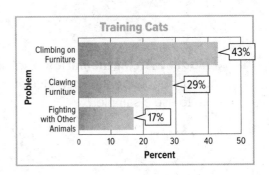

7. **MP Make a Prediction** The school librarian recorded the types of books students checked out on a typical day. Suppose there are 605 students enrolled at the school. Predict the number of students that prefer humor books. Compare this to the number of students at the school who prefer nonfiction.

_____

_____

_____

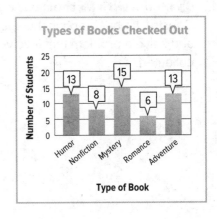

8. **MP** **Find the Error** A survey of a seventh-grade class showed that 4 out of every 10 students are taking a trip during spring break. There are 150 students in the seventh grade. Caitlyn is trying to determine how many of the seventh-grade students can be expected to take a trip during spring break. Find her mistake and correct it.

$$\frac{4}{10} = \frac{150}{x}$$

$$\frac{4}{10} = \frac{150}{375}$$

$$x = 375 \text{ students}$$

_____

_____

9. **MP** **Persevere with Problems** One letter tile is drawn from the bag and replaced 300 times. Predict how many times a consonant will *not* be picked.

_____

10. **MP** **Persevere with Problems** A survey found that 80% of teens enjoy going to the movies in their free time. Out of 5,200 teens, predict how many said that they do not enjoy going to the movies in their free time.

_____

11. **MP** **Model with Mathematics** Explain how to use a sample to predict what a group of people prefer. Then give an example of a situation in which it makes sense to use a sample.

_____

_____

_____

12. **MP** **Model with Mathematics** Design a survey to give to your classmates. Construct a bar graph in the space below to represent your data. Then write and solve a problem that involves a prediction based on the data you collected.

Show your work.

Extra Practice

Solve.

13. Luther won 12 of the last 20 video games he played. Find the probability of Luther winning the next game he plays. $\frac{3}{5}$, 0.6, or 60%

 Homework Help

$$P(winning) = \frac{number\ of\ games\ won}{number\ of\ games\ played}$$
$$= \frac{12}{20}\ or\ \frac{3}{5}$$

14. Refer to Exercise 13. Suppose Luther plays a total of 60 games with his friends over the next month. Predict how many of these games Luther will win. _____

15. Use the graph that shows the number of times teens volunteer.

How Often Teens Volunteer

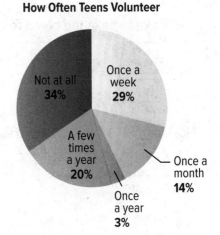

a. About 300,000 teens ages 12–14 live in Virginia. Predict the number of teens in this age group who volunteer a few times a year.

_____

b. Tennessee has about 250,000 teens ages 12–14. Predict the number of teens in this age group who volunteer once a week.

_____

c. About 240,000 teens ages 12–14 live in Missouri. Predict the number of teens in this age group who volunteer once a year.

_____

16. **MP Make a Prediction** The probability of Jaden making a free throw is 15%. Predict the number of free throws that he can expect to make if he attempts 40 free throws.

_____

Draw a line to match each situation with the appropriate equation or proportion.

17. 27 MP3s is what percent of 238 MP3s?

a. $n = 27 \cdot 2.38$

18. 238% of 27 is what number?

b. $\frac{27}{100} = \frac{p}{238}$

19. 27% of MP3 owners download music weekly. Predict how many MP3 owners out of 238 owners download music weekly.

c. $\frac{27}{238} = \frac{n}{100}$

Power Up! Test Practice

20. There were 515 students surveyed on how they spend time with their families. Which of the following estimates are accurate? Select all that apply.

☐ About 175 students spend time with their family eating dinner.

☐ About 72 students spend time with their family playing sports.

☐ About 50 students spend time with their family watching TV.

☐ About 38 students spend time with their family taking walks.

How Students Spend Time with Family	
Eating Dinner	34%
Watching TV	20%
Talking	14%
Playing Sports	14%
Talking Walks	4%
Other	14%

21. Yesterday a bakery baked 54 loaves of bread in 20 minutes. Today the bakery needs to bake 405 loaves of bread at the same rate. Select values to complete the model below to predict how long it will take to bake the bread today.

$$\frac{\boxed{}}{\boxed{}} = \frac{\boxed{}}{\boxed{}}$$

20
54
405
x

How long will it take to bake the bread today?

$\boxed{}$

Spiral Review

22. A magazine rack contains 5 sports magazines, 7 news magazines, and 10 fashion magazines. After a magazine is chosen, it is *not* replaced. Find the probability of randomly choosing two fashion magazines.

23. Each week, Ryan's mother has him randomly choose a chore that he must complete from the list shown. The first week, he chose washing the dishes. What is the probability that Ryan will choose washing the dishes two more weeks in a row?

Weekly Chores
Collecting the trash
Folding the laundry
Cleaning the house
Washing the dishes
Cutting the grass

24. In how many different orders can a person watch 3 different movies? Use a list to show the sample space.

Unbiased and Biased Samples

 Real-World Link Watch ▶

Entertainment A T.V. programming manager wants to conduct a survey to determine which reality television show is the favorite of viewers in a certain viewing area. He is considering the three samples shown. Draw an X through the two samples that would not fairly represent all of the people in the viewing area.

> **Sample 1**
> 100 people that are trying out for a reality show

> **Sample 2**
> 100 students at your middle school

> **Sample 3**
> Every 100th person at a shopping mall

 Essential Question

HOW do you know which type of graph to use when displaying data?

 Vocabulary

unbiased sample
simple random sample
systematic random sample
biased sample
convenience sample
voluntary response sample

Explain why the two samples that you crossed out do *not* fairly represent all of the people in the viewing area? Explain.

_____

_____

_____

_____

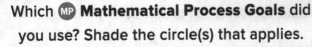

Which MP **Mathematical Process Goals did you use? Shade the circle(s) that applies.**

① Mathematical Problem Solving   ④ Mathematical Connections

② Mathematical Communication   ⑤ Mathematical Representations

③ Mathematical Reasoning

Biased and Unbiased Samples

To get valid results, a sample must be chosen very carefully. An **unbiased sample** is selected so that it accurately represents the entire population. Two ways to pick an unbiased sample are listed below.

Unbiased Samples		
Type	Description	Example
Simple Random Sample	Each item or person in the population is as likely to be chosen as any other.	Each student's name is written on a piece of paper. The names are placed in a bowl, and names are picked without looking.
Systematic Random Sample	The items or people are selected according to a specific time or item interval.	Every 20th person is chosen from an alphabetical list of all students attending a school.

In a **biased sample**, one or more parts of the population are favored over others. Two ways to pick a biased sample are listed below.

Biased Samples		
Type	Description	Example
Convenience Sample	A convenience sample consists of members of a population that are easily accessed.	To represent all the students attending a school, the principal surveys the students in one math class.
Voluntary Response Sample	A voluntary response sample involves only those who want to participate in the sampling.	Students at a school who wish to express their opinions complete an online survey.

Examples

Tutor

Determine whether the conclusion is valid. Justify your answer.

1. A random sample of students at a middle school shows that 10 students prefer listening to rock, 15 students prefer listening to hip hop, and 25 students prefer no music while they exercise. It can be concluded that half the students prefer no music while they exercise.

This is a simple random sample. So, the sample is unbiased and the conclusion is valid.

Determine whether each conclusion is valid. Justify your answer.

2. Every tenth person who walks into a department store is surveyed to determine his or her music preference. Out of 150 customers, 70 stated that they prefer rock music. The manager concludes that about half of all customers prefer rock music.

Since the population is every tenth customer of a department store, the sample is an unbiased, systematic random sample. The conclusion is valid.

3. The customers of a music store are surveyed to determine their favorite leisure time activity. The results are shown in the graph. The store manager concludes that most people prefer to listen to music in their leisure time.

Leisure Time Activities

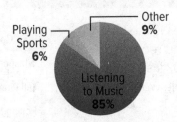

Other
9%

Playing
Sports
6%

Listening
to Music
85%

The customers of a music store probably like to listen to music in their leisure time. The sample is a biased, convenience sample since all of the people surveyed are in one specific location. The conclusion is not valid.

Got it? Do this problem to find out.

a. A radio station asks its listeners to indicate their preference for one of two candidates in an upcoming election. Seventy-two percent of the listeners who responded preferred candidate A, so the radio station announced that candidate A would win the election. Is the conclusion valid? Justify your answer.

Show your work.

a. _____

Use Sampling to Predict

A valid sampling method uses unbiased samples. If a sampling method is valid, you can make generalizations about the population.

Example

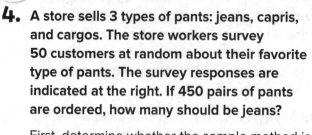

4. A store sells 3 types of pants: jeans, capris, and cargos. The store workers survey 50 customers at random about their favorite type of pants. The survey responses are indicated at the right. If 450 pairs of pants are ordered, how many should be jeans?

Type	Number
Jeans	25
Capris	15
Cargos	10

First, determine whether the sample method is valid. The sample is a simple random sample since customers were randomly selected. Thus, the sample method is valid.

$\frac{25}{50}$ or 50% of the customers prefer jeans. So, find 50% of 450.

$0.5 \times 450 = 225$, so about 225 pairs of jeans should be ordered.

Guided Practice

1. Zach is trying to decide which of three golf courses is the best. He randomly surveyed people at a sports store and recorded the results in the table. Is the sample method valid? If so, suppose Zach surveyed 150 more people. How many people would be expected to vote for Rolling Meadows? (Example 4)

Course	Number
Whispering Trail	10
Tall Pines	8
Rolling Meadows	7

_____

_____

2. To find how much money the average American family spends to cool their home, 100 Alaskan families are surveyed at random. Of the families, 85 said that they spend less than $75 per month on cooling. The researcher concluded that the average American family spends less than $75 on cooling per month. Is the conclusion valid? Explain. (Examples 1–3)

_____

_____

_____

_____

3. **Building on the Essential Question** How is using a survey one way to determine experimental probability?

_____

_____

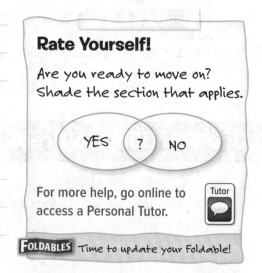

Rate Yourself!

Are you ready to move on?
Shade the section that applies.

YES   ?   NO

For more help, go online to access a Personal Tutor.

FOLDABLES Time to update your Foldable!

Independent Practice

Go online for Step-by-Step Solutions

eHelp

Determine whether each conclusion is valid. Justify your answer.
(Examples 1–3)

1 To evaluate the quality of their product, a manufacturer of cell phones checks every 50th phone off the assembly line. Out of 200 phones tested, 4 are defective. The manager concludes that about 2% of the cell phones produced will be defective.

Show your work.

_____

_____

2. To determine whether the students will attend an arts festival at the school, Oliver surveys his friends in the art club. All of Oliver's friends plan to attend. So, Oliver assumes that all the students at his school will also attend.

_____

_____

3 A random sample of people at a mall shows that 22 prefer to take a family trip by car, 18 prefer to travel by plane, and 4 prefer to travel by bus. Is the sample method valid? If so, how many people out of 500 would you expect to say they prefer to travel by plane? (Example 4)

_____

_____

Preferred Ways to Travel

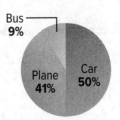

Bus 9%
Plane 41%
Car 50%

4. **MP Use Math Tools** Use the organizer to determine whether the conclusion is valid.

Step 1: Read the situation. → Marcus wants to predict the next student council president. He polls every fourth person from each grade level as they exit the cafeteria. In his poll, 65% chose Sophia. So, Marcus predicts Sophia will win the election.

Step 2: Determine the type of sample taken. → _____

Step 3: Determine if the conclusion is valid. → _____

5. **MP** **Persevere with Problems** How could the wording of a question or the tone of voice of the interviewer affect a survey? Provide an example.

_____

_____

_____

MP **Justify Conclusions** Determine whether each statement is *sometimes*, *always*, or *never* true. Explain your reasoning to a classmate.

6. A biased sample is valid.

_____

_____

7. A simple random sample is valid.

_____

_____

8. A voluntary response sample is valid.

_____

_____

9. **MP** **Find the Error** Marisol wants to determine how many students plan to attend the girls' varsity basketball game. Find her mistake and correct it.

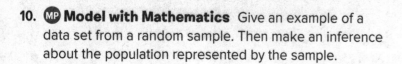
I will survey students at the boys' varsity basketball game.

_____

_____

_____

10. **MP** **Model with Mathematics** Give an example of a data set from a random sample. Then make an inference about the population represented by the sample.

_____

_____

_____

Extra Practice

Determine whether each conclusion is valid. Justify your answer.

11. To determine what people in California think about a proposed law, 5,000 people from the state are randomly surveyed. Of the people surveyed, 58% are against the law. The legislature concludes that the law should not be passed.

This is an unbiased, simple random sample because randomly selected Californians were surveyed. So, the conclusion is valid.

12. A magazine asks its readers to complete and return a questionnaire about popular television actors. The majority of those who replied liked one actor the most, so the magazine decides to write more articles about that actor.

_____

_____

13. The Student Council advisor asked every tenth student in the lunch line how they preferred to be contacted with school news. The results are shown in the table. Is this a random sample? If yes, suppose there are 684 students at the school. How many can be expected to prefer E-mail?

Method	Number
E-mail	16
Newsletter	12
Announcement	5
Telephone	3

_____

MP Justify Conclusions **Each of the following surveys results in a biased sample. For each situation, explain why the survey is biased. Then explain how you would change the survey to obtain an unbiased sample.**

14. A store manager sends an E-mail survey to customers who have registered at the store's Web site.

_____

_____

_____

15. A school district surveys the family of every tenth student to determine if they would vote in favor of the construction of a new school building.

_____

_____

_____

16. Maci surveyed all the members of her softball team about their favorite sport. Based on these results, Maci concludes that softball is the favorite sport among all her classmates. Explain why Maci's conclusion might *not* be valid. How could she change the survey to achieve a more valid conclusion?

Sport	Number of Members
Softball	12
Basketball	5
Soccer	3
Volleyball	8

17. Ms. Hernandez determined that 60% of the students in her classes brought an umbrella to school when the weather forecast predicted rain. She has a total of 150 students in her classes. Determine if each statement represents a valid or invalid conclusion.

a. On days when rain is forecasted, less than $\frac{2}{5}$ of her students bring an umbrella to school.   ☐ Valid   ☐ Invalid

b. On days when rain is forecasted, about 90 of her students bring an umbrella to school.   ☐ Valid   ☐ Invalid

c. On days when rain is forecasted, more than $\frac{1}{2}$ of her students bring an umbrella to school.   ☐ Valid   ☐ Invalid

Spiral Review

For Exercises 18 and 19, use the table that shows Alana's first six math test scores.

Test	1	2	3	4	5	6
Score	88%	92%	70%	96%	84%	96%

18. Find the mean, median, and mode of Alana's test scores. Round to the nearest tenth if necessary.

mean: _____   median: _____   mode: _____

19. Determine which measure of center best represents Alana's performance. Justify your reasoning.

_____

_____

Inquiry WHY is it important to analyze multiple samples of data before making predictions?

A hostess at a restaurant randomly hands out crayons to young children. There are three different color crayons: green (G), red (R), and blue (B). The server gives out the green crayon 40% of the time, the red crayon 40% of the time, and the blue crayon 20% of the time.

Hands-On Activity 1

When you draw a conclusion about a population from a sample of data, you are making *inferences* about that population. Sometimes, making inferences about a population from only one sample is not as accurate as using multiple samples of data.

Use a spinner to simulate the situation above.

Step 1   Create a spinner with five equal sections. Label two sections G. Label another two sections R and label one section B.

Step 2   Each spin of the spinner represents a young child receiving a crayon. Spin the spinner 20 times. Record the number of times each color of crayon was received in the column labeled Sample 1 in the table below. Repeat two more times. Record the results in the columns labeled Sample 2 and Sample 3 in the table.

Color	Sample 1 Frequency	Sample 2 Frequency	Sample 3 Frequency
Green			
Red			
Blue			

Compare the results of the 3 samples. Do you notice any differences?

_____

The most commonly used keyboard is the QWERTY keyboard. However, there is another type of keyboard called the Dvorak keyboard that is based on letter frequency. Complete the Activity below about letter frequencies.

Hands-On Activity 2

The table at the right contains fifteen randomly selected words from the English language dictionary.

Sample 1		
airport	juggle	sewer
blueberry	lemon	standard
costume	mileage	thread
doorstop	percentage	vacuum
instrument	print	whale

Step 1 Find the frequency of each letter. Record the frequencies in the Sample 1 rows of the tables below.

Letter	a	b	c	d	e	f	g	h	i	j	k	l	m
Sample 1 Frequency													
Sample 2 Frequency													
Sample 3 Frequency													

Letter	n	o	p	q	r	s	t	u	v	w	x	y	z
Sample 1 Frequency													
Sample 2 Frequency													
Sample 3 Frequency													

Step 2 Randomly select another 15 words from a dictionary. Record the frequency of the letters in the rows labeled Sample 2 in the tables above.

Step 3 Repeat Step 2. Record the frequency of the letters in the rows labeled Sample 3.

Investigate

Work with a partner to collect multiple samples based on the following situation.

Janet and Masao are making centerpieces for their school's fall dance. They randomly select a ribbon to use in each centerpiece. There are four different colors of ribbon to choose from: brown (B), green (G), orange (O), and yellow (Y).

1. **MP** **Model with Mathematics** Design a method to simulate how many times each ribbon will be selected. Describe your simulation.

   > Show your work.

   _____

   _____

2. Use the method you described in Exercise 1 to simulate the ribbon selection 20 times. Record the frequency of each color selection in the Sample 1 Frequency column of the table below.

Color	Sample 1 Frequency	Sample 2 Frequency	Sample 3 Frequency
Brown			
Green			
Orange			
Yellow			

3. Repeat the process described in Exercise 2 two more times. Record the frequencies of each color selection in the Sample 2 and Sample 3 columns.

4. Make an inference to determine which color was selected the most often in each sample.

   _____

5. The *relative frequency* of a color being selected is the ratio of the number of times the color was selected to the total number of selections. Find the relative frequency of an orange ribbon being selected for each sample.

   Sample 1: _____   Sample 2: _____   Sample 3: _____

6. Masao predicts that 5 out of 10 centerpieces will have an orange ribbon. How far off is Masao's prediction? Explain.

   _____

   _____

Work with a partner to answer the following questions. Refer to Activity 2.

7. What is the relative frequency for the letter *e* for each sample? Round to the nearest hundredth.

   Sample 1: _____   Sample 2: _____   Sample 3: _____

8. What is the mean relative frequency of the letter *e* for the three samples? the median relative frequency? Round to the nearest tenth if necessary.

   mean relative frequency: _____   median relative frequency: _____

9. **MP Use Math Tools** Research on the Internet to find the actual relative frequency of the letter *e* for words in the English language. How do your sample results compare to the actual relative frequency?

   _____

   _____

10. **MP Reason Inductively** Write a few sentences describing the inferences you can make about the frequency of letters in the words in the English language using your three samples.

    _____

    _____

    _____

Create

On Your Own

11. **MP Justify Conclusions** Research on the Internet to find the relative frequency of other letters in words in the English language. Write how your sample results compare to the actual frequencies. Note any differences.

    _____

    _____

    _____

12. **Inquiry** WHY is it important to analyze multiple samples of data before making predictions?

    _____

    _____

Misleading Graphs and Statistics

Real-World Link

Hockey The Stanley Cup is awarded annually to the champion team in the National Hockey League. The graph shows the total number of points scored in Stanley Cup playoff games by three players during their careers.

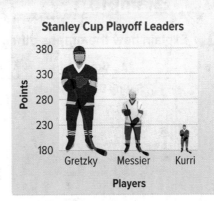

Stanley Cup Playoff Leaders

Points: 380, 330, 280, 230, 180

Players: Gretzky, Messier, Kurri

Essential Question

HOW do you know which type of graph to use when displaying data?

1. According to the size of the players, how many times more points does Messier appear to have than Kurri?

2. Do you think this is representative of the players' number of points? Explain.

3. What reason could someone have for intentionally creating a misleading Stanley Cup graph?

Which **MP** **Mathematical Process Goals** did you use? Shade the circle(s) that applies.

① Mathematical Problem Solving

② Mathematical Communication

③ Mathematical Reasoning

④ Mathematical Connections

⑤ Mathematical Representations

Identify a Misleading Graph

Graphs let readers analyze data easily, but are sometimes made to influence conclusions by misrepresenting the data.

 Example

 Tutor

1. **Explain how the graphs differ.**

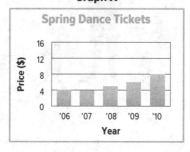

The graphs show the same data. However, the graphs differ in that Graph A uses an interval of 4, and Graph B uses an interval of 2.

Which graph appears to show a sharper increase in price?
Graph B makes it appear that the prices increased more rapidly even though the price increase is the same.

Which graph might the Student Council use to show that while ticket prices have risen, the increase is not significant? Why?
They might use Graph A. The scale used on the vertical axis of this graph makes the increase appear less significant.

Got it? **Do this problem to find out.**

a. The line graphs show monthly profits of a company from October to March. Which graph suggests that the business is extremely profitable? Is this a valid conclusion? Explain.

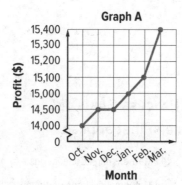

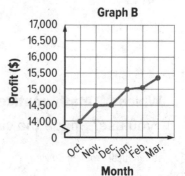

Show your work.

a. _____

Misleading Statistics

Statistics can also be used to influence conclusions.

Example

Tutor

2. An amusement park boasts that the average height of their roller coasters is 170 feet. Explain how this might be misleading.

Park Roller Coaster Heights	
Coaster	**Height (ft)**
Viper	109
Monster	135
Red Zip	115
Tornado	365
Riptide	126

Mean
$$\frac{109 + 135 + 115 + 365 + 126}{5} = \frac{850}{5}$$
$$= 170$$

Median   109, 115, 126, 135, 365

Mode   none

The average used by the park was the mean. This measure is much greater than most of the heights listed because of the coaster that is 365 feet. So, it is misleading to use this measure to attract visitors.

A more appropriate measure to describe the data is the median, 126 feet, which is closer to the height of most of the coasters.

> **Mode**
> The mode is the number or numbers that appear most often in a set of data.

Got it? Do this problem to find out.

b. Find the mean, median, and mode of the sofa prices shown in the table. Which measurement might be misleading in describing the average cost of a sofa? Explain.

Sofa Prices	
Sofa Style	**Cost**
leather	$1,700
reclining	$1,400
DIY assembly	$350
sectional	$1,600
micro-fiber	$1,400

Show your work.

b. _____

Copyright ... w-Hill Education

1. The graph suggests that Cy Young had three times as many wins as Jim Galvin. Is this a valid conclusion? Explain. (Example 1)

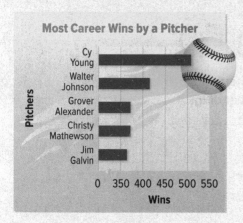

Most Career Wins by a Pitcher

_____

_____

_____

_____

_____

2. The graph at the right shows the results of a survey to determine students' favorite pets. Why is the graph misleading? (Example 1)

Favorite Pet

_____

_____

_____

3. The table lists the five largest land vehicle tunnels in the United States. Write a convincing argument for which measure of center you would use to emphasize the average length of the tunnels. (Example 2)

U.S. Vehicle Tunnels	Length (ft)
Anton Anderson Memorial	13,300
E. Johnson Memorial	8,959
Eisenhower Memorial	8,941
Allegheny	6,072
Liberty Tubes	5,920

_____

_____

_____

4. **Building on the Essential Question** Describe at least two ways in which the display of data can influence the conclusions reached.

_____

_____

_____

Rate Yourself!

How well do you understand misleading graphs and statistics? Circle the image that applies.

Clear   Somewhat   Not So
              Clear   Clear

For more help, go online to access a Personal Tutor.

Independent Practice

Go online for Step-by-Step Solutions

1 Which graph could be used to indicate a greater increase in monthly gas prices? Explain. (Example 1)

 Show your work.

_____

_____

_____

_____

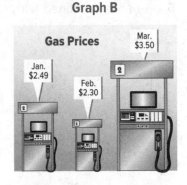

Graph A · Graph B

For Exercises 2 and 3, use the table. (Example 2)

2. Find the mean, median, and mode of the data. Which measure might be misleading in describing the average annual number of visitors who visit these sights? Explain.

_____

_____

_____

Annual Sight-Seeing Visitors	
Sight	**Visitors**
Cape Cod	4,600,000
Grand Canyon	4,500,000
Lincoln Memorial	4,000,000
Castle Clinton	4,600,000
Smoky Mountains	10,200,000

3 Which measure would be best if you wanted a value close to the most number of visitors? Explain.

_____

_____

4. MP Model with Mathematics Refer to the graphic novel frame below. Which measure of center should the students use? _____

_____

_____

For Exercises 5 and 6, create a display that would support each argument. The monthly costs to rent an apartment for the last five years are $500, $525, $560, $585, and $605.

5. Rent has remained fairly stable.

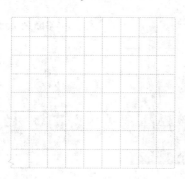

6. Rent has increased dramatically.

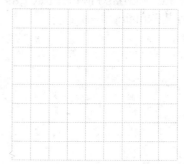

H.O.T. Problems Higher Order Thinking

7. **MP** **Reason Inductively** How could the graph you created in Exercise 5 help influence someone's decision to rent the apartment?

_____

_____

_____

8. **MP** **Persevere with Problems** Does adding values that are much greater or much less than the other values in a set of data affect the median of the set? Give an example to support your answer.

_____

_____

_____

9. **MP** **Reason Inductively** The circle graph shows the results of a survey. In what way is this graph misleading? Explain.

Favorite Time of Year

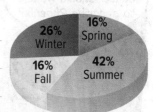

_____

_____

_____

Extra Practice

10. To determine how often his students are tardy, Mr. Kessler considered the attendance record for his first period class. Why is this graph misleading?

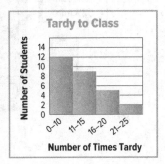

Tardy to Class

Number of Students: 14, 12, 10, 8, 6, 4, 2, 0
Number of Times Tardy: 0–10, 11–15, 16–20, 21–25

There are not equal intervals on the horizontal axis. So, the height of the bars is not representative of the sample.

11. The graph shows the height of a plant after 9 weeks of growth. Why is the graph misleading?

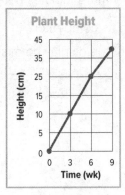

Plant Height

Height (cm): 45, 35, 25, 15, 10, 5, 0
Time (wk): 0, 3, 6, 9

_____

_____

_____

12. **MP** **Justify Conclusions** Each of the graphs below show the distance Romerio travels on his bike. Romerio wants to impress his friends with the distance he travels. Which graph should he show his friends? Explain.

Graph A

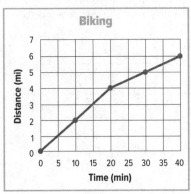

Biking

Distance (mi): 7, 6, 5, 4, 3, 2, 1, 0
Time (min): 0, 5, 10, 15, 20, 25, 30, 35, 40

Graph B

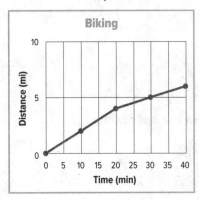

Biking

Distance (mi): 10, 5, 0
Time (min): 0, 5, 10, 15, 20, 25, 30, 35, 40

_____

_____

_____

13. The scores Emily received on her math tests were 80, 90, 85, 100, 100, and 84. Why might it be misleading for Emily to say that most of the time she receives a score of 100?

_____

_____

14. Phones For All uses the display shown at the right to compare the number of minutes that they offer per month versus their competitor.

Cell Phone Minutes

Phones for All
750 min

Phonetastic
525 min

a. How many more minutes per month does Phones For All offer than its competitor?

b. Why might the display be misleading?

15. The graph shows the average number of hours each week that certain students spend on extracurricular activities after school. Which of the following describe reasons why the graph may be misleading? Select all that apply.

☐ The graph does not show the number of hours each student spent on extracurricular activities.

☐ The intervals on the vertical scale are inconsistent.

☐ The graph's title is misleading.

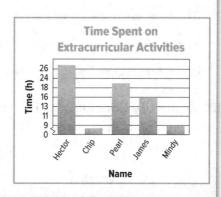

Time Spent on Extracurricular Activities

Time (h)

Name

Hector Chip Pearl James Mindy

Spiral Review

Draw a histogram to represent the set of data.

16.

Test Scores		
Percent	Tally	Frequency
50–59	|	1
60–69	||	2
70–79	||||	4
80–89	⦀⦀ |	11
90–99	⦀ |||	8

Show your work.

Case #1 Fishy Waters

Tess recently purchased a saltwater aquarium. She needs to add 1 tablespoon of sea salt for every 5 gallons of water.

Sea Salt Requirements						
Tablespoons of Sea Salt	1	2	3	4	5	6
Capacity of Tank (gallons)	5	10	15	20	25	30

How can she use a graph to show the number of tablespoons of salt required for a 50-gallon saltwater fish tank?

 Understand *What are the facts?*

You know the number of gallons of the tank. You need to show the number of tablespoons of sea salt.

 Plan *What is your strategy to solve this problem?*

Organize the rest of the data in a graph so you can easily see any trends.

 Solve *How can you apply the strategy?*

Continue the graph until you align horizontally with 50 gallons. Graph a point. What value of sea salt corresponds with the point?

 Check *Does the answer make sense?*

Find the unit rate of tablespoons of sea salt per gallon of water. Multiply the unit rate by the number of gallons to find the number of tablespoons of sea salt.

$$\frac{0.2 \text{ tbsp salt}}{1 \text{ gal water}} \times \frac{50 \text{ gal water}}{1} = \boxed{} \text{ tbsp salt} \checkmark$$

Analyze the Strategy [Tutor]

MP Make a Prediction Suppose the tank holds 32 gallons. Predict how much sea salt is required.

Case #2 Calories

The table shows the average number of Calories burned while sleeping for various numbers of hours. Assume the trend continues.

Make a graph to determine the approximate number of Calories that are burned by sleeping for 10 hours.

Calories Burned While Sleeping	
Hours	Calories
6	386
7	450
8	514
9	579

Understand

Read the problem. What are you being asked to find?

I need to find _____.

What information do you know?

There is an average of _____ Calories burned while sleeping for

6 hours and 514 Calories burned while sleeping for _____ hours.

Plan

Choose a problem-solving strategy.

I will use the _____ strategy.

Solve

Use your problem-solving strategy to solve the problem.

Continue the graph until it is aligned vertically with 10 hours. Graph a point. Find what value of Calories corresponds with the point. So, about _____ Calories are burned while sleeping for 10 hours.

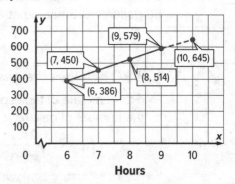

Check

Review the data in the table.

450 − 386 = 64; 514 − 450 = 64; 579 − 514 = 65. 645 − 579 = 66.

So, the answer seems reasonable.

Work with a small group to solve the following cases. Show your work on a separate piece of paper.

Collaborate

Case #3 Postage

The table shows the postage stamp rate from 1999 to 2009.

Make a graph of the data. Predict the year the postage rate will reach $0.52.

Postage Stamp Rates	
Year	Cost ($)
1999	0.33
2001	0.34
2002	0.37
2006	0.39
2007	0.41
2008	0.42
2009	0.44

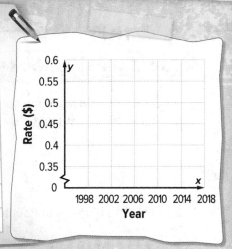

Case #4 Trains

The lengths of various train rides are 4, 1, 2, 3, 6, 2, 3, 2, 5, 8, and 4 hours.

Draw a box plot for the data set. What percent of the train rides are longer than 3 hours?

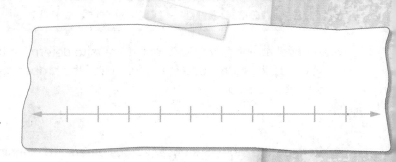

Case #5 Advertising

A local newspaper charges $14.50 for every three lines of a classified ad plus a 7% sales tax.

What is the cost of a 7-line ad? Round to the nearest hundredth.

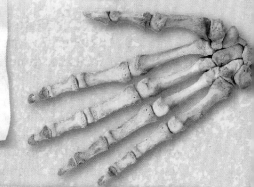

Use any strategy!

Case #6 Anatomy

Each human hand has 27 bones. There are 6 more bones in the fingers than in the wrist. There are 3 fewer bones in the palm than in the wrist.

How many bones are in each part of the hand?

Mid-Chapter Check

Vocabulary Check

1. **MP** **Be Precise** Define *sample*. Give an example of a sample of the students in a middle school.

_____

_____

2. Fill in the blank in the sentence below with the correct terms.

_____ and _____

are two types of unbiased samples.

Skills Check and Problem-Solving

3. A travel agent surveyed her customers to determine their favorite vacation locations. Use the table to find the probability of choosing a beach vacation.

Show your work.

_____

4. Refer to the table. Suppose 120 customers are planning vacations. Predict how many will plan a national park vacation.

_____

Vacation Locations	
Location	**Customers**
amusement park	2
beach	11
campground	8
national park	4

5. The number of points Emerson scored in 5 basketball games is 10, 8, 9, 8, and 30. Why might it be misleading for Emerson to say that she averages 13 points per game?

_____

_____

6. **MP** **Persevere with Problems** An online gaming site conducted a survey to determine the types of games people play online. The results are shown in the circle graph. If 1,500 people participated in the study, how many more would play card games than arcade games?

_____

Games People Play Online

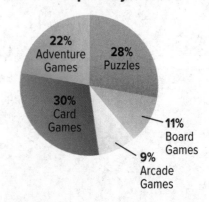

22% Adventure Games
28% Puzzles
30% Card Games
11% Board Games
9% Arcade Games

7. An owner of a restaurant wants to conduct a survey about possible menu changes. Give an example of a sampling method that would produce a valid sample.

_____

Real-World Link

Concerts Alicia researched the average price of concert tickets. The table shows the results.

Average Ticket Prices of Top 10 Money-Earning Concerts				
$83.87	$68.54	$51.53	$62.10	$59.58
$47.22	$66.58	$88.49	$50.63	$68.98

Vocabulary

histogram
frequency distribution

Virginia Standards
7.9a, b

1. Fill in the tally column and frequency column on the frequency table.

Average Ticket Prices of Top 10 Money-Earning Concerts		
Price	**Tally**	**Frequency**
$25.00–$49.99		
$50.00–$74.99		
$75.00–$99.99		

2. What does each tally mark represent? _____

3. What is one advantage of using the frequency table?

_____

_____

4. What is one advantage of using the first table?

_____

_____

Which (MP) **Mathematical Process Goals did you use? Shade the circle(s) that applies.**

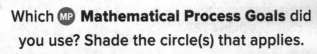

① Mathematical Problem Solving   ④ Mathematical Connections

② Mathematical Communication   ⑤ Mathematical Representations

③ Mathematical Reasoning

Interpret Data

Data from a frequency table can be displayed as a histogram. A **histogram** is a type of bar graph used to display numerical data that have been organized into equal intervals. These intervals allow you to see the **frequency distribution** of the data, or how many pieces of data are in each interval.

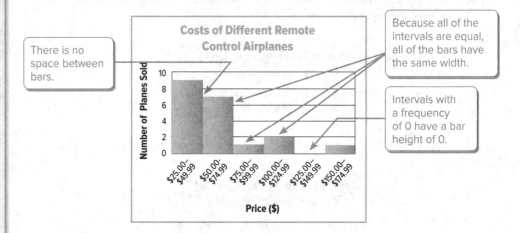

There is no space between bars.

Because all of the intervals are equal, all of the bars have the same width.

Intervals with a frequency of 0 have a bar height of 0.

Example

Tutor

1. **Refer to the histogram above. Describe the histogram. How many remote control airplanes cost at least $100?**

There are $9 + 7 + 1 + 2 + 1$ or 20 prices, in dollars, recorded. More remote control airplanes had prices between $25.00 and $49.99 than any other range. There were no airplanes recorded with a price between $125.00 and $149.99.

Two remote control airplanes had prices between $100.00–$124.99 and one remote control airplane had a price between $150.00–$174.99. So, $2 + 1$, or 3, remote control airplanes had prices that were at least $100.

Show your work.

Got it? Do this problem to find out.

a. Refer to the histogram above. How many remote control airplanes cost less than $75?

a. _____

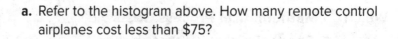

Construct a Histogram

You can use data from a table to construct a histogram.

Example

Watch ▶ Tutor 💬

2. The table shows the number of daily visitors to selected state parks. Draw a histogram to represent the data.

Daily Visitors to Selected State Parks

108	209	171	152	236
165	244	263	212	161
327	185	192	226	137
193	235	207	382	241

Step 1 Make a frequency table to organize the data. Use a scale from 100 through 399 with an interval of 50.

Daily Visitors to Selected State Parks

Visitors	Tally	Frequency
100–149	||	2
150–199	ⅡⅡ ||	7
200–249	ⅡⅡ |||	8
250–299	|	1
300–349	|	1
350–399	|	1

Scales and Intervals

It is important to choose a scale that includes all of the numbers in the data set. The interval should organize the data to make it easy to compare.

Step 2 Draw and label a horizontal and vertical axis. Include a title. Show the intervals from the frequency table on the horizontal axis. Label the vertical axis to show the frequencies.

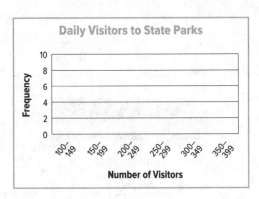

STOP and Reflect

When is a histogram more useful than a table with individual data? Explain below.

Step 3 For each interval, draw a bar whose height is given by the frequencies.

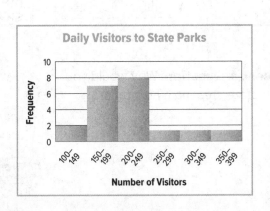

b. The table at the right shows a set of test scores. Choose intervals, make a frequency table, and construct a histogram to represent the data.

Test Scores						
72	97	80	86	92	98	88
76	79	82	91	83	90	76
81	94	96	92	72	83	85
65	91	92	68	86	89	97

Test Scores		
Score	Tally	Frequency

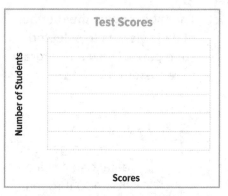

Test Scores

Number of Students

Scores

Guided Practice

1. The frequency table below shows the number of books read on vacation by the students in Mrs. Angello's class. (Examples 1 and 2)

   a. Draw a histogram to represent the data.

   b. Describe the histogram. _____

   _____

   c. How many students read six or more books? _____

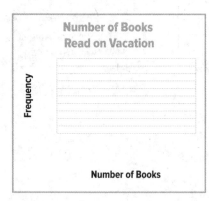

Number of Books Read on Vacation

Frequency

Number of Books

Number of Books Read		
Books	Tally	Frequency
0–2	⠅⠅|	6
3–5	⠅⠅ ⠅⠅	10
6–8	⠅⠅||	7
9–11	|||	3
12–14	||||	4

2. **Building on the Essential Question** Why would you create a frequency table before creating a histogram?

_____

_____

_____

Rate Yourself!

Are you ready to move on? Shade the section that applies.

YES   ?   NO

For more help, go online to access a Personal Tutor.

FOLDABLES Time to update your Foldable!

Independent Practice

Go online for Step-by-Step Solutions eHelp

For Exercises 1–4, use the histogram at the right. (Example 1)

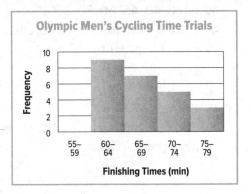

1. Describe the histogram. _____

_____

2. Which interval has 7 cyclists? _____

3 Which interval represents the greatest number of cyclists?

_____

4. How many cyclists had a time less than 70 minutes?

_____

Draw a histogram to represent the set of data. (Example 2)

5.

Number of States Visited by Students in Marty's Class		
Number of States	Tally	Frequency
0–4	ⅢⅢ ⅢⅢ	9
5–9	ⅢⅢ	3
10–14	ⅢⅢ	5
15–19	ⅢⅢ	3
20–24	ⅢⅢ Ⅰ	6
25–29	Ⅰ	1

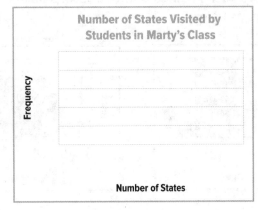

Number of States Visited by Students in Marty's Class

MP Use Math Tools For Exercises 6 and 7, refer to the histograms below.

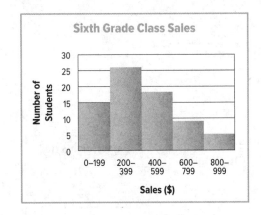

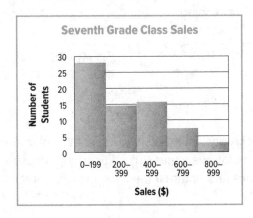

6. About how many students from both grades earned $600 or more?

_____

7 Which grade had more students earn between $400 and $599?

_____

8. **MP** **Be Precise** The following data provides the number of Calories of various types of frozen bars. {25, 35, 200, 280, 80, 80, 90, 40, 45, 50, 50, 60, 90, 100, 120, 40, 45, 60, 70, 350}

a. Draw a histogram to represent the data.

b. Find the measures of center.

_____

_____

c. Can you find the measures of center only from the histogram? Explain.

_____

_____

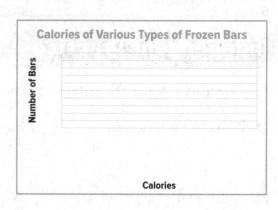

Calories of Various Types of Frozen Bars

H.O.T. Problems Higher Order Thinking

9. **MP** **Persevere with Problems** Give a set of data that could be represented by both histograms below.

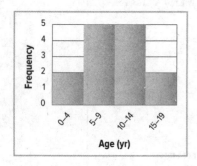

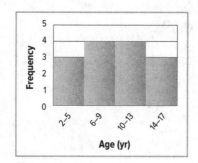

10. **MP** **Justify Conclusions** Identify the interval that is not equal to the other three. Explain your reasoning.

| 15–19 | 30–34 | 40–45 | 45–49 |

_____

11. **MP** **Reason Inductively** The table shows a set of plant heights. Describe two different sets of intervals that can be used in representing the set in a histogram. Compare and contrast the two sets of intervals.

Plant Heights (in.)		
12	7	15
8	24	41
16	18	27
43	33	11
24	10	22

_____

_____

_____

_____

Extra Practice

For Exercises 12–16, use the histogram.

12. Describe the histogram. The ages of 30 players were collected. One player is older than 35, the rest are 35 or younger.

> **Homework Help** → Add each of the frequencies to find the total players.
> 6 + 11 + 4 + 8 + 1 = 30

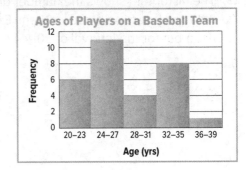

Ages of Players on a Baseball Team

13. Which interval represents the greatest number of players?

_____

14. Which interval has 4 players? _____

15. How many players are younger than 28? _____

16. How many players have ages in the interval 32–35? _____

MP Model with Mathematics Draw a histogram to represent the set of data.

17.

Number of Homeruns in a Season		
Homeruns	**Tally**	**Frequency**
0–9	ЖН ЖН II	12
10–19	ЖН ЖН	10
20–29	ЖН IIII	9
30–39	ЖН IIII	9
40–49	ЖН I	6

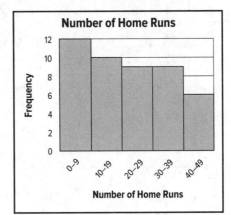

Number of Home Runs

18. **MP Find the Error** Pilar is analyzing the frequency table below. Find her mistake and correct it.

Distances from Home to School (mi)	Tally	Frequency
0.1–0.5	ЖН II	7
0.6–1.0	III	3
1.1–1.5	ЖН	5
1.6–2.0	III	3

15 people live less than 1.5 miles from school.

_____

_____

19. The histogram shows the number of goals scored by the top players on a soccer team. Explain why there is not a bar for the interval of 30–44 goals.

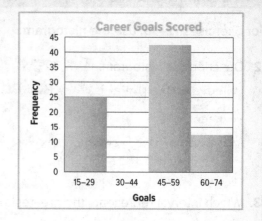

20. The table shows the number of sit-ups each member of a gym class completed in one minute. Choose an appropriate scale and intervals and construct a histogram of the data.

Number of Sit-Ups in One Minute				
30	15	34	22	28
20	25	26	31	29
27	30	19	22	28
32	31	27	23	26

Spiral Review

Divide.

21. $126 \div 3 =$ _____

22. $477 \div 9 =$ _____

23. $162 \div 6 =$ _____

24. $327 \div 5 =$ _____

25. $195 \div 2 =$ _____

26. $842 \div 4 =$ _____

27. Jamie, Tucker, and Lucinda bought a bag of apples. Jamie kept 0.25 of the apples, and Lucinda kept 0.5 of the apples. Who kept more of the apples?

_____

Select an Appropriate Display

Essential Question

HOW do you know which type of graph to use when displaying data?

 Virginia Standards
7.9c

Animals The displays show the maximum speed of six animals.

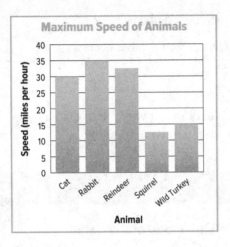

Maximum Speed of Animals

Speed (miles per hour): 40, 35, 30, 25, 20, 15, 10, 5, 0

Animal: Cat, Rabbit, Reindeer, Squirrel, Wild Turkey

Animal Speeds	
Speeds	**Number of Animals**
1–5	
6–10	
11–15	
16–20	
21–25	
26–30	
31–35	

1. Use the bar graph to fill in the "Number of Animals" column in the table.

2. Which display allows you to find a rabbit's maximum speed?

_____

3. In which display is it easier to find the number of animals with a maximum speed of 15 miles per hour or less? Explain.

_____

_____

_____

Which MP Mathematical Process Goals did you use? Shade the circle(s) that applies.

① Mathematical Problem Solving   ④ Mathematical Connections

② Mathematical Communication   ⑤ Mathematical Representations

③ Mathematical Reasoning

Statistical Displays

Type of Display	Best used to
Bar Graph	show the number of items in specific categories
Box Plot	show measures of variation for a set of data, also useful for very large sets of data
Histogram	show frequency of data divided into equal intervals
Line Graph	show change over a period of time
Line Plot	show how many times each number occurs

Data can often be displayed in several different ways. The display you choose depends on your data and what you want to show.

Example

1. **Which display allows you to tell the mode of the data?**

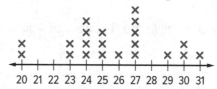

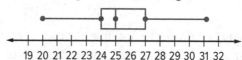

The line plot shows each night's data. The number of orders that occurs most frequently is 27. The box plot shows the spread of the data, but does not show individual data so it does not show the mode.

Got it? Do this problem to find out.

a. Which of the above displays allows you to easily find the median of the data?

a. _____

Examples

Tutor

2. A survey compared different brands of hair shampoo. The table shows the number of first-choice responses for each brand. Select an appropriate type of display to compare the number of responses. Justify your choice.

Favorite Shampoo Survey			
Brand	Responses	Brand	Responses
A	35	D	24
B	12	E	8
C	42	F	11

These data show the number of responses for each brand. A bar graph would be the best display to compare the responses.

STOP and Reflect

What type of data are best represented in a bar graph? Explain below.

3. Make the appropriate display of the data.

Step 1 Draw and label horizontal and vertical axes. Add a title.

Step 2 Draw a bar to represent the number of responses for each brand.

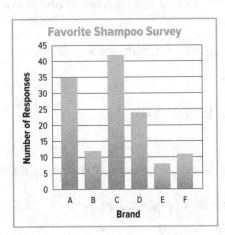

Favorite Shampoo Survey

Got it? Do these problems to find out.

Show your work.

The table shows the quiz scores of Mr. Vincent's math class.

Math Quiz Scores											
70	70	75	80	100	85	85	65	75	85	95	90
90	100	85	90	90	95	80	85	90	85	90	75

b. Select an appropriate type of display to allow you to count the number of students with a score of 85. Explain your choice.

c. Make the appropriate display of the data.

b. _____

Show your work.

1. Which display makes it easier to determine the greatest number of calendars sold? Justify your reasoning. (Example 1)

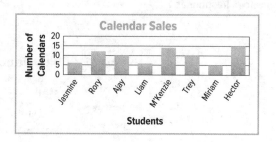 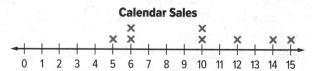

_____

Select an appropriate type of display for data gathered about each situation. Justify your reasoning. (Example 2)

2. the favorite cafeteria lunch item of the sixth-grade students _____

_____

3. the temperature from 6 A.M. to 12:00 P.M. _____

_____

4. Select and make an appropriate display for the following data. (Example 3)

Number of Push-Ups Done by Each Student											
15	20	8	11	6	25	32	12	14	16	21	25
18	35	40	20	25	15	10	5	18	20	31	28

 Show your work.

5. @ **Building on the Essential Question** Why is it important to choose the appropriate display for a set of data?

_____

Rate Yourself!

How confident are you about selecting an appropriate display? Shade the ring on the target.

I'm on target.

I need help.

For more help, go online to access a Personal Tutor.

Tutor

Independent Practice

Go online for Step-by-Step Solutions

1 Which display makes it easier to compare the maximum speeds of Top Thrill Dragster and Millennium Force? Justify your reasoning. (Example 1)

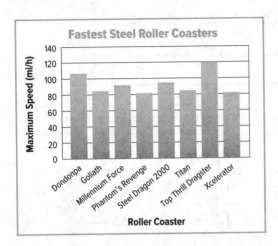

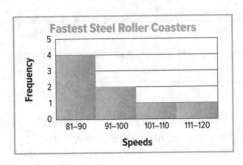

_____

Select an appropriate type of display for data gathered about each situation. Justify your reasoning. (Example 2)

2. the test scores each student had on a language arts test

_____

3. the median age of people who voted in an election

_____

MP Use Math Tools Select and make an appropriate type of display for the situation. (Example 3)

4.

South American Country	Water Area (km^2)	South American Country	Water Area (km^2)
Argentina	47,710	Guyana	18,120
Bolivia	15,280	Paraguay	9,450
Chile	12,290	Peru	5,220
Ecuador	6,720	Venezuela	30,000

5. **MP Use Math Tools** Use the Internet or another source to find a set of data that is displayed in a bar graph, line graph, frequency table, or circle graph. Was the most appropriate type of display used? What other ways might these same data be displayed? _____

6. **MP** **Be Precise** Fill in the graphic organizer below.

Display	What it shows
line plot	
histogram	
box plot	
bar graph	

7 Display the data in the bar graph using another type of display. Compare the advantages of each display.

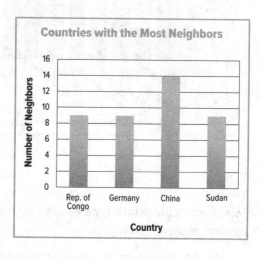

Countries with the Most Neighbors

Show your work.

H.O.T. Problems Higher Order Thinking

8. **MP** **Construct an Argument** Determine whether the following statement is *true* or *false*. If true, explain your reasoning. If false, give a counterexample.

Any set of data can be displayed using a line graph.

9. **MP** **Persevere with Problems** Which type of display allows you to easily find the mode of the data? Explain your reasoning.

10. **MP** **Reason Inductively** The table shows the number of each type of plant at a botanical garden. The director of the garden would like to add cacti so that the relative frequency of the plant is 50%. How many cactus plants should the director add?

Type of Plant	Frequency
Rose	13
Cactus	18
Palm	4
Ferns	15

Extra Practice

11. Which display makes it easier to see the median distance? Justify your reasoning.

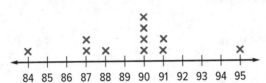

Winning Distance of Men's Olympic Javelin Throw Winners 1968–2008

Winning Distances of Olympic Javelin Throw

Homework Help

box plot; The median is easily seen on the box plot as the line in the box.

Select an appropriate type of display for data gathered about each situation. Justify your reasoning.

12. the amount of sales a company has over 6 months

_____

13. the prices of five different brands of tennis shoes at an athletic store

_____

14. the amount in a savings acount over a year

_____

15. the shape of the distribution of a team's football scores for one season

_____

MP Model with Mathematics Select and make an appropriate type of display for the situation.

Show your work.

16.

Number of Counties in Various Southern States	
67	67
95	82
33	64
63	29
46	100
75	77
95	105

17. The table shows the heights of 15 different dogs. Complete each statement with the most appropriate type of data display.

Height of Dogs (in.)				
24	26	22	22	23
24	25	24	23	23
18	26	25	22	24

a. A _____ would be most appropriate to show the data divided into equal intervals.

b. A _____ would be most appropriate to show how many times each height occurs.

c. A _____ would be most appropriate to show the distribution and spread of the data.

18. Match each situation to the type of display that would best represent it.

the favorite subject of the students in Mrs. Ling's homeroom _____

the weight a puppy gains in one year _____

the number of hits Dylan got in each game this baseball season _____

the number of each type of sandwich a deli sells during lunch _____

| bar graph |
| histogram |
| line graph |
| line plot |

Spiral Review

Divide.

19. $36 \div 12 =$ _____

20. $108 \div 12 =$ _____

21. $138 \div 23 =$ _____

22. $204 \div 17 =$ _____

23. $192 \div 12 =$ _____

24. $390 \div 15 =$ _____

25. $324 \div 36 =$ _____

26. $540 \div 36 =$ _____

27. $792 \div 12 =$ _____

28. Measure the pencil below to the nearest centimeter. Then represent your measurement in meters. _____

Inquiry HOW do you determine a measureable attribute?

Each item in a backpack has different attributes, such as color, size, and weight. Some of the attributes of the objects can be measured.

Hands-On Activity

You can choose the appropriate unit and tool to measure an object.

Step 1 Select an object in your classroom such as a desk, book, backpack, or trash can.

Step 2 List all of the measureable attributes of your object in the Step 3 table, for example length, weight or mass, time, or capacity.

Step 3 Select an appropriate tool and measure each attribute. Record each measure using appropriate units in the table below.

Object	Attribute	Tool	Measurement

Step 4 Choose a different object with at least one attribute that requires the use of a different tool to measure. Then repeat steps 1–3.

Object	Attribute	Tool	Measurement

Step 5 Write and solve a real-world problem in which one of your measurements is needed to solve the problem.

_____

_____

Investigate

Work with a partner. Choose an attribute common to several similar objects and use the appropriate unit and tool to measure.

1. Choose a set of objects and a measurable attribute.

   _____

2. Measure the attribute and record the results in a table. Then create a display of the data.

Analyze and Reflect

3. **MP Model with Mathematics** Write a few sentences describing your data. Include the number of observations, how the data was measured, and the overall pattern of the data. _____

   _____

   _____

   _____

   _____

4. **MP Make a Conjecture** Explain how the way you measured the objects influenced the shape of the display. _____

   _____

   _____

Create

5. **Inquiry** HOW do you determine a measureable attribute?

   _____

   _____

21ST CENTURY CAREER
in Market Research

Market Research Analyst

Do you think that gathering and analyzing information about people's opinions, tastes, likes, and dislikes sounds interesting? If so, then you should consider a career in market research. Market research analysts help companies understand what types of products and services consumers want. They design Internet, telephone, or mail response surveys and then analyze the data, identify trends, and present their conclusions and recommendations. Market research analysts must be analytical, creative problem-solvers, have strong backgrounds in mathematics, and have good written and verbal communication skills.

College & Career READINESS

Is This the Career for You?

Are you interested in a career as a market research analyst? Take some of the following courses in high school.

◆ Algebra
◆ Calculus
◆ Computer Science
◆ English
◆ Statistics

Find out how math relates to a career in Market Research.

ⓂP Keeping Your Eye on the Target Market!

Use the results of the survey in the table below to solve each problem.

1. At Hastings Middle School, 560 of the students use social networking sites. Predict how many of them use the sites to make plans with friends. _____

2. Suppose 17.9 million teens use online social networks. Predict how many will be using the sites to make new friends.

   _____

3. According to the survey, what percent of a teen's networking site friends are people they regularly see? _____

4. Landon randomly selects a friend from his social networking site. What is the probability that it is someone he never sees in person? Write as a percent. _____

5. Paris wants to leave a message on 8 of her friends' social networking sites. In how many ways can she leave a message on her friends' sites? _____

Survey Results: Teens and Social Networking	
Reason to Use Social Networks	**Percent of Respondents**
Stay in touch with friends	91%
Make plans with friends	72%
Make new friends	49%
Friends on Social Networking Sites	**Average Number**
People who are regularly seen	43
People who are occasionally seen	23
People who are never seen in person	33
Total	99

ⓂP Career Project

It's time to update your career portfolio! Use the Internet or another source to research a career as a market research analyst. Write a paragraph that summarizes your findings.

_____

_____

_____

_____

_____

> What skills would you need to improve to succeed in this career?
> • _____
> • _____
> • _____
> • _____
> • _____

Vocabulary Check

Complete the crossword puzzle using the vocabulary list at the beginning of the chapter.

Across

2. sample involving only those who want to participate (two words)

5. the group being studied

8. sample in which members of a population are easily accessed

9. part of a group

10. sample in which one or more parts of the population are favored over other parts

Down

1. random sample in which items are selected according to a specific time or interval

3. random sample in which each item is as likely to be chosen as any other item

4. a method of collecting information

6. a type of bar graph used to display numerical data that have been organized into equal intervals

7. sample that represents the entire population

Use Your FOLDABLES

Use your Foldable to help review the chapter.

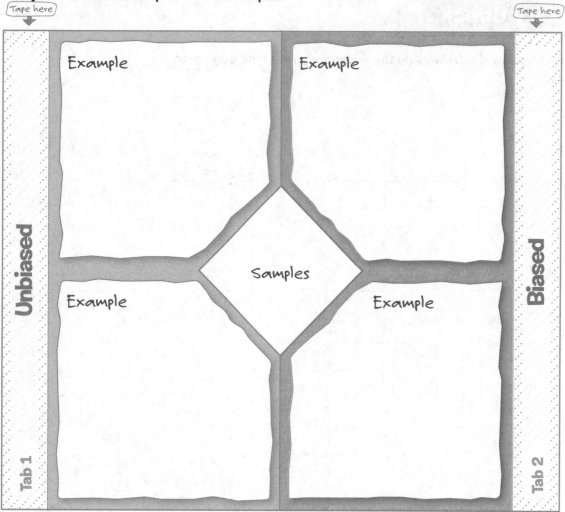

Tape here

Tape here

Unbiased

Tab 1

Biased

Tab 2

Example

Example

Example

Example

Samples

Got it?

Match each phrase with the correct term.

1. a method of collecting information

2. the group being studied

3. when one or more parts of the population is favored

4. a sample that involves only those who want to participate

a. voluntary response sample

b. biased sample

c. survey

d. population

e. convenience sample

Class Evaluation

Mr. Fuentes is analyzing his student's grades over the last three years. He has had approximately 65 students each year. To simplify his analysis, he has decided to use a random sample of data from only ten students from 2012 and 2013. He had no records of the grades from 2014, so he asked students to bring in transcripts. He used the first few transcripts he received for his 2014 data.

Student Grades									
2012	?	58	86	78	82	79	84	83	82	72
2013	83	85	85	85	87	87	88	90	91	91
2014	79	83	84	88	88	90	93	93	94	95

Write your answers on another piece of paper. Show all of your work to receive full credit.

Part A
Is the above information likely to be a legitimate representation of all the students of each respective year? Is the 2012 data biased or unbiased? Explain your answers.

Part B
In the year 2012, one of the grades is missing. If the mean was 80.1, what is the missing grade?

Part C
Considering the years 2013 and 2014, in which year were the grades the most consistent? Which of the two years had the better scores? What type of display would best show the data? Justify your responses.

Part D
Mr. Fuentes wants to submit the data from one year for a Teacher of the Year award. Choose a year. Could the data be seen as misleading? Explain.

Reflect

 Answering the Essential Question

Use what you learned about statistics to complete the graphic organizer.

Bar Graph

Line Graph

Essential Question

HOW do you know which type of graph to use when displaying data?

Double Dot Plot

Double Box Plot

Answer the Essential Question. HOW do you know which type of graph to use when displaying data?

Glossary/Glosario

The eGlossary contains words and definitions in the following 13 languages:

Arabic	Cantonese	Hmong	Spanish	Urdu
Bengali	English	Korean	Tagalog	Vietnamese
Brazilian Portuguese	Haitian Creole	Russian		

English	Español

Aa

absolute value The distance between a number and zero on a number line.

accuracy The degree of closeness of a measurement to the true value.

acute angle An angle with a measure greater than 0° and less than 90°.

acute triangle A triangle having three acute angles.

Addition Property of Equality If you add the same number to each side of an equation, the two sides remain equal.

Additive Identity Property The sum of any number and zero is the number.

additive inverse Two integers that are opposites. The sum of an integer and its additive inverse is zero.

adjacent angles Angles that share a common vertex, a common side, and do not overlap. In the figure, the adjacent angles are ∠5 and ∠6.

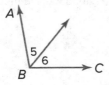

valor absoluto Distancia entre un número y cero en la recta numérica.

exactitud Cercanía de una medida a su valor verdadero.

ángulo agudo Ángulo que mide más de 0° y menos de 90°.

triángulo acutángulo Triángulo con tres ángulos agudos.

propiedad de adición de la igualdad Si sumas el mismo número a ambos lados de una ecuación, los dos lados permanecen iguales.

propiedad de identidad de la suma La suma de cualquier número y cero es el mismo número.

inverso aditivo Dos enteros opuestos.

ángulos adyacentes Ángulos que comparten un vértice, un lado común y no se traslapan. En la figura, los ángulos adyacentes son ∠5 y ∠6.

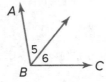

algebraic expression A combination of variables, numbers, and at least one operation.

expresión algebraica Una combinación de variables, números y por lo menos una operación.

algebra A branch of mathematics that involves expressions with variables.

álgebra Rama de las matemáticas que trata de las expresiones con variables.

alternate exterior angles Exterior angles that lie on opposite sides of the transversal. In the figure, transversal t intersects lines ℓ and m. $\angle 1$ and $\angle 7$, and $\angle 2$ and $\angle 8$ are alternate exterior angles. If line ℓ and m are parallel, then these pairs of angles are congruent.

ángulos alternos externos Ángulos externos que se encuentran en lados opuestos de la transversal. En la figura, la transversal t interseca las rectas ℓ y m. $\angle 1$ y $\angle 7$, y $\angle 2$ y $\angle 8$ son ángulos alternos externos. Si las rectas ℓ y m son paralelas, entonces estos ángulos son pares de ángulos congruentes.

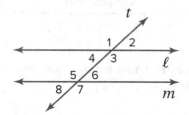

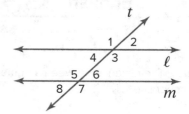

analyze To use observations to describe and compare data.

analizar Usar observaciones para describir y comparar datos.

angle of rotation The degree measure of the angle through which a figure is rotated.

ángulo de rotación Medida en grados del ángulo sobre el cual se rota una figura.

angle Two rays with a common endpoint form an angle. The rays and vertex are used to name the angle.

ángulo Dos rayos con un extremo común forman un ángulo. Los rayos y el vértice se usan para nombrar el ángulo.

$\angle ABC$, $\angle CBA$, or $\angle B$

$\angle ABC$, $\angle CBA$ o $\angle B$

arc One of two parts of a circle separated by a central angle.

arco Una de dos partes de un círculo separadas por un ángulo central.

arithmetic sequence A sequence in which the difference between any two consecutive terms is the same.

sucesión aritmética Sucesión en la cual la diferencia entre dos términos consecutivos es constante.

Associative Property The way in which three numbers are grouped when they are added or multiplied does not change their sum or product.

propiedad asociativa La forma en que se agrupan tres números al sumarlos o multiplicarlos no altera su suma o producto.

average The sum of two or more quantities divided by the number of quantities; the mean.

promedio La suma de dos o más cantidades dividida entre el número de cantidades; la media.

bar notation In repeating decimals, the line or bar placed over the digits that repeat. For example, $2.\overline{63}$ indicates that the digits 63 repeat.

notación de barra Línea o barra que se coloca sobre los dígitos que se repiten en decimales periódicos. Por ejemplo, $2.\overline{63}$ indica que los dígitos 63 se repiten.

base Any side of a parallelogram.

base Cualquier lado de un paralelogramo.

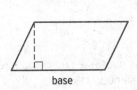
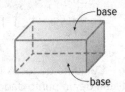

base

base

base

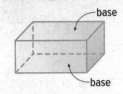
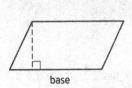

base

base

base

biased sample A sample drawn in such a way that one or more parts of the population are favored over others.

muestra sesgada Muestra en que se favorece una o más partes de una población.

bivariate data Data with two variables, or pairs of numerical observations.

datos bivariantes Datos con dos variables, o pares de observaciones numéricas.

box plot A method of visually displaying a distribution of data values by using the median, quartiles, and extremes of the data set. A box shows the middle 50% of the data.

diagrama de caja Un método de mostrar visualmente una distribución de valores usando la mediana, cuartiles y extremos del conjunto de datos. Una caja muestra el 50% del medio de los datos.

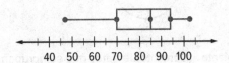

40 50 60 70 80 90 100

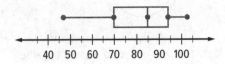

40 50 60 70 80 90 100

center of dilation The center point from which dilations are performed.

centro de la homotecia Punto fijo en torno al cual se realizan las homotecias.

center of rotation A fixed point around which shapes move in a circular motion to a new position.

centro de rotación Punto fijo alrededor del cual se giran las figuras en movimiento circular alrededor de un punto fijo.

center The point from which all points on circle are the same distance.

centro El punto desde el cual todos los puntos en una circunferencia están a la misma distancia.

central angle An angle that intersects a circle in two points and has its vertex at the center of the circle.

ángulo central Ángulo que interseca un círculo en dos puntos y cuyo vértice es el centro del círculo.

chord A segment with endpoints that are on a circle.

cuerda Segmento cuyos extremos están sobre un círculo.

circle graph A graph that shows data as parts of a whole. In a circle graph, the percents add up to 100.

Area of Oceans

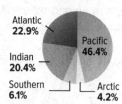

Atlantic
22.9%

Pacific
46.4%

Indian
20.4%

Southern
6.1%

Arctic
4.2%

gráfica circular Gráfica que muestra los datos como partes de un todo. En una gráfica circular los porcentajes suman 100.

Área de superficie de los océanos

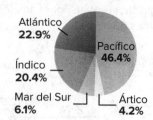

Atlántico
22.9%

Pacífico
46.4%

Índico
20.4%

Mar del Sur
6.1%

Ártico
4.2%

circle The set of all points in a plane that are the same distance from a given point called the center.

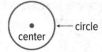

circle

center

círculo Conjunto de todos los puntos en un plano que equidistan de un punto dado llamado centro.

círculo

centro

circumference The distance around a circle.

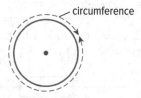

circumference

circunferencia Distancia en torno a un círculo.

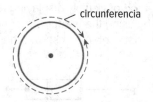

circunferencia

cluster Data that are grouped closely together.

agrupamiento Conjunto de datos que se agrupan.

coefficient The numerical factor of a term that contains a variable.

coeficiente Factor numérico de un término que contiene una variable.

common denominator A common multiple of the denominators of two or more fractions. 24 is a common denominator for $\frac{1}{3}$, $\frac{5}{8}$, and $\frac{3}{4}$ because 24 is the LCM of 3, 8, and 4.

común denominador El múltiplo común de los denominadores de dos o más fracciones. 24 es un denominador común para $\frac{1}{3}$, $\frac{5}{8}$ y $\frac{3}{4}$ porque 24 es el mcm de 3, 8 y 4.

common difference The difference between any two consecutive terms in an arithmetic sequence.

diferencia común La diferencia entre cualquier par de términos consecutivos en una sucesión aritmética.

Commutative Property The order in which numbers are added or multiplied does not change the sum or product.

propiedad commutativa La forma en que se suman o multiplican dos números no altera su suma o producto.

compatible numbers Numbers that are easy to use to perform computations mentally.

números compatibles Números que son fáciles de usar para realizar computations mentales.

complementary angles Two angles are complementary if the sum of their measures is 90°.

1
2

∠1 and ∠2 are complementary angles.

ángulos complementarios Dos ángulos son complementarios si la suma de sus medidas es 90°.

1
2

∠1 y ∠2 son complementarios.

complementary events   The events of one outcome happening and that outcome not happening. The sum of the probabilities of an event and its complement is 1 or 100%. In symbols, $P(A) + P(\text{not } A) = 1$.

complex fraction   A fraction $\frac{A}{B}$ where A or B are fractions and B does not equal zero.

composite figure   A figure made of triangles, quadrilaterals, semicircles, and other two-dimensional figures.

composite solid   An object made up of more than one type of solid.

composition of transformations   The resulting transformation when a transformation is applied to a figure and then another transformation is applied to its image.

compound event   An event consisting of two or more simple events.

compound interest   Interest paid on the initial principal and on interest earned in the past.

cone   A three-dimensional figure with one circular base connected by a curved surface to a single vertex.

congruent angles   Angles that have the same measure.

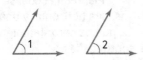

∠1 and ∠2 are congruent angles.

eventos complementarios   Los eventos de un resultado que ocurre y ese resultado que no ocurre. La suma de las probabilidades de un evento y su complemento es 1 ó 100. En símbolos $P(A) + P(\text{no } A) = 1$.

fracción compleja   Una fracción $\frac{A}{B}$ en la cual A o B son fracciones y B no es igual a cero.

figura compuesta   Figura formada por triángulos, cuadriláteros, semicírculos y otras figuras bidimensionales.

sólido complejo   Cuerpo compuesto de más de un tipo de sólido.

composición de transformaciones   Transformación que resulta cuando se aplica una transformación a una figura y luego se le aplica otra transformación a su imagen.

evento compuesto   Un evento que consiste en dos o más eventos simples.

interés compuesto   Interés que se paga por el capital inicial y sobre el interés ganado en el pasado.

cono   Una figura tridimensional con una circlular base conectada por una superficie curva para un solo vértice.

ángulos congruentes   Ángulos que tienen la misma medida.

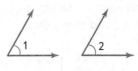

∠1 y ∠2 son congruentes.

congruent figures Figures that have the same size and same shape and corresponding sides and angles with equal measure.

figuras congruentes Figuras que tienen el mismo tamaño y la misma forma y los lados y los ángulos correspondientes tienen igual medida.

congruent segments Sides with the same length.

segmentos congruentes Lados con la misma longitud.

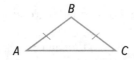

Side $\overline{AB}$ is congruent to side $\overline{BC}$.

$\overline{AB}$ es congruente a $\overline{BC}$.

congruent Having the same measure; if one image can be obtained by another by a sequence of rotations, reflections, or translations.

congruente Que tienen la misma medida; si una imagen puede obtenerse de otra por una secuencia de rotaciones, reflexiones o traslaciones.

constant of proportionality A constant ratio or unit rate of two variable quantities. It is also called the constant of variation.

constante de proporcionalidad Una razón constante o tasa por unidad de dos cantidades variables. También se llama constante de variación.

constant of variation The constant ratio in a direct variation. It is also called the constant of proportionality.

constante de variación Una razón constante o tasa por unidad de dos cantidades variables. También se llama constante de proporcionalidad.

constant rate of change The rate of change between any two points in a linear relationship is the same or *constant.*

tasa constante de cambio La tasa de cambio entre dos puntos cualesquiera en una relación lineal permanece igual o *constante.*

constant A term that does not contain a variable.

constante Término que no contiene ninguna variable.

continuous data Data that take on any real number value. It can be determined by considering what numbers are reasonable as part of the domain.

datos continuos Datos que asumen cualquier valor numérico real. Se pueden determinar al considerar qué números son razonables como parte del dominio.

convenience sample A sample which includes members of the population that are easily accessed.

muestra de conveniencia Muestra que incluye miembros de una población fácilmente accesibles.

converse The converse of a theorem is formed when the parts of the theorem are reversed. The converse of the Pythagorean Theorem can be used to test whether a triangle is a right triangle. If the sides of the triangle have lengths a, b, and c, such that $c^2 = a^2 + b^2$, then the triangle is a right triangle.

recíproco El recíproco de un teorema se forma cuando se invierten las partes del teorema. El recíproco del teorema de Pitágoras puede usarse para averiguar si un triángulo es un triángulo rectángulo. Si las longitudes de los lados de un triángulo son a, b y c, tales que $c^2 = a^2 + b^2$, entonces el triángulo es un triángulo rectángulo.

coordinate plane A plane in which a horizontal number line and a vertical number line intersect at their zero points. Also called a coordinate grid.

plano de coordenadas Plano en el cual se han trazado dos rectas numéricas, una horizontal y una vertical, que se intersecan en sus puntos cero. También conocido como sistema de coordenadas.

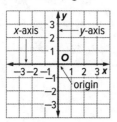

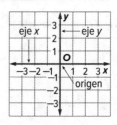

coplanar Lines or points that lie in the same plane.

corresponding angles Angles that are in the same position on two parallel lines in relation to a transversal.

corresponding parts Parts of congruent or similar figures that match.

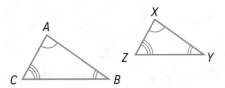

corresponding sides The sides of similar figures that are in the same relative position.

counterexample A specific case which proves a statement false.

cross product The product of the numerator of one ratio and the denominator of the other ratio. The cross products of any proportion are equal.

cross section The cross section of a solid and a plane.

cube root One of three equal factors of a number. If $a^3 = b$, then a is the cube root of b. The cube root of 64 is 4 since $4^3 = 64$.

cubed The product in which a number is a factor three times. Two cubed is 8 because $2 \times 2 \times 2 = 8$.

cubic units Used to measure volume. Tells the number of cubes of a given size it will take to fill a three-dimensional figure.

3 cubic units

cylinder A three-dimensional figure with two parallel congruent circular bases connected by a curved surface.

---

coplanar Líneas o puntos situados en el mismo plano.

ángulos correspondientes Ángulos que están en la misma posición sobre dos rectas paralelas en relación con la transversal.

partes correspondientes Partes de figuras congruentes o semejantes que coinciden.

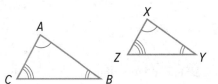

lados correspondientes Lados de figuras semejantes que estan en la misma posición.

contraejemplo Caso específico que demuestra la falsedad de un enunciado.

producto cruzado Producto del numerador de una razón por el denominador de la otra razón. Los productos cruzados de cualquier proporción son iguales.

sección transversal Intersección de un sólido con un plano.

raíz cúbica Uno de tres factores iguales de un número. Si $a^3 = b$, entonces a es la raíz cúbica de b. La raíz cúbica de 64 es 4, dado que $4^3 = 64$.

al cubo El producto de un número por sí mismo, tres veces. Dos al cubo es 8 porque $2 \times 2 \times 2 = 8$.

unidades cúbicas Se usan para medir el volumen. Indican el número de cubos de cierto tamaño que se necesitan para llenar una figura tridimensional.

3 unidades cúbicas

cilindro Una figura tridimensional con dos paralelas congruentes circulares bases conectados por una superficie curva.

Dd

data Information, often numerical, which is gathered for statistical purposes.

decagon A polygon having ten sides.

deductive reasoning A system of reasoning that uses facts, rules, definitions, or properties to reach logical conclusions.

defining a variable Choosing a variable and a quantity for the variable to represent in an expression or equation.

degree A unit used to measure temperature and angles.

dependent events Two or more events in which the outcome of one event affects the outcome of the other event(s).

dependent variable The variable in a relation with a value that depends on the value of the independent variable.

derived unit A unit that is derived from a measurement system base unit, such as length, mass, or time.

diagonal A line segment whose endpoints are vertices that are neither adjacent nor on the same face.

diameter The distance across a circle through its center.

diameter

dilation A transformation that enlarges or reduces a figure by a scale factor.

dimensional analysis The process of including units of measurement when you compute.

datos Información, con frecuencia numérica, que se recoge con fines estadísticos.

decágono Un polígono con diez lados.

razonamiento deductivo Sistema de razonamiento que emplea hechos, reglas, definiciones o propiedades para obtener conclusions lógicas.

definir una variable El eligir una variable y una cantidad que esté representada por la variable en una expresión o en una ecuacion.

grado Unidad que se usa para medir la temperatura y los àngulos.

eventos dependientes Dos o más eventos en que el resultado de un evento afecta el resultado de otro u otros eventos.

variable dependiente La variable en una relación cuyo valor depende del valor de la variable independiente.

unidad derivada Unidad derivada de una unidad básica de un sistema de medidas como por ejemplo, la longitud, la masa o el tiempo.

diagonal Segmento de recta cuyos extremos son vértices que no son ni adyacentes ni yacen en la misma cara.

diámetro Segmento que pasa por el centro de un círculo y lo divide en dos partes iguales.

diámetro

homotecia Transformación que produce la ampliación o reducción de una imagen por un factor de escala.

análisis dimensional Proceso que incluye las unidades de medida al hacer cálculos.

direct variation A relationship between two variable quantities with a constant ratio.

discount The amount by which the regular price of an item is reduced.

discrete data Data with space between possible data values. Graphs are represented by dots.

disjoint events Events that cannot happen at the same time.

Distance Formula The distance d between two points with coordinates (x_1, y_1) and (x_2, y_2) is given by the formula

$$d = \sqrt{(x_1 - x_2)^2 + (y_1 - y_2)^2}.$$

distribution A way to show the arrangement of data values.

Distributive Property To multiply a sum by a number, multiply each addend of the sum by the number outside the parentheses. For any numbers a, b, and c, $a(b + c) = ab + ac$ and $a(b - c) = ab - ac$.

Example: $2(5 + 3) = (2 \times 5) + (2 \times 3)$ and $2(5 - 3) = (2 \times 5) - (2 \times 3$

Division Property of Equality If you divide each side of an equation by the same nonzero number, the two sides remain equal.

Division Property of Inequality When you divide each side of an inequality by a negative number, the inequality symbol must be reversed for the inequality to remain true.

domain The set of input values for a function or a set of x-coordinates in a relation.

dot plot A diagram that shows the frequency of data on a number line. Also known as a line plot.

double dot plot A method of visually displaying a distribution of two sets of data values where each value is shown as a dot above a number line.

variación directa Relación entre las cantidades de dos variables que tienen una tasa constante.

descuento Cantidad que se le rebaja al precio regular de un artículo.

datos discretos Datos con espacios entre posibles valores de datos. Las gráficas están representadas por puntos.

eventos disjuntos Eventos que no pueden ocurrir al mismo tiempo.

fórmula de la distancia La distancia d entre dos puntos con coordenadas (x_1, y_1) y (x_2, y_2) viene dada por la fórmula

$$d = \sqrt{(x_1 - x_2)^2 + (y_1 - y_2)^2}.$$

distribución Una manera de mostrar la agrupación de valores.

propiedad distributiva Para multiplicar una suma por un número, multiplíquese cada sumando de la suma por el número que está fuera del paréntesis. Sean cuales fuere los números a, b, y c, $a(b + c) = ab + ac$ y $a(b - c) = ab - ac$.

Ejemplo: $2(5 + 3) = (2 \cdot 5) + (2 \cdot 3)$ y $2(5 - 3) = (2 \cdot 5) - (2 \cdot 3)$

propiedad de igualdad de la división Si divides ambos lados de una ecuación entre el mismo número no nulo, los lados permanecen iguales.

propiedad de desigualdad en la división Cuando se divide cada lado de una desigualdad entre un número negativo, el símbolo de desigualdad debe invertirse para que la desigualdad siga siendo verdadera.

dominio El conjunto de valores de entrada para una función o un conjunto de coordenadas x en una relaciòn.

doble diagrama de caja Dos diagramas de caja sobre la misma recta numérica.

doble diagrama de puntos Un método de mostrar visualmente una distribución de dos conjuntos de valores donde cada valor se muestra como un punto arriba de una recta numérica.

Ee

edge The line segment where two faces of a polyhedron intersect.	**arista** El segmento de línea donde se cruzan dos caras de un poliedro.

 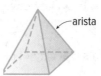

enlargement An image larger than the original.	**ampliación** Imagen más grande que la original.
equals sign A symbol of equality, =.	**signo de igualdad** Símbolo que indica igualdad, =.
equation A mathematical sentence showing two expressions are equal. An equation contains an equals sign, =.	**ecuación** Enunciado matemático que muestra que dos expresiones son iguales. Una ecuación contiene el signo de igualdad, =.
equation A mathematical sentence that contains an equals sign, =, stating that two quantities are equal.	**ecuación** Enunciado matemático que contiene el signo de igualdad = indicando que dos cantidades son iguales.
equiangular A polygon in which all angles are congruent.	**equiangular** Polígono en el cual todos los ángulos son congruentes.

equilateral triangle A triangle having three congruent sides.	**triángulo equilátero** Triángulo con tres lados congruentes.

equilateral In a polygon, all of the sides are congruent.	**equilátero** En un polígono, todos los lados son congruentes.
equivalent equations Two or more equations with the same solution.	**ecuaciones equivalentes** Dos o más ecuaciones con la misma solución.
equivalent expressions Expressions that have the same value regardless of the value(s) of the variable(s).	**expresiones equivalentes** Expresiones que poseen el mismo valor, sin importar los valores de la(s) variable(s).
equivalent ratios Ratios that express the same relationship between two quantities.	**razones equivalentes** Razones que expresan la misma relación entre dos cantidades.
evaluate To find the value of an algebraic expression by replacing variables with numbers.	**evaluar** Calcular el valor de una expresión sustituyendo las variables por número.
event An outcome is a possible result.	**evento** Un resultado posible.

experimental probability   An estimated probability based on the relative frequency of positive outcomes occurring during an experiment. It is based on what *actually* occurred during such an experiment.

exponential form   Numbers written with exponents.

exponential function   A nonlinear function in which the base is a constant and the exponent is an independent variable.

exponent   In a power, the number that tells how many times the base is used as a factor. In 5^3, the exponent is 3. That is, $5^3 = 5 \times 5 \times 5$.

exterior angles   The four outer angles formed by two lines cut by a transversal.

probabilidad experimental   Probabilidad estimada que se basa en la frecuencia relativa de los resultados positivos que ocurren durante un experimento. Se basa en lo que *en realidad* ocurre durante dicho experimento.

forma exponencial   Números escritos usando exponentes.

función exponencial   Función no lineal en la cual la base es una constante y el exponente es una variable independiente.

exponente   En una potencia, el número que indica las veces que la base se usa como factor. En 5^3, el exponente es 3. Es decir, $5^3 = 5 \times 5 \times 5$.

ángulo externo   Los cuatro ángulos exteriores que se forman cuando una transversal corta dos rectas.

Ff

face   A flat surface of a polyhedron.

face

cara   Una superficie plana de un poliedro.

cara

factor the expression   The process of writing numeric or algebraic expressions as a product of their factors.

factored form   An expression expressed as the product of its factors.

factors   Two or more numbers that are multiplied together to form a product.

factor   To write a number as a product of its factors.

fair game   A game where each player has an equally likely chance of winning.

first quartile   For a data set with median M, the first quartile is the median of the data values less than M.

five-number summary   A way of characterizing a set of data that includes the minimum, first quartile, median, third quartile, and the maximum.

formal proof   A two-column proof containing statements and reasons.

factorizar la expresión   El proceso de escribir expresiones numéricas o algebraicas como el producto de sus factores.

forma factorizada   Una expresión expresada como el producto de sus factores.

factores   Dos o más números que se multiplican entre sí para formar un producto.

factorizar   Escribir un número como el producto de sus factores.

juego justo   Juego donde cada jugador tiene igual posibilidad de ganar.

primer cuartil   Para un conjunto de datos con la mediana M, el primer cuartil es la mediana de los valores menores que M.

resumen de los cinco números   Una manera de caracterizar un conjunto de datos que incluye el mínimo, el primer cuartil, la mediana, el tercer cuartil y el máximo.

demostración formal   Demostración endos columnas contiene enunciados y razonamientos.

formula   An equation that shows the relationship among certain quantities.

fórmula   Ecuación que muestra la relación entre ciertas cantidades.

fraction   A number that represents part of a whole or part of a set. $\frac{1}{2}, \frac{1}{3}, \frac{1}{4}, \frac{3}{4}$

fracción   Número que representa parte de un todo o parte de un conjunto. $\frac{1}{2}, \frac{1}{3}, \frac{1}{4}, \frac{3}{4}$

frequency distribution   How many pieces of data are in each interval.

distribución de frecuencias   Cantidad de datos asociada con cada intervalo.

frequency table   A table that shows the number of pieces of data that fall within the given intervals.

tabla de frecuencias   Tabla que muestra el número de datos en cada intervalo.

function rule   An expression that describes the relationship between each input and output.

regla de funciones   Expresión que describe la relación entre cada valor de entrada y de salida.

function table   A table organizing the input, rule, output, domain, rule, and range of a function.

tabla de funciones   Tabla que organiza la entrada, regla, salida, dominio, regla y rango de una función.

function   A relation in which each member of the domain (input value) is paired with exactly one member of the range (output value).

función   Relación en la cual a cada elemento del dominio (valor de entrada) le corresponde exactamente un único elemento del rango (valor de salida).

Fundamental Counting Principle   Uses multiplication of the number of ways each event in an experiment can occur to find the number of possible outcomes in a sample space.

principio fundamental de contar   Método que usa la multiplicación del número de maneras en que cada evento puede ocurrir en un experimento, para calcular el número de resultados posibles en un espacio muestral.

Gg

gap   An empty space or interval in a set of data.

laguna   Espacio o intervalo vacío en un conjunto de datos.

geometric sequence   A sequence in which each term after the first is found by multiplying the previous term by a constant.

sucesión geométrica   Sucesión en la cual cada término después del primero se determina multiplicando el término anterior por una constante.

gram   A unit of mass in the metric system equivalent to 0.001 kilogram. The amount of matter an object can hold.

gramo   Unidad de masa en el sistema métrico que equivale a 0.001 de kilogramo. La cantidad de materia que puede contener un objeto.

graph   The process of placing a point on a number line or on a coordinate plane at its proper location.

graficar   Proceso de dibujar o trazar un punto en una recta numérica o en un plano de coordenadas en su ubicación correcta.

gratuity   Also known as a tip. It is a small amount of money in return for a service.

gratificación   También conocida como propina. Es una cantidad pequeña de dinero en retribución por un servicio.

Greatest Common Factor (GCF)   The greatest of the common factors of two or more numbers. The greatest common factor of 12, 18, and 30 is 6.

máximo común divisor (MCD)   El mayor de los factores comunes de dos o más números. El máximo común divisor de 12, 18 y 30 es 6.

Hh

half-plane   The part of the coordinate plane on one side of the boundary.

height   The shortest distance from the base of a parallelogram to its opposite side.

height

hemisphere   One of two congruent halves of a sphere.

heptagon   A polygon having seven sides.

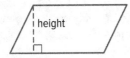

hexagon   A polygon having six sides.

histogram   A type of bar graph used to display numerical data that have been organized into equal intervals.

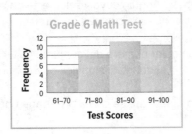

hypotenuse   The side opposite the right angle in a right triangle.

hipotenusa

---

semiplano   Parte del plano de coordenadas en un lado de la frontera.

altura   La distancia más corta desde la base de un paralelogramo hasta su lado opuesto.

altura

hemisferio   Una de dos mitades congruentes de una esfera.

heptágono   Polígono con siete lados.

hexágono   Polígono con seis lados.

histograma   Tipo de gráfica de barras que se usa para exhibir datos que se han organizado en intervalos iguales.

hipotenusa   El lado opuesto al ángulo recto de un triángulo rectángulo.

hipotenusa

Ii

Identity Properties   Properties that state that the sum of any number and 0 equals the number and that the product of any number and 1 equals the number.

propiedades de identidad   Propiedades que establecen que la suma de cualquier número y 0 es igual al número y que el producto de cualquier número y 1 es igual al número.

Identity Property of Zero The sum of an addend and zero is the addend. Example: $5 + 0 = 5$

identity An equation that is true for every value for the variable.

image The resulting figure after a transformation.

independent events Two or more events in which the outcome of one event does not affect the outcome of the other event(s).

independent variable The variable in a function with a value that is subject to choice.

Indirect measurement Finding a measurement using similar figures to find the length, width, or height of objects that are too difficult to measure directly.

inductive reasoning Reasoning that uses a number of specific examples to arrive at a plausible generalization or prediction. Conclusions arrived at by inductive reasoning lack the logical certainty of those arrived at by deductive reasoning.

inequality A mathematical sentence that uses $<$, $>$, $\neq$, $\leq$, or $\geq$, comparing two unequal quantities.

informal proof A paragraph proof.

inscribed angle An angle that has its vertex on the circle. Its sides contain chords of the circle.

integer Any number from the set {... -4, -3, -2, -1, 0, 1, 2, 3, 4 ...} where ... means *continues without end*.

interest The amount of money paid or earned for the use of money.

interior angle An angle inside a polygon or the four inside angles formed by two lines cut by a transversal.

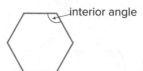
interior angle

interquartile range A measure of variation in a set of numerical data, the interquartile range is the distance between the first and third quartiles of the data set.

propiedad de identidad del cero La suma de un sumando y cero es igual al sumando. Ejemplo: $5 + 0 = 5$

identidad Ecuación que es verdad para cada valor de la variable.

imagen Figura que resulta después de una transformación.

eventos independientes Dos o más eventos en los cuales el resultado de uno de ellos no afecta el resultado de los otros eventos.

variable independiente Variable en una función cuyo valor está sujeto a elección.

medición indirectia Hallar una medicion usando figuras semejantes para calcular el largo, ancho o altura de objetos que son dificiles de medir directamente.

razonamiento inductivo Razonamiento que usa varios ejemplos especificos para lograr una generalización o una predicción plausible. Las conclusions obtenidas por razonamiento inductivo carecen de la certeza lógica de aquellas obtenidas por razonamiento deductivo.

desigualdad Enunciado matemático que utiliza $<$, $>$, $\neq$, $\leq$, o $\geq$, comparaciòn de dos cantidades desiguales.

demonstración informal Demonstración en forma de párrafo.

ángulo inscrito Ángulo cuyo vértice está en el círculo y cuyos lados contienen cuerdas del círculo.

entero Cualquier número del conjunto {... -4, -3, -2, -1, 0, 1, 2, 3, 4 ...} donde ... significa que *continúa sin fin*.

interés Cantidad que se cobra o se paga por el uso del dinero.

ángulo interno Ángulo dentro de un polígono o los cuatro àngulos interiores formados por dos lineas cortadas por una transversal.

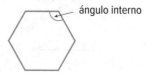
ángulo interno

rango intercuartil El rango intercuartil, una medida de la variación en un conjunto de datos numéricos, es la distancia entre el primer y el tercer cuartil del conjunto de datos.

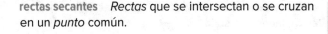

intersecting lines   *Line*s that meet or cross at a common *point*.

rectas secantes   *Rectas* que se intersectan o se cruzan en un *punto* común.

interval   The difference between successive values on a scale.

intervalo   La diferencia entre valores sucesivos de una escala.

inverse operations   Pairs of operations that undo each other. Addition and subtraction are inverse operations. Multiplication and division are inverse operations.

peraciones inversas   Pares de operaciones que se anulan mutuamente. La adición y la sustracción son operaciones inversas. La multiplicación y la división son operaciones inversas.

inverse variation   A relationship where the product of *x* and *y* is a constant *k*. As *x* increases in value, *y* decreases in value, or as *y* decreases in value, *x* increases in value.

variación inversa   Relación en la cual el producto de *x* y *y* es una constante *k*. A medida que aumenta el valor de *x*, disminuye el valor de *y* o a medida que disminuye el valor de *y*, aumenta el valor de *x*.

irrational number   A number that cannot be expressed as the quotient $\frac{a}{b}$, where a and b are integers and $b \neq 0$.

números irracionales   Número que no se puede expresar como el cociente $\frac{a}{b}$, donde a y b son enteros y $b \neq 0$.

isosceles triangle   A triangle having at least two congruent sides.

triángulo isósceles   Triángulo que tiene por lo menos dos lados congruentes.

Kk

---

kilogram   The base unit of mass in the metric system. One kilogram equals 1,000 grams.

kilogramo   Unidad básica de masa del sistema métrico. Un kilogramo equivale a 1,000 gramos.

Ll

---

lateral area   The sum of the areas of the lateral faces of a solid.

área lateral   La suma de las áreas de las caras laterales de un sólido.

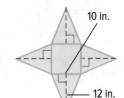

10 in.

12 in.

10 pulg

12 pulg

lateral area $= 4\left(\frac{1}{2} \times 10 \times 12\right) = 240$ square inches

área lateral $= 4\left(\frac{1}{2} \times 10 \times 12\right) = 240$ pulgadas cuadradas

lateral face   Any flat surface that is not a base.

cara lateral   Cualquier superficie plana que no es la base.

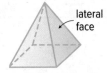

lateral face

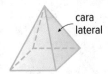

cara lateral

lateral surface area   The sum of the areas of all of the lateral faces of a solid.

área de superficie lateral   Suma de las áreas de todas las caras de un sólido.

least common denominator (LCD)   The least common multiple of the denominators of two or more fractions. You can use the LCD to compare fractions.

mínimo común denominador (mcd)   El menor de los múltiplos de los denominadores de dos o más fracciones. Puedes usar el mínimo común denominador para comparar fracciones.

least common multiple (LCM)   The smallest whole number greater than 0 that is a common multiple of each of two or more numbers. The LCM of 2 and 3 is 6.

mínimo común múltiplo (mcm)   El menor número entero, mayor que 0, múltiplo común de dos o más números. El mcm de 2 y 3 es 6.

leaves   The digits of the least place value of data in a stem-and-leaf plot.

hoja   En un diagrama de tallo y hojas, los dígitos del menor valor de posición.

legs   The two sides of a right triangle that form the right angle.

catetos   Los dos lados de un triángulo rectángulo que forman el ángulo recto.

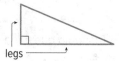

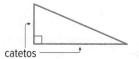

like fractions   Fractions that have the same denominators.

fracciones semejantes   Fracciones que tienen el mismo denominador.

like terms   Terms that contain the same variables raised to the same power. Example: 5*x* and 6*x* are like terms.

términos semejante   Términos que contienen las mismas variables elevadas a la misma potencia. Ejemplo: 5*x* y 6*x* son *términos semejante*.

line graph   A type of statistical graph using lines to show how values change over a period of time.

gráfica lineal   Tipo de gráfica estadística que usa segmentos de recta para mostrar cómo cambian los valores durante un período de tiempo.

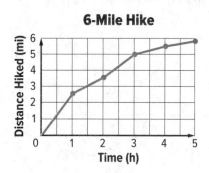

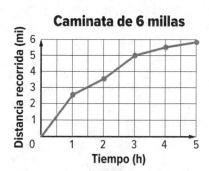

line of best fit   A line that is very close to most of the data points in a scatter plot.

recta de mejor ajuste   Recta que más se acerca a la mayoría de puntos de los datos en un diagrama de dispersión.

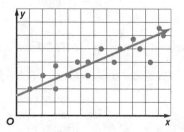

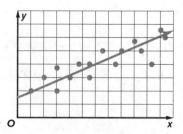

line of reflection   The line over which a figure is reflected.

line of symmetry   A line that divides a figure into two halves that are reflections of each other.

line of symmetry

line plot   A diagram that shows the frequency of data on a number line. Also known as a dot plot.

line segment   A part of a *line* that connects two points.

line symmetry   A figure has line symmetry if a line can be drawn so that one half of the figure is a mirror image of the other half.

linear equation   An equation with a graph that is a straight line.

linear expression   An algebraic expression in which the variable is raised to the first power, and variables are not multiplied nor divided.

linear function   A function in which the graph of the solution forms a straight line.

linear relationship   A relationship for which the graph is a straight line.

linear   To fall in a straight line.

line   A set of *points* that form a straight path that goes on forever in opposite directions.

literal equation   An equation or formula that has more than one variable.

liter   The base unit of capacity in the metric system. The amount of dry or liquid material an object can hold.

línea de reflexión   Línea a través de la cual se refleja una figura.

eje de simetría   Recta que divide una figura en dos mitades especulares.

eje de simetría

esquema lineal   Diagrama que muestra la frecuencia de los datos sobre una recta numérica.

segmento de recta   Parte de una *recta* que conecta dos puntos.

simetría lineal   Una figura tiene simetría lineal si se puede trazar una recta de manera que una mitad de la figura sea una imagen especular de la otra mitad.

ecuación lineal   Ecuación cuya gráfica es una recta.

expresión lineal   Expresión algebraica en la cual la variable se eleva a la primera potencia.

función lineal   Función en la que la gráfica de la solución forma una línea recta.

relación lineal   Una relación para la cual la gráfica es una línea recta.

lineal   Que cae en una línea recta.

recta   Conjunto de *puntos* que forman una trayectoria recta sin fin en direcciones oputestas.

ecuación literal   Ecuación o fórmula con más de una variable.

litro   Unidad básica de capacidad del sistema métrico. La cantidad de materia líquida o sólida que puede contener un objeto.

Mm

markdown   An amount by which the regular price of an item is reduced.

rebaja   Una cantidad por la cual el precio regular de un artículo se reduce.

markup   The amount the price of an item is increased above the price the store paid for the item.

mean absolute deviation   The average of the absolute values of differences between the mean and each value in a data set.

mean   The sum of the data divided by the number of items in the set.

measures of center   Numbers that are used to describe the center of a set of data. These measures include the mean, median, and mode.

measures of variation   A measure used to describe the distribution of data.

median   A measure of center in a set of numerical data. The median of a list of values is the value appearing at the center of a sorted version of the list—or the mean of the two central values, if the list contains an even number of values.

meter   The base unit of length in the metric system.

metric system   A decimal system of measures. The prefixes commonly used in this system are kilo-, centi-, and milli-.

mode   The number or numbers that appear most often in a set of data. If there are two or more numbers that occur most often, all of them are modes.

monomial   A number, a variable, or a product of a number and one or more variables.

Multiplication Property of Equality   If you multiply each side of an equation by the same nonzero number, the two sides remain equal.

Multiplication Property of Inequality   When you multiply each side of an inequality by a negative number, the inequality symbol must be reversed for the inequality to remain true.

Multiplicative Identity Property   The product of any number and one is the number.

margen de utilidad   Cantidad de aumento en el precio de un artículo por encima del precio que paga la tienda por dicho artículo.

desviación media absoluta   El promedio de los valores absolutos de diferencias entre el medio y cada valor de un conjunto de datos.

media   La suma de datos dividida entre el número total de artículos.

medidas del centro   Numéros que se usan para describir el centro de un conjunto de datos. Estas medidas incluyen la media, la mediana y la moda.

medidas de variación   Medida usada para describir la distribución de los datos.

mediana   Una medida del centro en un conjunto de datos numéricos. La mediana de una lista de valores es el valor que aparece en el centro de una versión ordenada de la lista, o la media de los dos valores centrales si la lista contiene un número par de valores.

metro   Unidad fundamental de longitud del sistema métrico.

sistema métrico   Sistema decimal de medidas. Los prefijos más comunes son kilo-, centi- y mili-.

moda   El número o números que aparece con más frecuencia en un conjunto de datos. Si hay dos o más números que ocurren con más frecuencia, todosellos son modas.

monomio   Un número, una variable o el producto de un número por una o más variables.

propiedad de multiplicación de la igualdad   Si multiplicas ambos lados de una ecuación por el mismo número no nulo, lo lados permanecen iguales.

propiedad de desigualdad en la multiplicación   Cuando se multiplica cada lado de una desigualdad por un número negativo, el símbolo de desigualdad debe invertirse para que la desigualdad siga siendo verdadera.

propiedad de identidad de la multiplicación   El producto de cualquier número y uno es el mismo número.

multiplicative inverses   Two numbers with a product of 1. For example, the multiplicative inverse of $\frac{2}{3}$ is $\frac{3}{2}$.

inversos multiplicativo   Dos números cuyo producto es 1. El inverso multiplicativo de $\frac{2}{3}$ es $\frac{3}{2}$.

Multiplicative Property of Zero   The product of any number and zero is zero.

propiedad del cero en la multiplicación   El producto de cualquier número y cero es cero.

Nn

negative exponent   Any nonzero number to the negative n power. It is the multiplicative inverse of its nth power.

exponente negativo   Cualquier número que no sea cero a la potencia negativa de n. Es el inverso multiplicativo de su *en*ésimo potencia.

negative integer   An integer that is less than zero. Negative integers are written with a — sign.

entero negativo   Número menor que cero. Se escriben con el signo —.

net   A two-dimensional pattern of a three-dimensional figure.

red   Patrón bidimensional de una figura tridimensional.

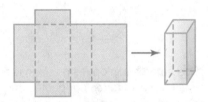

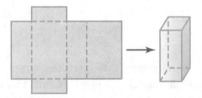

nonagon   A polygon having nine sides.

enágono   Polígono que tiene nueve lados.

nonlinear function   A function whose rate of change is not constant. The graph of a nonlinear function is not a straight line.

función no lineal   Función cuya tasa de cambio no es constante. La gráfica de una función no lineal no es una recta.

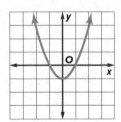

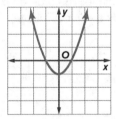

nonproportional   The relationship between two ratios with a rate or ratio that is not constant.

no proporcional   Relación entre dos razones cuya tasa o razón no es constante.

null set   The empty set.

conjunto nulo   El conjunto vacío.

numerical expression   A combination of numbers and operations.

expresión numérica   Una combinación de números y operaciones.

obtuse angle Any angle that measures greater than 90° but less than 180°.

ángulo obtuso Cualquier ángulo que mide más de 90° pero menos de 180°.

obtuse triangle A triangle having one obtuse angle.

triángulo obtusángulo Triángulo que tiene un ángulo obtuso.

octagon A polygon having eight sides.

octágono Polígono que tiene ocho lados.

opposites Two integers are opposites if they are represented on the number line by points that are the same distance from zero, but on opposite sides of zero. The sum of two opposites is zero.

opuestos Dos enteros son opuestos si, en la recta numérica, están representados por puntos que equidistan de cero, pero en direcciones opuestas. La suma de dos opuestos es cero.

order of operations The rules to follow when more than one operation is used in a numerical expression.

orden de las operaciones Reglas a seguir cuando se usa más de una operación en una expresión numérica.

ordered pair A pair of numbers used to locate a point in the coordinate plane. The ordered pair is written in this form: (*x*-coordinate, *y*-coordinate).

par ordenado Par de números que se utiliza para ubicar un punto en un plano de coordenadas. Se escribe de la siguiente forma: (coordenada *x*, coordenada *y*).

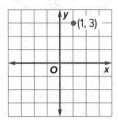

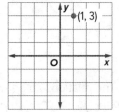

origin The point of intersection of the *x*-axis and *y*-axis in a coordinate plane. The origin as at (0,0)

origen Punto en que el eje *x* y el eje *y* se intersecan en un plano de coordenadas. El origen como en (0,0)

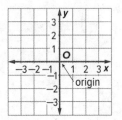

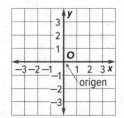

outcome Any one of the possible results of an action. For example, 4 is an outcome when a number cube is rolled.

outlier A data value that is either much *greater* or much *less* than the median.

resultado Cualquiera de los resultados posibles de una acción. Por ejemplo, 4 puede ser un resultado al lanzar un cubo numerado.

valor atípico Valor de los datos que es mucho *mayor* o mucho *menor* que la mediana.

paragraph proof A paragraph that explains why a statement or conjecture is true.

prueba por párrafo Párrafo que explica por qué es verdadero un enunciado o una conjetura.

parallel lines Lines in the same plane that never intersect or cross. The symbol ∥ means parallel.

rectas paralelas Rectas que yacen en un mismo plano y que no se intersecan. El símbolo ∥ significa paralela a.

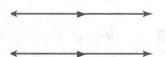

parallelogram A quadrilateral with opposite sides parallel and opposite sides congruent.

paralelogramo Cuadrilátero cuyos lados opuestos son paralelos y congruentes.

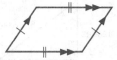

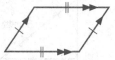

parallel Lines that never intersect no matter how far they extend.

paralelo Rectas que nunca se intersecan sea cual sea su extensión.

peak The most frequently occurring value in a line plot.

pico El valor que ocurre con más frecuencia en un diagrama de puntos.

pentagon A polygon having five sides.

pentágono Polígono que tiene cinco lados.

percent equation An equivalent form of a percent proportion in which the percent is written as a decimal. part = percent • whole

ecuación porcentual Ecuación que describe la relación entre la parte, el todo y el por ciento. parte = por ciento • todo

percent error A ratio that compares the inaccuracy of an estimate (amount of error) to the actual amount.

porcentaje de error Una razón que compara la inexactitud de una estimación (cantidad del error) con la cantidad real.

percent of change A ratio that compares the change in quantity to the original amount.

$$\text{percent of change} = \frac{\text{amount of change}}{\text{original amount}}$$

porcentaje de cambio Razón que compara el cambio en una cantidad a la cantidad original.

$$\text{procentaje de cambio} = \frac{\text{cantidad de cambio}}{\text{cantidad original}}$$

percent of decrease   A negative percent of change.

percent of increase   A positive percent of change.

percent proportion   One ratio or fraction that compares part of a quantity to the whole quantity. The other ratio is the equivalent percent written as a fraction with a denominator of 100.

$$\frac{\text{part}}{\text{whole}} = \frac{\text{percent}}{100}$$

percent   A ratio that compares a number to 100.

perfect cube   A rational number whose cube root is a whole number. 27 is a perfect cube because its cube root is 3.

perfect squares   Numbers with square roots that are whole numbers. 25 is a perfect square because the square root of 25 is 5.

perimeter   The distance around a figure.

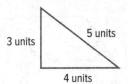

$$P = 3 + 4 + 5 = 12 \text{ units}$$

permutation   An arrangement, or listing, of objects in which order is important.

perpendicular lines   Two lines that intersect to form right angles.

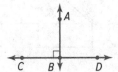

pi   The ratio of the circumference of a circle to its diameter. The Greek letter π represents this number. The value of pi is always 3.1415926... .

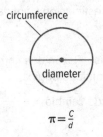

$$\pi = \frac{C}{d}$$

porcentaje de disminución   Porcentaje de cambio negativo.

porcentaje de aumento   Porcentaje de cambio positivo.

proporción porcentual   Razón o fracción que compara parte de una cantidad a toda la cantidad. La otra razón es el porcentaje equivalente escrito como fracción con 100 de denominador.

$$\frac{\text{parte}}{\text{todo}} = \frac{\text{porcentaje}}{100}$$

por ciento   Razón en que se compara un número a 100.

cubo perfecto   Número racional cuya raíz cúbica es un número entero. 27 es un cubo perfecto porque su raíz cúbica es 3.

cuadrados perfectos   Números cuya raíz cuadrada es un número entero. 25 es un cuadrado perfecto porque la raíz cuadrada de 25 es 5.

perímetro   La distancia alrededor de una figura.

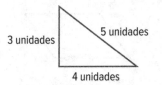

$$P = 3 + 4 + 5 = 12 \text{ unidades}$$

permutación   Arreglo o lista de objetos en la cual el orden es importante.

rectas perpendiculares   Dos rectas que se intersecan formando ángulos rectos.

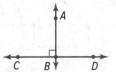

pi   Razón de la circunferencia de un círculo al diámetro del mismo. La letra griega π representa este número. El valor de pi es siempre 3.1415926... .

$$\pi = \frac{C}{d}$$

plane   A two-dimensional flat surface that extends in all directions.

point-slope form   An equation of the form $y - y_1 = m(x - x_1)$, where m is the slope and (x_1, y_1) is a given point on a nonvertical line.

point   An exact location in space that is represented by a dot.

polygon   A simple, closed figure formed by three or more line segments.

polyhedron   A three-dimensional figure with faces that are polygons.

population   The entire group of items or individuals from which the samples under consideration are taken.

positive integer   A number that is greater than zero. It can be written with or without a + sign.

powers   Numbers expressed using exponents. The power 3_2 is read *three to the second power,* or *three squared.*

precision   The ability of a measurement to be consistently reproduced.

preimage   The original figure before a transformation.

principal   The amount of money invested or borrowed.

prism   A three-dimensional figure with at least three rectangular lateral faces and top and bottom faces parallel.

plano   Superficie bidimensional que se extiende en todas direcciones.

forma punto-pendiente   Ecuación de la forma $y - y_1 = m(x - x_1)$ donde m es la pendiente y $(x_1 - y_1)$ es un punto dado de una recta no vertical.

punto   Ubicación exacta en el espacio que se representa con un marca puntual.

polígono   Figura simple y cerrada formada por tres o más segmentos de recta.

poliedro   Una figura tridimensional con caras que son polígonos.

población   El grupo total de individuos o de artículos del cual se toman las muestras bajo estudio.

entero positivo   Número que es mayor que cero y se puede escribir con o sin el signo +.

potencias   Números que se expresan usando exponentes. La potencia 3_2 se lee *tres a la segunda potencia* o *tres al cuadrado.*

precisión   Capacidad de una medida a ser reproducida consistentemente.

preimagen   Figura original antes de una transformación.

capital   Cantidad de dinero que se invierte o que se toma prestada.

prisma   Figura tridimensional que tiene por lo menos tres caras laterales rectangulares y caras paralelas superior e inferior.

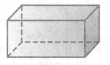

probability model A model used to assign probabilities to outcomes of a chance process by examining the nature of the process.

probability The chance that some event will happen. It is the ratio of the number of favorable outcomes to the number of possible outcomes.

proof A logical argument in which each statement that is made is supported by a statement that is accepted as true.

properties Statements that are true for any number or variable.

property A statement that is true for any numbers.

proportional The relationship between two ratios with a constant rate or ratio.

proportion An equation stating that two ratios or rates are equivalent.

pyramid A polyhedron with one base that is a polygon and three or more triangular faces that meet at a common vertex.

Pythagorean Theorem In a right triangle, the square of the length of the hypotenuse c is equal to the sum of the squares of the lengths of the legs a and b.
$$a^2 + b^2 = c^2$$

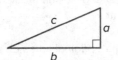

modelo de probabilidad Un modelo usado para asignar probabilidades a resultados de un proceso aleatorio examinando la naturaleza del proceso.

probabilidad La posibilidad de que suceda un evento. Es la razón del número de resultados favorables al número de resultados posibles.

prueba Argumento lógico en el cual cada enunciado hecho se respalda con un enunciado que se acepta como verdadero.

propiedades Enunciados que son verdaderos para cualquier número o variable.

propiedad Enunciado que se cumple para cualquier número.

proporcional Relación entre dos razones con una tasa o razón constante.

proporción Ecuación que indica que dos razones o tasas son equivalentes.

pirámide Un poliedro con una base que es un polígono y tres o más caras triangulares que se encuentran en un vértice común.

Teorema de Pitágoras En un triángulo rectángulo, el cuadrado de la longitud de la hipotenusa es igual a la suma de los cuadrados de las longitudes de los catetos.
$$a^2 + b^2 = c^2$$

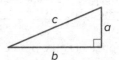

Qq

quadrants The four sections of the coordinate plane separated by the x-axis and y-axis.

cuadrantes Las cuatro secciones del plano de coordenadas separadas por el eje x y el eje y.

quadratic function   A function in which the greatest power of the variable is 2.

función cuadrática   Función en la cual la potencia mayor de la variable es 2.

quadrilateral   A closed figure having four sides and four angles.

cuadrilátero   Figura cerrada que tiene cuatro lados y cuatro ángulos.

qualitative graph   A graph used to represent situations that do not necessarily have numerical values.

gráfica cualitativa   Gráfica que se usa para representar situaciones que no tienen valores numéricos necesariamente.

quantitative data   Data that can be given a numerical value.

datos cualitativos   Datos que se pueden dar un valor numérico.

quartile   A value that divides the data set into four equal parts.

cuartil   Valor que divide el conjunto de datos en cuatro partes iguales.

radical sign   The symbol used to indicate a nonnegative square root, $\sqrt{}$

signo radical   Símbolo que se usa para indicar una raíz cuadrada no negativa, $\sqrt{}$.

radius   The distance from the center of a circle to any point on the circle.

radio   Distancia desde el centro de un círculo hasta cualquier punto del mismo.

random   Outcomes occur at random if each outcome occurs by chance. For example, rolling a number on a number cube occurs at random.

azar   Los resultados ocurren aleatoriamente si cada resultado ocurre por casualidad. Por ejemplo, sacar un número en un cubo numerado ocurre al azar.

range   The difference between the greatest number (maximum) and the least number (minimum) in a set of data The set of y coordinates in a relation.

rango   La diferencia entre el número mayor (máximo) y el número menor (mínimo) en un conjunto de datos. El conjunto de coordenadas y en una relaciòn.

rate of change   A rate that describes how one quantity changes in relation to another. A rate of change is usually expressed as a unit rate.

tasa de cambio   Tasa que describe cómo cambia una cantidad con respecto a otra. Por lo general, se expresa como tasa unitaria.

rate   A ratio comparing two quantities with different kinds of units.

tasa   Razón que compara dos cantidades que tienen diferentes tipos de unidades.

ratio table   A table with columns filled with pairs of numbers that have the same ratio.

tabla de razones   Tabla cuyas columnas contienen pares de números que tienen una misma razón.

rational numbers   The set of numbers that can be written in the form $\frac{a}{b}$, where a and b are integers and $b \neq 0$. All integers, fractions, mixed numbers, and percents are rational numbers.

números racionales   Conjunto de números que puede escribirse en la forma $\frac{a}{b}$, donde a y b son números enteros y $b \neq 0$. Todos los enteros, fracciones, nùmeros mixtos y porcentajes son nùmeros racionales.

Examples: $1 = \frac{1}{1}, \frac{2}{9}, -2.3 = -2\frac{3}{10}$

Ejemplos: $1 = \frac{1}{1}, \frac{2}{9}, -2.3 = -2\frac{3}{10}$

ratio A comparison of two quantities by division. The ratio of 2 to 3 can be stated as 2 out of 3, 2 to 3, 2 : 3, or $\frac{2}{3}$.

ray A line that has one endpoint and goes on forever in only one direction.

real numbers A set made up of rational and irrational numbers.

reciprocals The multiplicative inverse of a number. Any two numbers that have a product of 1.

Since $\frac{5}{6} \times \frac{6}{5} = 1$, $\frac{5}{6}$ and $\frac{6}{5}$ are reciprocals.

rectangle A parallelogram having four right angles.

rectangular prism A prism that has two parallel congruent bases that are rectangles.

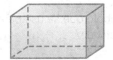

reduction An image smaller than the original.

reflection The mirror image produced by flipping a figure over a line. Also called a flip.

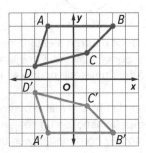

regular polygon A polygon that has all sides congruent and all angles congruent.

regular pyramid A pyramid whose base is a regular polygon and in which the segment from the vertex to the center of the base is the altitude.

relation Any set of ordered pairs.

razón Comparación de dos cantidades mediante división. La razón de 2 a 3 puede escribirse como 2 de cada 3, 2 a 3, 2 : 3, 2 : 3, or $\frac{2}{3}$.

rayo Recta con un extremo y la cual se extiende infinitamente en una sola dirección.

números reales Conjunto de números racionales e irracionales.

recíproco El inverso multiplicativo de un nùmero. Cualquier par de números cuyo producto es 1.

Como $\frac{5}{6} \times \frac{6}{5} = 1$, $\frac{5}{6}$ y $\frac{6}{5}$ son recíprocos.

rectángulo Paralelogramo con cuatro ángulos rectos.

prisma rectangular Un prisma con dos bases paralelas congruentes que son rectángulos.

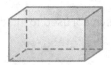

reducción Imagen más pequeña que la original.

reflexión Transformación en la cual una figura se voltea sobre una recta. También se conoce como simetría de espejo. Tambièn se llama flip.

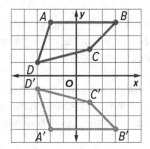

polígono regular Polígono con todos los lados y todos los ángulos congruentes.

pirámide regular Pirámide cuya base es un polígono regular y en la cual el segmento desde el vértice hasta el centro de la base es la altura.

relación Cualquier conjunto de pares ordenados.

relative frequency   The ratio of the number of experimental successes to the total number of experimental attempts.

frecuencia relativa   Razón del número de éxitos experimentales al número total de intentos experimentales.

remote interior angles   The angles of a triangle that are not adjacent to a given exterior angle.

ángulos internos no adyacentes   Ángulos de un triángulo que no son adya centes a un ángulo exterior dado.

repeating decimal   Decimal form of a rational number.

decimal periódico   Forma decimal de un número racional.

rhombus   A parallelogram having four congruent sides.

rombo   Paralelogramo que tiene cuatro lados congruentes.

right angle   An angle that measures exactly 90°.

ángulo recto   Ángulo que mide exactamente 90°.

right triangle   A triangle having one right angle.

triángulo rectángulo   Triángulo que tiene un ángulo recto.

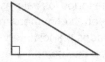

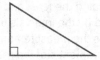

rise   The vertical change between any two points on a line.

elevación   El cambio vertical entre cualquier par de puntos en una recta.

rotational symmetry   A type of symmetry a figure has if it can be rotated less than 360° about its center and still look like the original.

simetría rotacional   Tipo de simetría que tiene una figura si se puede girar menos que 360° en torno al centro y aún sigue viéndose como la figura original.

rotation   A transformation in which a figure is turned about a fixed point.

rotación   Transformación en la cual una figura se gira alrededor de un punto fijo.

run   The horizontal change between any two points on a line.

carrera   El cambio horizontal entre cualquier par de puntos en una recta.

Ss

sales tax   An additional amount of money charged on certain goods and services.

impuesto sobre las ventas   Cantidad de dinero adicional que se cobra por ciertos artículos y servicios.

sample space   The set of all possible outcomes of a probability experiment.

espacio muestral   Conjunto de todos los resultados posibles de un experimento probabilístico.

sample   A randomly selected group chosen for the purpose of collecting data.

muestra   Grupo escogido al azar o aleatoriamente que se usa con el propósito de recoger datos.

scale drawing   A drawing that is used to represent objects that are too large or too small to be drawn at actual size.

scale factor   The ratio of the lengths of two corresponding sides of two similar polygons.

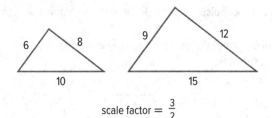

$$\text{scale factor} = \frac{3}{2}$$

scale model   A model used to represent objects that are too large or too small to be built at actual size.

scalene triangle   A triangle having no congruent sides.

scale   The set of all possible values of a given measurement, including the least and greatest numbers in the set, separated by the intervals used. Gives the ration that compares the measurements of a drawing or model to the measurement s of the real object.

scaling   To multiply or divide two related quantities by the same number.

scatter plot   A graph that shows the relationship between a data set with two variables graphed as ordered pairs on a coordinate plane.

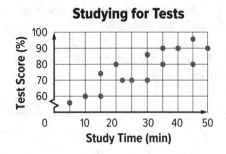

scientific notation   A compact way of writing numbers with absolute values that are very large or very small. In scientific notation, 5,500 is 5.5×10^3

selling price   The amount the customer pays for an item.

dibujo a escala   Dibujo que se usa para representar objetos que son demasiado grandes o demasiado pequeños como para dibujarlos de tamaño natural.

factor de escala   La razón de las longitudes de dos lados correspondientes de dos polígonos semejantes.

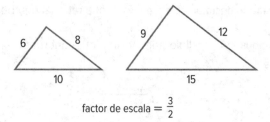

$$\text{factor de escala} = \frac{3}{2}$$

modelo a escala   Réplica de un objeto real, el cual es demasiado grande o demasiado pequeño como para construirlo de tamaño natural.

triángulo escaleno   Triángulo sin lados congruentes.

escala   Conjunto de todos los valores posibles de una medida dada, incluyendo el número menor y el mayor del conjunto, separados por los intervalos usados. Proporciona la ración que compara las mediciones de un dibujo o modelo con la medida s del objeto real.

homotecia   Multiplicar o dividir dos cantidades relacionadas entre un mismo número.

diagrama de dispersión   Gráfica que muestra la relación entre un conjunto de datos con dos variables graficadas como pares ordenados en un plano de coordenadas.

notación científica   Manera abreviada de escribir números con valores absolutos que son muy grandes o muy pequeños. En notación científica, 5,500 es 5.5×10^3.

precio de venta   Cantidad de dinero que paga un consumidor por un artículo.

semicircle Half of a circle. The formula for the area of a semicircle is $A = \frac{1}{2}\pi r^2$. The arc measuring 180°

sequence A list of numbers in a specific order, such as 0, 1, 2, 3, or 2, 4, 6, 8.

similar figures Figures that have the same shape but not necessarily the same size.

similar polygons Polygons that have the same shape.

similar solids Solids with the same shape. Their corresponding linear measures are proportional, but not necessarily the same size.

similar If one image can be obtained from another by a sequence of transformations and dilations.

simple event One outcome or a collection of outcomes.

simple interest The amount paid or earned for the use of money. The formula for simple interest is $I = prt$.

simple random sample An unbiased sample where each item or person in the population is as likely to be chosen as any other.

simplest form An algebraic expression that has no like terms and no parentheses.

simplify To perform all possible operations in an expression.

simulation An experiment that is designed to model the action in a given situation.

skew lines Lines that do not intersect and are not coplanar.

slant height The altitude or height of each lateral face of a pyramid.

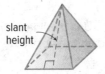

semicírculo Medio círculo La fórmula para el área de un semicírculo es $A = \frac{1}{2}\pi r^2$. El arco que mide 180°.

sucesión Lista de números en un orden específico como, por ejemplo, 0, 1, 2, 3 ó 2, 4, 6, 8.

figuras semejantes Figuras que tienen la misma forma, pero no necesariamente el mismo tamaño.

polígonos semejantes Polígonos con la misma forma.

sólidos semejantes Sólidos con la misma forma. Sus medidas lineales correspondientes son proporcionales, pero no necesariamente del mismo tamaño.

similar Si una imagen puede obtenerse de otra mediante una secuencia de transformaciones y dilataciones.

eventos simples Un resultado o una colección de resultados.

interés simple Cantidad que se paga o que se gana por el uso del dinero. La fórmula para calcular el interés simple es $I = prt$.

muestra aleatoria simple Muestra de una población que tiene la misma probabilidad de escogerse que cualquier otra.

forma reducida Expresión algebraica que carece de términos semejantes y de paréntesis.

simplificar Realizar todas las operaciones posibles en una expresión.

simulacro Un experimento diseñado para modelar la acción en una situación dada.

rectas alabeadas Rectas que no se intersecan y que no son coplanares.

altura oblicua La longitud de la altura de cada cara lateral de una pirámide.

slope-intercept form   An equation written in the form $y = mx + b$, where m is the slope and b is the y-intercept.

forma pendiente intersección   Ecuación de la forma $y = mx + b$, donde m es la pendiente y b es la intersección y.

slope   The rate of change between any two points on a line. The ratio of the rise, or vertical change, to the run, or horizontal change. The slope tells you how steep the line is.

pendiente   Razón de cambio entre cualquier par de puntos en una recta. La razón de la altura, o cambio vertical, a la carrera, o cambio horizontal. La pendiente te dice lo empinado que está la línea.

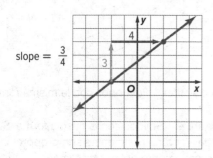

$$\text{slope} = \frac{3}{4}$$

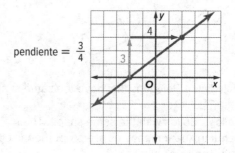

$$\text{pendiente} = \frac{3}{4}$$

solid   A three-dimensional figure formed by intersecting planes.

sólido   Figura tridimensional formada por planos que se intersecan.

solution   The value of a variable that makes an equation true. The solution of $12 = x + 7$ is 5.

solución   Valor de la variable de una ecuación que hace verdadera la ecuación. La solución de $12 = x + 7$ es 5.

solve   To replace a variable with a value that results in a true sentence.

resolver   Reemplazar una variable con un valor que resulte en un enunciado verdadero.

sphere   The set of all points in space that are a given distance from a given point called the center.

esfera   Conjunto de todos los puntos en el espacio que están a una distancia dada de un punto dado llamado centro.

square root   One of the two equal factors of a number. If $a^2 = b$, then a is the square root of b. A square root of 144 is 12 since $12^2 = 144$.

raíz cuadrada   Uno de dos factores iguales de un número. Si $a^2 = b$, la a es la raíz cuadrada de b. Una raíz cuadrada de 144 es 12 porque $12^2 = 144$.

squared   The product of a number and itself. 36 is the square of 6.

raíz cuadrada   El producto de un número por sí mismo. 36 es el cuadrado de 6.

square   A parallelogram having four right angles and four congruent sides.

cuadrado   Paralelogramo con cuatro ángulos rectos y cuatro lados congruentes.

standard deviation   A measure of variation that describes how the data deviates from the mean of the data.

desviación estándar   Una medida de variación que describe cómo los datos se desvía de la media de los datos.

standard form   An equation written, without exponents, in the form $Ax + By = C$.

forma estándar   Una ecuación, sin exponentes, escrita en la forma $Ax + By = C$.

statistical question   A question that anticipates and accounts for a variety of answers.

statistics   The study of collecting, organizing, and interpreting data.

stem-and-leaf plot   A system where data are organized from least to greatest. The digits of the least place value usually form the leaves, and the next place-value digits form the stems.

Stem	Leaf
1	2 4 5
2	1 2 3 3 9
3	0 4 6 7
4	

4 | 7 = 47

stems   The digits of the greatest place value of data in a stem-and-leaf plot.

straight angle   An angle that measures exactly 180°.

substitution   An algebraic model that can be used to find the exact solution of a system of equations.

Subtraction Property of Equality   If you subtract the same number from each side of an equation, the two sides remain equal.

Subtraction Property of Inequality   If you subtract the same number from each side of an inequality, the inequality remains true.

supplementary angles   Two angles are supplementary if the sum of their measures is 180°.

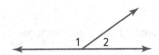

∠1 and ∠2 are supplementary angles.

surface area   The sum of the areas of all the surfaces (faces) of a three-dimensional figure.
$S.A. = 2\ell h + 2\ell w + 2hw$

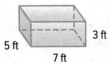

5 ft   3 ft   7 ft

$S.A. = 2(7 \times 3) + 2(7 \times 5) + 2(3 \times 5)$
$= 142$ square feet

cuestión estadística   Una pregunta que se anticipa y da cuenta de una variedad de respuestas.

estadística   Estudio que consiste en recopilar, organizar e interpretar datos.

diagrama de tallo y hojas   Sistema donde los datos se organizan de menor a mayor. Por lo general, los dígitos de los valores de posición menores forman las hojas y los valores de posición más altos forman los tallos.

Tallo	Hojas
1	2 4 5
2	1 2 3 3 9
3	0 4 6 7
4	

4 | 7 = 47

tallo   Los dígitos del mayor valor de posición de los datos en un diagrama de tallo y hojas.

ángulo llano   Ángulo que mide exactamente 180°.

sustitución   Modelo algebraico que se puede usar para calcular la solución exacta de un sistema de ecuaciones.

propiedad de sustracción de la igualdad   Si restas el mismo número de ambos lados de una ecuación, los dos lados permanecen iguales.

propiedad de desigualdad en la resta   Si se resta el mismo número a cada lado de una desigualdad, la desigualdad sigue siendo verdadera.

ángulos suplementarios   Dos ángulos son suplementarios si la suma de sus medidas es 180°.

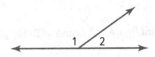

∠1 y ∠2 son ángulos suplementarios.

área de superficie   La suma de las áreas de todas las superficies (caras) de una figura tridimensional.
$S.A. = 2\ell h + 2\ell w + 2hw$

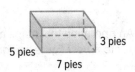

5 pies   3 pies   7 pies

$S.A. = 2(7 \times 3) + 2(7 \times 5) + 2(3 \times 5)$
$= 142$ pies cuadrados

survey A question or set of questions designed to collect data about a specific group of people, or population.

encuesta Pregunta o conjunto de preguntas diseñadas para recoger datos sobre un grupo específico de personas o población.

symmetric distribution Data that are evenly distributed.

distribución simétrica Datos que están distribuidos.

symmetric A description of the shape of a distribution in which the left side of the distribution looks like the right side.

simétrico Una descripción de la forma de una distribución en la que el lado izquierdo de la distribución se parece el lado derecho.

system of equations A set of two or more equations with the same variables.

sistema de ecuaciones Sistema de ecuaciones con las mismas variables.

systematic random sample A sample where the items or people are selected according to a specific time or item interval.

muestra aleatoria sistemática Muestra en que los elementos o personas se eligen según un intervalo de tiempo o elemento específico.

Tt

terminating decimal A decimal is called terminating if its repeating digit is 0.

decimal finito Un decimal se llama finito si el dígito que se repite es 0.

term A number, variable, or a product or quotient of numbers and variables separated by a plus or minus signs.

término Un número, una variable, o un producto o cociente de números y variables separados por un signo más o menos.

theorem A statement or conjecture that can be proven.

teorema Un enunciado o conjetura que puede probarse.

theoretical probability The ratio of the number of ways an event can occur to the number of possible outcomes. It is based on what *should* happen when conducting a probability experiment.

probabilidad teórica Razón del número de maneras en que puede ocurrir un evento al número de resultados posibles. Se basa en lo que *debería* pasar cuando se conduce un experimento probabilístico.

third quartile For a data set with median M, the third quartile is the median of the data values greater than M.

tercer cuartil Para un conjunto de datos con la mediana M, el tercer cuartil es la mediana de los valores mayores que M.

three-dimensional figure A figure with length, width, and height.

figura tridimensional Figura que tiene largo, ancho y alto.

tip Also known as a gratuity, it is a small amount of money in return for a service.

propina También conocida como gratificación; es una cantidad pequeña de dinero en recompensa por un servicio.

total surface area The sum of the areas of the surfaces of a solid.

área de superficie total La suma del área de las superficies de un sólido.

transformation An operation that maps a geometric figure, preimage, onto a new figure, image.

transformación Operación que convierte una figura geométrica, la pre-imagen, en una figura nueva, la imagen.

translation A transformation that slides a figure from one position to another without turning.

traslación Transformación en la cual una figura se desliza de una posición a otra sin hacerla girar.

transversal   The third line formed when two parallel lines are intersected.

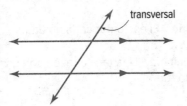
transversal

transversal   Tercera recta que se forma cuando se intersecan dos rectas paralelas.

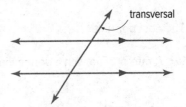
transversal

trapezoid   A quadrilateral with one pair of parallel sides.

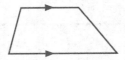

trapecio   Cuadrilátero con un único par de lados paralelos.

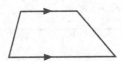

tree diagram   A diagram used to show the total number of possible outcomes in a probability experiment.

diagrama de árbol   Diagrama que se usa para mostrar el número total de resultados posibles en un experimento de probabilidad.

triangle   A figure formed by three line segments that intersect only at their endpoints.

triángulo   Figura formada por tres segmentos de recta que se intersecan sólo en sus extremos.

triangular prism   A prism that has two parallel congruent bases that are triangles.

prisma triangular   Un prisma que tiene dos bases congruentes paralelas que triángulos.

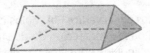

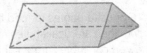

two-column proof   A formal proof that contains statements and reasons organized in two columns. Each step is called a statement, and the properties that justify each step are called reasons.

demostración de dos columnas   Demonstración formal que contiene enunciados y razones organizadas en dos columnas. Cada paso se llama enunciado y las propiedades que lo justifican son las razones.

two-step equation   An equation having two different operations.

ecuación de dos pasos   Ecuación que contiene dos operaciones distintas.

two-step inequality   An inequality than contains two operations.

desigualdad de dos pasos   Desigualdad que contiene dos operaciones.

two-way table   A table that shows data that pertain to two different categories.

tabla de doble entrada   Una tabla que muestra datos que pertenecen a dos categorías diferentes.

Uu

unbiased sample   A sample that is selected so that it is representative of the entire population.

muestra no sesgada   Muestra que se selecciona de modo que sea representativa de la población entera.

unfair game   A game where there is not a chance of each player being equally likely to win.

juego injusto   Juego donde cada jugador no tiene la misma posibilidad de ganar.

uniform probability model   A probability model which assigns equal probability to all outcomes.

modelo de probabilidad uniforme   Un modelo de probabilidad que asigna igual probabilidad a todos los resultados.

unit price   The cost per unit.

precio unitario   El costo por cada unidad.

unit rate/ratio   A rate or ratio with a denominator of 1.

tasa/razón unitaria   Una tasa o razón con un denominador de 1.

univariate data   Data with one variable.

datos univariante   Datos con una variable.

unlike fractions   Fractions with different denominators.

fracciones con distinto denominador   Fracciones cuyos denominadores son diferentes.

variable   A symbol, usually a letter, used to represent a number in mathematical expressions or sentences.

variable   Símbolo, por lo general una letra, que se usa para representar un número en expresiones o enunciados matemáticos.

vertex   A vertex of an angle is the common endpoint of the rays forming the angle.

vértice   El vértice de un ángulo es el extremo común de los rayos que lo forman.

vertical angles   Opposite angles formed by the intersection of two lines. Vertical angles are congruent. In the figure, the vertical angles are $\angle 1$ and $\angle 3$, and $\angle 2$ and $\angle 4$.

ángulos opuestos por el vértice   Ángulos congruentes que se forman de la intersección de dos rectas. En la figura, los ángulos opuestos por el vértice son $\angle 1$ y $\angle 3$, y $\angle 2$ y $\angle 4$.

visual overlap   A visual demonstration that compares the centers of two distributions with their variation, or spread.

superposición visual   Una demostración visual que compara los centros de dos distribuciones con su variación, o magnitud.

volume   The measure of the space occupied by a solid. Standard measures are cubic units such as in^3 or ft^3.

volumen   Medida del espacio que ocupa un sólido. Las medidas estándares son las unidades cúbicas, como pulg^3 o pies^3.

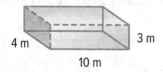

$$V = 10 \times 4 \times 3 = 120 \text{ cubic meters}$$

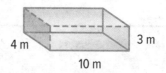

$$V = 10 \times 4 \times 3 = 120 \text{ metros cúbicos}$$

voluntary response sample   A sample which involves only those who want to participate in the sampling.

muestra de respuesta voluntaria   Muestra que involucra sólo aquellos que quieren participar en el muestreo.

Xx

x-axis   The horizontal line of the two perpendicular number lines in a coordinate plane.

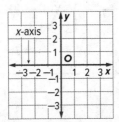

**eje *x*   La recta horizontal de las dos rectas numéricas perpendiculares en un plano de coordenadas.

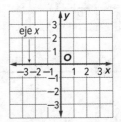

x-coordinate   The first number of an ordered pair. It corresponds to a number on the *x*-axis.

x-intercept   The *x*-coordinate of the point where the line crosses the *x*-axis.

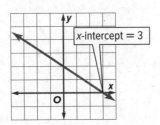

**coordenada *x*   El primer número de un par ordenado. Corresponde a un número en el eje *x*.

**intersección *x*   La coordenada *x* del punto donde cruza la gráfica el eje *x*.

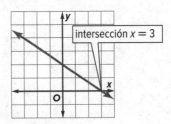

Yy

y-axis   The vertical line of the two perpendicular number lines in a coordinate plane.

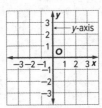

**eje *y*   La recta vertical de las dos rectas numéricas perpendiculares en un plano de coordenadas.

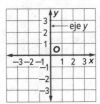

y-coordinate   The second number of an ordered pair. The *y*-coordinate corresponds to a number on the *y*-axis.

**coordenada *y*   El segundo número de un par ordenado, el cual corresponde a un número en el eje *y*.

y-intercept   The *y*-coordinate of the point where the line crosses the *y*-axis.

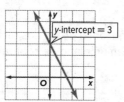

intersección y   La coordenada *y* del punto donde cruza la gráfica el eje *y*.

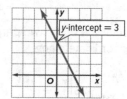

Zz

zero pair   The result when one positive counter is paired with one negative counter. The value of a zero pair is 0.

par nulo   Resultado de hacer coordinar una ficha positiva con una negativa. El valor de un par nulo es 0.

Chapter 5 Equations and Inequalities

Page 384 Chapter 5 Are You Ready?

1. $p + 3$ **3.** $g + 10$ **5.** 17 **7.** 1 **9.** 35

Pages 393–394 Lesson 5-1 Independent Practice

1. 7 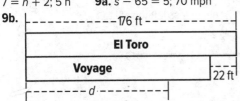17 **5.** −1

7.

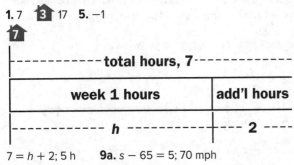

total hours, 7

week 1 hours	add'l hours
h	2

$7 = h + 2$; 5 h   **9a.** $s − 65 = 5$; 70 mph

9b.

176 ft

El Toro	
Voyage	22 ft
d	

$d + 22 = 176$; 154 ft   **9c.** The solution of each equation is 197; Colossos is 197 feet tall.   **11.** $115 + 115 + 65 + x = 360$; 65   **13.** She should have subtracted 5 from each side; −13   **15.** $x + 2 = 8$; The solution for the other equations is −6.

Pages 395–396 Lesson 5-1 Extra Practice

17. −9 **19.** −12 **21.** 7

23.

x points

Chicago Bull points	
Miami Heat points	13 points
79 points	

$x − 13 = 79$; 92 points   **25.** $−1 + (−3) + s + 2 = 0$; +2   **27.** −1.25 **29.** 12.3 **31.** 5.8 **33.** $−\frac{1}{12}$ **35a.** True **35b.** False **35c.** True **37.** −20 **39.** 60 **41.** −36 **43.** $3h = −3$; $h = −1$

Pages 403–404 Lesson 5-2 Independent Practice

1. 7 **3.** 8 **5.** 80 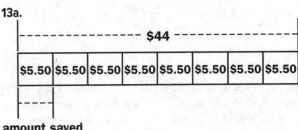−5 **9.** −90 **11** $205 = \frac{d}{3}$; 615 mi

13a.

$44

$5.50	$5.50	$5.50	$5.50	$5.50	$5.50	$5.50	$5.50

amount saved in 1 hour

13b. $5.5x = 44$ **13c.** Sample answer: Divide each side by 5.5. Then simplify. $x = 8$ **15.** True; Sample answer: Multiply each side of the equation by $\frac{1}{5}$ instead of dividing each side by 5.

17. Sample answer: Multiply both sides by x, then divide both sides of the equation by 6; −5.

Pages 405–406 Lesson 5-2 Extra Practice

19. 4 **21.** 70 **23.** −120 **25.** $50 = 25t$; 2 s **27.** 8 in. **29.** $3\frac{1}{3}$ **31.** $1\frac{1}{100}$ **33.** $\frac{13}{4}$ **35.** 4 **37.** 2.1 **39.** $\frac{21}{4}$ or $5\frac{1}{4}$

Pages 413–414 Lesson 5-3 Independent Practice

1. 5 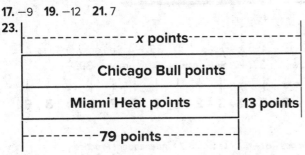3 **5.** $\frac{20}{3}$ or $6\frac{2}{3}$ **7** $\frac{3}{4}p = 46.50$; $62 **9.** Emily's homeroom class; Sample answer: Write and solve the equations $0.75e = 15$ and $\frac{2}{3}s = 12$; $e = 20$ and $s = 18$; Since 20 > 18, Emily's homeroom class has more students.   **11.** 20; Sample answer: Solve $8 = \frac{m}{4}$ to find that $m = 32$. So, replace m with 32 to find $32 − 12 = 20$.   **13.** Sample answer: Multiply each side by 2. Then divide each side by $(b_1 + b_2)$. So, $\frac{2A}{b_1 + b_2} = h$.

Pages 415–416 Lesson 5-3 Extra Practice

15. 7 **17.** −3.8 **19.** $−\frac{125}{12}$ or $−10\frac{5}{12}$

21.

$\frac{7}{15}$ of elevation, 140 ft

20	20	20	20	20	20	20	20	20	20	20	20	20	20	20

total elevation, x ft

$140 = \frac{7}{15}x$; 300 ft

23. a train that travels 100 miles in $\frac{2}{3}$ hour; a train that travels 90 miles in $\frac{3}{5}$ hour **25.** 22 **27.** 2 **29.** $3 \times $0.25 + 5 \times 0.50; $3.25

Pages 425–426   Lesson 5-4   Independent Practice

1. 3   **3** 7   **5.** −3

7.

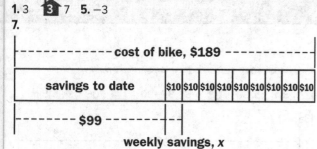

cost of bike, $189		
savings to date		$10 $10 $10 $10 $10 $10 $10 $10 $10
$99		

weekly savings, *x*

$189 = 10x + 99$; 9 weeks

9. 2.25   **11 a.** −9°C   **b.** 92.2°F   **13.** No, none of the Fahrenheit temperatures convert to the same temperature in Celsius. Only −40°F = −40°C.   **15.** Sample answer: Cameron found the area of a trapezoid to be 52 square inches. One base was 12 inches long and the other was 14 inches long. What is the height *h* of the trapezoid?; 4 in.

Pages 427–428   Lesson 5-4   Extra Practice

17. −4   **19.** 4   **21.** 36

23a.

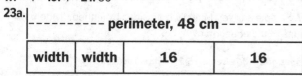

perimeter, 48 cm			
width	width	16	16

23b. $48 = 32 + 2w$; 8 cm   **23c.** Sample answer: Using either method, you would subtract first and then divide
25. $c = 30 + 0.05m$; 395 mi   **27.** $6 \cdot 10 + 6 \cdot n$ or $60 + 6n$
29. $5(x + 7)$ **31.** $10(t + 3)$

Pages 437–438   Lesson 5-5   Independent Practice

1. 6   **3** −14   **5.** −3.2   **7** $3(\ell + 5) = 60$; 15 in.
9a. $12(m − 2.57) = 0.36$ **9b.** Sample answer: I first divided each side by 12 and then added 2.57 to each side; $2.60.
11. Sample answer: Marisol should have divided by six before subtracting three; $6(x + 3) = 21$, $x + 3 = 3.5$, $x = 3.5 − 3$, $x = 0.5$ **13.** $3(x − 8) = 12$; Sample answer: Valeria bought a new collar for each of her three dogs. She paid $8 for each necklace. Suppose she had $12 left. How much money did Valeria have initially to spend on each dog collar?; $12 per collar

Pages 439–440   Lesson 5-5   Extra Practice

15. 16   **17.** −2   **19.** 78   **21.** $5\frac{3}{4}$ or 5.75

23. $1.20\left(n + 2\frac{1}{2}\right) = 4.50$; 1.25 or $1\frac{1}{4}$ pounds   **25.** Divide both sides by *p*; Add *q* to both sides.   **27.** −4   **29.** 4   **31.** −3
33. 2   **35.** −3, −2, −1, 0

Page 443   Problem-Solving Investigation   Work Backward

Case 3. 1,250 ft   **Case 5.** 6:25 A.M.

Pages 453–454   Lesson 5-6   Independent Practice

1. $h \le −8$ **3** $5 < n$ **5.** $x > −1$
7. $m \ge −6$;

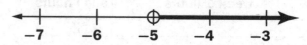

9 $n + 4 > 13$; $n > 9$ **11.** $p + 17 \le 26$; $p \le 9$; Nine additional players or fewer can make the team.
13a. $42 + x \ge 74$; $x \ge 32$ **13b.** $74 + y \ge 110$; $y \ge 36$
15. Sample answer: $x + 3 < 25$ **17.** no; Sample answer: The solution is $x \ge −1$, so the graph should have a closed dot above −1 and the arrow should point to the right, not the left.

Pages 455–456   Lesson 5-6   Extra Practice

19. $m \le 4.3$
21. $−5 < a$

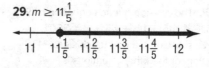

23. $n − 8 < 10$; $n < 18$ **25.** $68 + c \le 125$; $c \le 57$; The salesman has 57 cars or less left to sell.
27. $2\frac{2}{3} > x$ or $x < 2\frac{2}{3}$

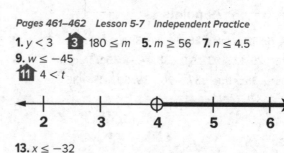

29. $m \ge 11\frac{1}{5}$

31. $n \ge −4\frac{3}{16}$

33. $x + 4 \le 7$; $−7 \ge x − 10$ **35.** −4; See answer 39 for graph.   **37.** −2; See answer 39 for graph.   **39.** −6;

Pages 461–462   Lesson 5-7   Independent Practice

1. $y < 3$ **3** $180 \le m$ **5.** $m \ge 56$ **7.** $n \le 4.5$
9. $w \le −45$
11 $4 < t$

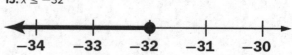

13. $x \le −32$

15. Sample answer: $y > 4.5$　**17.** $n < 12$　**19.** at least a 15

21a.

21b. yes; It represents the solutions that satisfy both inequalities.　**21c.** $4 \le b \le 13$

21d.

Pages 463–464　Lesson 5-7　Extra Practice

23. $y > -5$　**25.** $p \ge -6$　**27.** $-40 < y$ or $y > -40$
29. $w > 13$

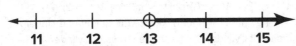

31. $-20 \ge t$ or $t \le -20$

33. $4n \ge -12$; $n \ge -3$　**35a.** False　**35b.** True　**35c.** False
37. 2　**39.** -2.5　**41.** 12

Pages 469–470　Lesson 5-8　Independent Practice

1 Yes; the rate of change between cost and time for each hour is a constant 3¢ per hour.　**3.** Yes; the rate of change between vinegar and oil for each cup of oil is a constant $\frac{3}{8}$ cup vinegar per cup of oil.　**5** Yes; the rate of change between the actual distance and the map distance for each inch on the map is a constant 7.5 mi/in.　**7.** Yes; the ratio of the cost to time is a constant 3¢ per hour, so the relationship is proportional.　**9.** Yes; the ratio of actual distance to map distance is a constant $\frac{15}{2}$ miles per inch, so the relationship is proportional.

11. Sample answer:

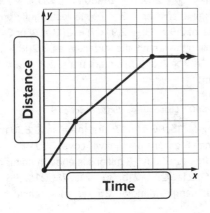

13a. no; Sample answer: $\frac{3.50}{1} \neq \frac{4.00}{2}$
13b. yes; Sample answer: $\frac{2.50}{1} = \frac{5.00}{2} = \frac{7.50}{3} = \frac{10.00}{4}$

Pages 471–472　Lesson 5-8　Extra Practice

15. No; the rate of change from 1 to 2 hours, $\frac{24-12}{2-1}$ or 12 per hour, is not the same as the rate of change from 3 to 4 hours, $\frac{60-36}{4-3}$ or 24 per hour, so the rate of change is not constant.
17. -50 mph; the distance decreased by 50 miles every hour.
19. 0.5; $\frac{1}{2}$ of retail price.　**21a.** False　**21b.** True　**21c.** True
23. 750 kB/min　**25.** 6.6 m/s

Pages 479–480　Lesson 5-9　Independent Practice

1 $-\frac{5}{8}$　**3.** $-\frac{3}{4}$　**5.** 2　**7** -4　**9.** yes; $\frac{1}{15} < \frac{1}{12}$
11. Jacob did not use the x-coordinates in the same order as the y-coordinates.
$$m = \frac{3-2}{4-0}$$
$$m = \frac{1}{4}$$
13a. Sample answer: (1, 1), (2, 6), (3, 11)　**13b.** Sample answer: (1, 1), (6, 2), (11, 3)　**13c.** Sample answer: (1, 1), (0, 6), (−1, 11)

Pages 481–482　Lesson 5-9　Extra Practice

15. 3　**17.** -3　**19.** 2　**21.** $\frac{1}{5}$　**23.** (0, 4); (4, 1); $-\frac{3}{4}$
25. $\frac{30}{180} = \frac{x}{240}$; 40 minutes　**27.** 15　**29.** 7.5　**31.** -60

Pages 487–488　Lesson 5-10　Independent Practice

1. 3; 4　**3.** -3; -4　**5** $y = \frac{5}{6}x + 8$　**7.** $y = \frac{5}{4}x - 12$

9.

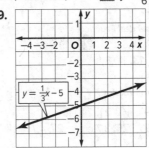

11

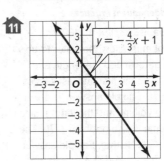

13. 0; Sample answer: A line that has a y-intercept but no x-intercept is a horizontal line. **15.** Quadrants I, II, and IV; if a y-intercept is graphed at (0, b), where b is positive, and then a line is drawn through the point so that it has a negative slope, the line will pass through Quadrants I, II, and IV.

Pages 489–490   Lesson 5-10   Extra Practice

17. −5; 2   **19.** 2; 8   **21.** $y = -2x + 3$
23.

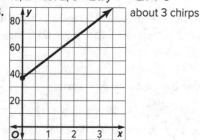 about 3 chirps

25. $y = 8x + 5$ **27.** 8; 20; y-intercept; slope   **29.** −2
31. yes; $\frac{4}{1}$ or 4

Page 496   Chapter Review   Key Concept Check

1. solution   **3.** equivalent equations

Chapter 6 Measure Figures

Page 502   Chapter 6   Are You Ready?

1. 42 sq m   **3.** 76.5 sq mm

Pages 507–508   Lesson 6-1   Independent Practice

1. 64 cm^2 **3.** 220.5 cm^2 **5** 38.6 ft^2 **7** 119.5 ft^2
9. 77 cm^2 **11.** 44.6 ft^2; 30.3 ft   **13.** 110.8 ft^2

Pages 509–510   Lesson 6-1   Extra Practice

15. 87.5 m^2 **17.** 180 cm^2 **19.** 9 cm^2 **21.** 240 ft^2
23a. 36   **23b.** 14.14   **23c.** 92.56   **25.** 3.7 cm^2 **27.** 4.7 m

Pages 515–516   Lesson 6-2   Independent Practice

1 192 m^3 **3** 108 m^3 **5a.** 96 ft^3; 128 ft^3; 168 ft^3;
160 ft^3; 120 ft^3 **5b.** The height must allow the water to be deep enough for someone to get wet and the length and width must allow a person to fit. So the first and last sets of dimensions would not work.   **7a.** Sample answer: There is a direct relationship between the volume and the length. Since the length is doubled, the volume is also doubled.   **7b.** The volume is eight times greater.   **7c.** Neither; Sample answer: doubling the height will result in a volume of 4 · 4 · 10 or 160 in^3; doubling the width will result in a volume of 4 · 8 · 5 or 160 in^3.

Pages 517–518   Lesson 6-2   Extra Practice

11. 236.3 cm^3 **13.** 20.4 mm^3 **15.** 306.52 = 19.4h; 15.8 m
17. $166\frac{1}{4}$ yd^3 **19.** 2 in. by 1.5 in. by 0.5 in.; 3 in. by 1 in. by 0.5 in.   **21.** 25.8 m   **23.** 29.2 cm

Pages 525–526   Lesson 6-3   Independent Practice

1 141.4 in^3 **3** 831.9 lb   **5a.** bag: 132 in^3; candle: 29.5 in^3 **5b.** 102.5 in^3 **5c.** 13 packages   **7.** Sample answer: The shorter cylinder, because the radius is larger and that is the squared value in the formula.   **9a.** 2:1   **9b.** 4:1

Pages 527–528   Lesson 6-3   Extra Practice

11 2,770.9 yd^3 **13.** 81.7 ounces   **15.** 8 in.
17a. $V = \pi(1)^2(1)$; $V = \pi(1)^2(2)$; $V = \pi(2)^2(1)$; $V = \pi(2)^2(2)$
17b. The height of Cylinder B is twice the height of Cylinder A. The radius of Cylinder C is twice the radius of Cylinder A. The radius and height of Cylinder D are twice the radius and height of Cylinder A.
17c.

	Radius (cm)	Height (cm)	Volume (cm^3)
Cylinder A	1	1	3.14 cm^3
Cylinder B	1	2	6.28 cm^3
Cylinder C	2	1	12.57 cm^3
Cylinder D	2	2	25.13 cm^3

17d. When the radius is doubled, the volume is four times the original volume. When the height is doubled, the volume is twice the original volume. When the radius and height are doubled, the volume is eight times the original volume.
19. The volume of the container is exactly 20.25π cubic inches; The volume of the container to the nearest tenth is about 63.6 cubic inches.   **21.** 201.1 cm^2 **23.** 28.3 in^2
25. 50.3 m^2.

Pages 537–538   Lesson 6-4   Independent Practice

1 314 cm^2 **3** 207 in^2 **5.** 180 in^2 **7.** S.A. = $6x^2$
9. False; Sample answer: A 9 × 7 × 13 rectangular prism has a surface area of 2(9 × 13) + 2(9 × 7) + 2(13 × 7) or 542 square units. Doubling the length, the surface area is 2(18 × 13) + 2(18 × 7) + 2(13 × 7) or 902 square units. 2 × 542 ≠ 902
11. 1,926 cm^2

Pages 539–540   Lesson 6-4   Extra Practice

13. 833.1 mm^2 **15.** 96 ft^2 **17.** Yes; there are 2,520 ft^2 of fencing. Since 8 gallons of paint will cover 350 · 8 or 2,800 ft^2 and 2,800 ft^2 > 2,520 ft^2, 8 gallons is enough paint.
19. 64.5 in^2 **21a.** 12.5   **21b.** 50   **21c.** 71   **21d.** 196
23. triangle; triangle; triangle   **25.** rectangle; circle; oval

Pages 547–548   Lesson 6-5   Independent Practice

1 88.0 mm^2 **3.** 272.0 mm^2 **5.** 113.1 in^2 **7.** 1,068.1 yd^2
9 241.3 in^2 **11.** No, the surface area of the side of the cylinder will double, but the area of the bases will not.
13. $A = 2\pi rh + \pi r^2$; Sample answer: The baker will not ice the bottom of the cake, so you only need to include the area of one of the bases in the equation.

Pages 549–550   Lesson 6-5   Extra Practice

15 1,105.8 cm^2; 1,508.0 cm^2 **17.** 763.4 in^2
19. Sample answer: $2 \cdot 3 \cdot 4^2 + 2 \cdot 3 \cdot 4 \cdot 4$ or 192 m^2
21. about 85.7%   **23a.** 562   **23b.** 653   **23c.** II; 91; I
25. 23.08 ft^2

Page 553   Problem-Solving Investigation   Solve a Simpler Problem

Case 3. 80 chairs   **Case 5.** 7,763,270.6 mi^2; Sample answer: The area of Asia is about 17,251,712.4 mi^2 and the area of North America is about 9,488,441.8 mi^2. 17,251,712.4 − 9,488,441.8 = 7,763,270.6

Pages 563–564   Lesson 6-6   Independent Practice

1 2.3 m^3 **3.** 2,600 ft^2 **5** 0.5 ft^3 **7.** 10.4 m^2
9. 100 in^3 **13.** less than; Sample answer: The combined surface area of the two prisms is 180 in^2. Since they share a common surface, the area of that surface is not included in the total surface area.

Pages 565–566   Lesson 6-6   Extra Practice

15. 100 in^3 **17.** 280.2 cm^2 **19a.** 1.68 ft^3 **19b.** 19.28 ft^2
21.

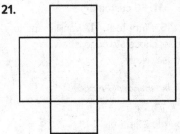

23.

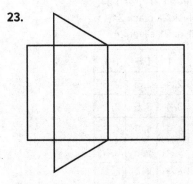

Pages 575–576   Lesson 6-7   Independent Practice

1 yes; Sample answer: A rotation, a translation of 4 units down, and a dilation with a scale factor of $\frac{3}{2}$ maps $\triangle XYW$ onto $\triangle VUW$.   **3** 6.75 in. by 11.25 in.; yes   **5.** Sample answer: translation of 1 unit to the right and 1 unit down followed by a dilation with a scale factor of 4   **7.** Product of dilation(s) should equal 1.   **9.** false; Sample answer: If you perform the dilation after a translation, the translation is multiplied by the same scale factor.

Pages 577–578   Lesson 6-7   Extra Practice

11. no; The ratios of the side lengths are not equal.   **13.** 7.5 ft by 6 ft; yes   **15a.** False   **15b.** True   **15c.** False

17.

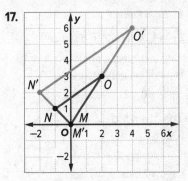

$M'(0, 0)$, $N'(-2, 2)$, $O'(4, 6)$

19.

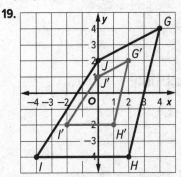

$G'(2, 2)$, $H'(1, -2)$, $I'(-1, -2)$, $J'(0, 1)$

Pages 583–584   Lesson 6-8   Independent Practice

1 No; The corresponding angles are congruent, but $\frac{3}{7} \neq \frac{4}{8}$.   **3** translation and dilation; 4.5   **5a.** Figure 1: 96 cm^2; Figure 2: 294 cm^2 **5b.** Sample answer: The scale factor of the side lengths is $\frac{14}{8}$ or $\frac{7}{4}$. The ratio of the areas is $\frac{49}{16}$. The ratio of the areas is the scale factor of the side lengths squared.   **7.** 400 ft   **9.** false; Sample answer: In rectangles, all corresponding angles are congruent but not all sides are proportional. Rectangle A is not similar to Rectangle B, since $\frac{4}{4} \neq \frac{1}{2}$.

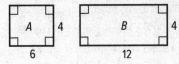

Pages 585–586   Lesson 6-8   Extra Practice

13. No; the corresponding angles are congruent, but $\frac{5}{4} \neq \frac{8}{6}$.
15. 70 ft   **17a.** True   **17b.** True   **17c.** False   **19.** $\frac{1}{24}$
21. $\frac{1}{2}$ **23.** $\frac{1}{7,920}$

Pages 591–592   Lesson 6-9   Independent Practice

1. The triangles are not similar.   **3.** 200 ft   **5** 37.5 m
7 $\frac{136}{34} = \frac{h}{1.5}$; 6 feet tall   **11.** Sample answer: The length of the tall object's shadow, the length of the shadow of a nearby object with a height that is directly measurable, and the height of the nearby object.

13. 90 ft   **15.** 6 m   **17a.** $\frac{h}{ED} = \frac{BC}{DC}$ **17b.** The distance from the mirror to the person, the distance from the mirror to the base of the flag, the height of the person's eyes.
19. Sample answer: $\frac{6\text{ ft}}{3\text{ ft}} = \frac{h\text{ ft}}{25\text{ ft}}$; 50   **21.** Yes; the corresponding angles are congruent and $\frac{5}{10} = \frac{4}{8}$.

1. solids   **3.** indirect   **5.** scale   **7.** similar

1. similar polygon   **3.** height

Chapter 7 Probability

1. $\frac{1}{3}$ **3.** $\frac{2}{3}$ **5.** 30   **7.** 24

1. $\frac{1}{4}$, 25%, or 0.25   **3** $\frac{1}{1}$, 100%, or 1   **5** $\frac{1}{5}$, 0.2, or 20%; Sample answer: Since 80% arrive on time, that means that 20% do not arrive on time.   **7.** Picking a black jelly bean is impossible since the probability of picking a black jelly bean is 0%.   **9a.** $\frac{1}{8}$, 0.125, 12.5%; $\frac{1}{2}$, 0.5, 50%   **9b.** $\frac{3}{4}$, 0.75, 75%
11. 70%, $\frac{1}{3}$; Sample answer: 70% and $\frac{1}{3}$ are probabilities that are not complementary because $0.7 + 0.\overline{3} \neq 1$. The other sets of probability are complementary.

13. $\frac{1}{5}$, 20%, or 0.2   **15.** $\frac{7}{10}$, 70%, or 0.7   **17.** $\frac{1}{2}$, 50%, or 0.5
19. $\frac{3}{5}$, 60%, or 0.6   **21.** The complement of selecting a girl is selecting a boy. The probability of the complement is $\frac{37}{100}$, 0.37, or 37%.   **23.** $\frac{124}{125}$, 99.2%, or 0.992; It is very likely that card 13 will *not* be chosen.   **25.** $P(\text{orange}) = \frac{1}{5}$; $P(\text{green}) = \frac{2}{5}$ **27.** >
29. $\frac{3}{25}$; $\frac{1}{5}$; Bryan misses more foul shots than Dwayne.

1 **a.** $\frac{1}{5}$; The experimental probability is close to the theoretical probability of $\frac{1}{6}$.   **b.** $\frac{9}{10}$; The experimental probability is close to the theoretical probability of $\frac{5}{6}$.
3a. 162 people   **3b.** about 134 people   **5** **a.** $\frac{1}{3}$
b. $\frac{6}{25}$; $\frac{13}{50}$
c.

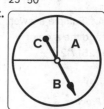

Sample answer: Section B should be one half of the spinner and sections A and C should each be one fourth of the spinner.
7. Yes; Sample answer: $\dfrac{5\text{ sharpened}}{10\text{ unsharpened}} = \dfrac{20\text{ sharpened}}{x\text{ unsharpened}}$. So, $x = 40$.

9. $\frac{9}{20}$; The experimental probability of $\frac{9}{20}$ is close to the theoretical probability of $\frac{1}{2}$.   **11.** 50 customers
13. experimental; 40; less   **15.** $P(\text{not red})$ **17.** vanilla sundae, vanilla cone, chocolate sundae, chocolate cone, strawberry sundae, strawberry cone; equally likely

1. H1, H2, H3, H4, H5, T1, T2, T3, T4, T5
3 purple 10, purple 18, purple 21, purple 24, green 10, green 18, green 21, green 24, black 10, black 18, black 21, black 24, silver 10, silver 18, silver 21, silver 24
5. $\frac{1}{36}$;

1, 1	1, 2	1, 3	1, 4	1, 5	1, 6
2, 1	2, 2	2, 3	2, 4	2, 5	2, 6
3, 1	3, 2	3, 3	3, 4	3, 5	3, 6
4, 1	4, 2	4, 3	4, 4	4, 5	4, 6
5, 1	5, 2	5, 3	5, 4	5, 5	5, 6
6, 1	6, 2	6, 3	6, 4	6, 5	6, 6

7 $P(\text{Player 1}) = \frac{6}{8}$ or $\frac{3}{4}$; $P(\text{Player 2}) = \frac{2}{8}$ or $\frac{1}{4}$; RRB, RYB, RRY, RYY, BRB, BYB, BYY, BRY   **9.** The first outcome in the I bracket should be IC.

Pages 633–634   Lesson 7-3   Extra Practice

11.

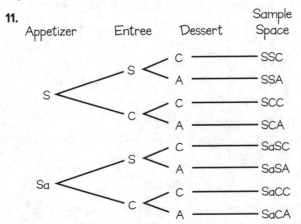

Appetizer   Entree   Dessert   Sample Space

- S — C — SSC
- S — A — SSA
- C — C — SCC
- C — A — SCA
- Sa — S — C — SaSC
- Sa — S — A — SaSA
- Sa — C — C — SaCC
- Sa — C — A — SaCA

13a. 16 combinations   **13b.** $\frac{1}{16}$

13c.

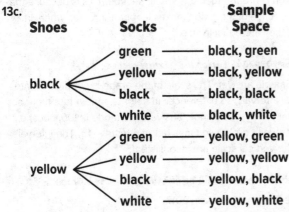

Shoes   **Socks**   **Sample Space**

- black — green — black, green
- black — yellow — black, yellow
- black — black — black, black
- black — white — black, white
- yellow — green — yellow, green
- yellow — yellow — yellow, yellow
- yellow — black — yellow, black
- yellow — white — yellow, white

8 combinations

15. (Ava, Brooke); (Greg, Brooke); (Antoine, Mario)   **17.** $\frac{1}{8}$
19. $\frac{1}{2}$ **21.** $\frac{1}{3}$; There are 2 numbers out of 6 on a number cube that are greater than 4. $\frac{2}{6} = \frac{1}{3}$

Pages 639–640   Lesson 7-4   Independent Practice

1 Sample answer: Spin a spinner with 4 equal-size sections 50 times.   **3** Sample answer: Spin a spinner divided into 3 equal sections and roll a number cube. Repeat the simulation until all types of cookies are obtained.   **5.** Sample answer: Use 3 red marbles to represent winning and 7 blue marbles to represent losing. Draw 1 marble 4 times, replacing the marble each time.   **7.** Sample answer: a survey of 100 people voting on whether or not to enact a tax increase, where each person is equally likely to vote yes or no. Toss a coin 100 times.
9. Sample answer: sometimes; The spinner must have equal-sized sections.

Pages 641–642   Lesson 7-4   Extra Practice

11. Sample answer: Use a spinner with 5 equal sections to represent the 5 discounts. Spin 4 times to represent 4 customers receiving cards.   **13.** Sample answer: Toss a coin. Heads represents one color and tails represents the other color. Repeat until both colors are selected.   **15.** Sample answer: Spin a spinner with 4 equal sections. Each section represents one of the magazines. Repeat the simulation until all possible magazines are selected.   **17.** Spin a spinner with equal size spaces labeled A, B, C, D, E, and F. Let spinning A represent winning a prize and let spinning other letters represent not winning a prize; Roll a number cube. Let rolling a 1 represent winning a prize and let rolling a 2, 3, 4, 5, or 6 represent not winning a prize.

Page 649   Problem-Solving Investigation   Act It Out

Case 3. 31   **Case 5.** unfair; Sample answer: There are 20 out of 36 outcomes that are multiples of 3 and only 15 that are multiples of 4. Jason has a greater chance of winning.

Pages 655–656   Lesson 7-5   Independent Practice

1 12   **3.** 84   **5.** 6 possible routes; $\frac{1}{6}$ or about 17%
7. $\frac{1}{50}$; very unlikely   **9** No; the number of selections is $32 \cdot 11$ or 352, which is less than 365.   **11.** 10 groups, 8 activities have 80 outcomes; the other two have 72 outcomes.   **13.** 6^x

Pages 657–658   Lesson 7-5   Extra Practice

15. 8   **17.** 27   **19.** 16   **21.** $\frac{4}{48}$ or $\frac{1}{12}$; Sample answer: There are $3 \cdot 4 \cdot 4$ or 48 different possible outcomes of a phone plan. There are $1 \cdot 4 \cdot 1$ or 4 different possible outcomes of a phone plan that includes Brand B and has a headset.   **23.** $108 = 9 \times c \times 2$; 6 colors   **25.** $\frac{1}{2}$ **27.** Sample answer: Assign each number of a number cube to a toy. Roll the number cube. Repeat until all numbers are rolled.

Pages 663–664   Lesson 7-6   Independent Practice

1 24   **3.** 840   **5.** 40,320   **7.** 120 ways   **9** 6
11. Sample answer: The number of ways you can order 3 books on a shelf is $3 \cdot 2 \cdot 1$ or 6.   **13a.** 15   **13b.** 120
13c. 10   **13d.** 28

Pages 665–666   Lesson 7-6   Extra Practice

15. 60   **17.** 120   **19.** $\frac{1}{90}$ **21.** $\frac{1}{120}$ **23a.** False   **23b.** True
23c. True   **25.** $\frac{29}{30}$ **27.** WB, WG, RB, RG, GB, GG

Page 669 Chapter Review Vocabulary Check

1. sample space **3.** theoretical

Page 670 Chapter Review Key Concept Check

1. experimental probability **3.** compound event

Chapter 8 Statistics

Page 676 Chapter 8 Are You Ready?

1. Rihanna **3.** 75

Pages 681–682 Lesson 8-1 Independent Practice

1. $\frac{3}{10}$, 0.3, or 30% **3** $\frac{2}{25}$, 0.08, or 8% **5** 9 students
7. About 143 students prefer humor books, and the number of students that prefer nonfiction is 88. So, there are about 55 more students who prefer humor books to nonfiction books.
9. about 100 times **11.** Sample answer: Randomly select a part of the group to get a sample. Determine their preferences and use the results to determine the percent of the total group. It makes sense to use a sample when surveying the population of a city.

Pages 683–684 Lesson 8-1 Extra Practice

13. $\frac{3}{5}$, 0.6, or 60% **15a.** about 60,000 **15b.** about 72,500
15c. about 7,200 **17.** $\frac{27}{238} = \frac{n}{100}$ **19.** $\frac{27}{100} = \frac{p}{238}$
21. $\frac{54}{20} = \frac{405}{x}$; 150 minutes or 2.5 hours **23.** $\frac{1}{25}$

Pages 689–690 Lesson 8-2 Independent Practice

1 The conclusion is valid. This is an unbiased systematic random sample. **3** This is a simple random sample. So, the sample is valid; about 205 people. **5.** Sample answer: Questions should be asked in a neutral manner. For example, the question "You really don't like Brand X, do you?" might not get the same answer as the question "Do you prefer Brand X or Brand Y?" **7.** Sometimes; Sample answer: The sample needs to represent the entire population to be valid. **9.** Sample answer: The sample will be biased because it is a convenience sample. Marisol will be asking only basketball fans.

Pages 691–692 Lesson 8-2 Extra Practice

11. This is an unbiased, simple random sample because randomly selected Californians were surveyed. So, the conclusion is valid. **13.** This is an unbiased, systematic random sample. So, the conclusion is valid; 304 students. **15.** The survey results in a convenience sample; Sample answer: The school district should survey every tenth family living within the school district's boundaries. **17a.** Invalid **17b.** Valid **17c.** Valid **19.** median; Sample answer: She scored better than the mean on four of the tests. She scored lower than the mode on four of the tests.

Pages 701–702 Lesson 8-3 Independent Practice

1 Graph B; Sample answer: The ratio of the area of the gas pumps in the graph on the right are not proportional to the cost of gas. **3** The median or the mode because they are much closer in value to most of the data.

5.

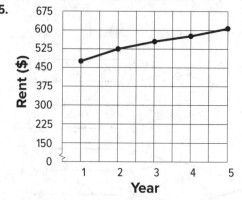

7. Sample answer: Since the graph makes it seem as if rent has been stable, a person may choose to become a tenant.
9. Sample answer: The graph makes it appear that the Fall section is greater than the Spring section. This is because the perspective of the graph makes it appear greater, when, in fact, they are equal in size.

Pages 703–704 Lesson 8-3 Extra Practice

11. Sample answer: The scale of the graph is not divided into equal intervals, so differences in heights appear less than they actually are. **13.** Sample answer: The mode is 100, but she only received 100 two times out of 6 tests. **15.** The intervals on the vertical scale are inconsistent.

Page 707 Problem-Solving Investigation Use a Graph

Case 3. Sample answer: 2017

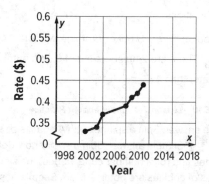

Case 5. $36.20

Pages 713–714 *Lesson 8-4* *Independent Practice*

1. Sample answer: 24 cyclists participated. No one finished with a time lower than 60 minutes. 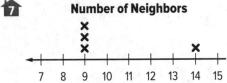 **3** 60–64 minutes

5.

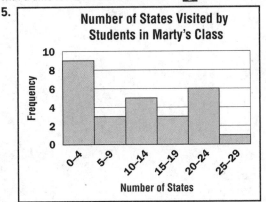

Number of States Visited by Students in Marty's Class

7 6th grade **9.** Sample answer: ages of students at summer camp: 3, 4, 5, 7, 7, 8, 8, 10, 10, 11, 13, 14, 15, 15 **11.** Sample answer: One set of intervals would be from 0 to 45, with intervals of 5. Another set would be from 0 to 50 with intervals of 10. If smaller intervals are used, less data values will be in each interval, therefore making the bars of the histogram shorter.

Pages 715–716 *Lesson 8-4* *Extra Practice*

13. 24–27 yrs **15.** 17

17.

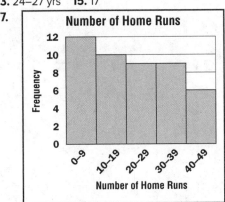

Number of Home Runs

19. Sample answer: There were no players who scored between 30 and 44 goals in their career. **21.** 42 **23.** 27 **25.** 97.5 **27.** Lucinda

Pages 721–722 *Lesson 8-5* *Independent Practice*

1 bar graph; The bar graph shows the maximum speeds, not just the interval in which the data occurs. **3.** box plot; A box plot easily displays the median.

7 **Number of Neighbors**

```
        ×
        ×
        ×  ×              ×
   ┬──┬──┬──┬──┬──┬──┬──┬──┬─▶
   7  8  9  10 11 12 13 14 15
```

Sample answer: The line plot allows you to easily see how many countries have a given number of neighbors. The bar graph, however, allows you to see the number of neighbors for each given country. **9.** Sample answer: line plot; You can easily locate the values with the most Xs to find the mode.

Pages 723–724 *Lesson 8-5* *Extra Practice*

11. box plot; The median is easily seen on the box plot as the line in the box. **13.** bar graph; A bar graph allows for the prices to be compared. **15.** Sample answer: box plot; A box plot easily shows the spread of data. **17a.** histogram **17b.** line plot **17c.** box plot **19.** 3 **21.** 6 **23.** 16 **25.** 9 **27.** 66

Page 729 *Chapter Review* *Vocabulary Check*

Across
5. population **9.** sample
Down
1. systematic **3.** simple **7.** unbiased

Page 730 *Chapter Review* *Key Concept Check*

1. survey **3.** biased sample

Index

Mm

Nn

Zz

Index

$$=$$

Equation Mat   WM1

Work Mats

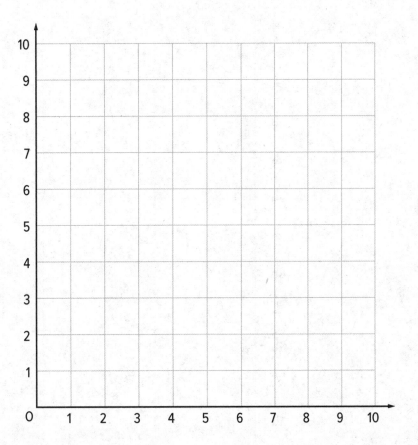

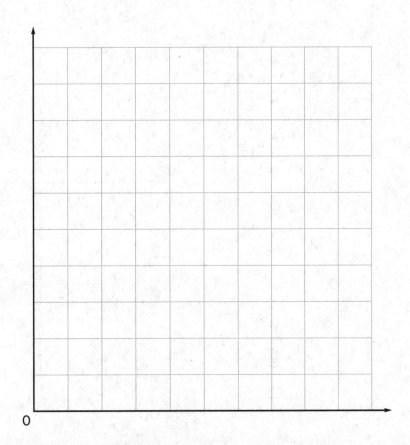

0 1 2 3 4 5 6 7 8 9

−11 −10 −9 −8 −7 −6 −5 −4 −3 −2 −1 0 1 2 3 4 5 6 7 8 9 10 11

What Are Foldables and How Do I Create Them?

Foldables are three-dimensional graphic organizers that help you create study guides for each chapter in your book.

Step 1 Go to the back of your book to find the Foldable for the chapter you are currently studying. Follow the cutting and assembly instructions at the top of the page.

Step 2 Go to the Key Concept Check at the end of the chapter you are currently studying. Match up the tabs and attach your Foldable to this page. Dotted tabs show where to place your Foldable. Striped tabs indicate where to tape the Foldable.

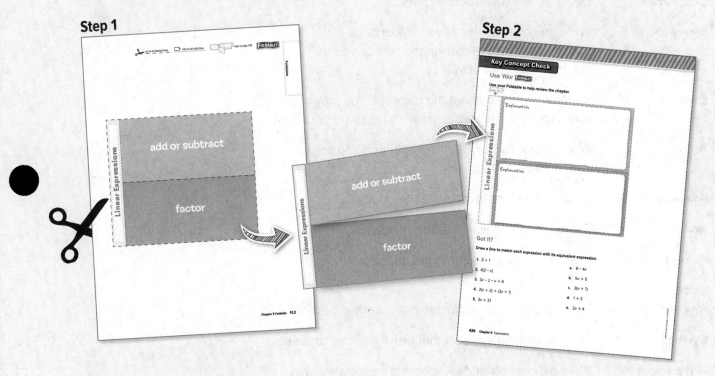

How Will I Know When to Use My Foldable?

When it's time to work on your Foldable, you will see a Foldables logo at the bottom of the **Rate Yourself!** box on the Guided Practice pages. This lets you know that it is time to update it with concepts from that lesson. Once you've completed your Foldable, use it to study for the chapter test.

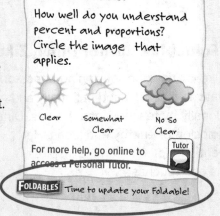

Rate Yourself!

How well do you understand percent and proportions? Circle the image that applies.

Clear   Somewhat Clear   No So Clear

For more help, go online to access a Personal Tutor.

FOLDABLES Time to update your Foldable!

How Do I Complete My Foldable?

No two Foldables in your book will look alike. However, some will ask you to fill in similar information. Below are some of the instructions you'll see as you complete your Foldable. **HAVE FUN** learning math using Foldables!

Instructions and what they mean

Best Used to...	Complete the sentence explaining when the concept should be used.
Definition	Write a definition in your own words.
Description	Describe the concept using words.
Equation	Write an equation that uses the concept. You may use one already in the text or you can make up your own.
Example	Write an example about the concept. You may use one already in the text or you can make up your own.
Formulas	Write a formula that uses the concept. You may use one already in the text.
How do I ...?	Explain the steps involved in the concept.
Models	Draw a model to illustrate the concept.
Picture	Draw a picture to illustrate the concept.
Solve Algebraically	Write and solve an equation that uses the concept.
Symbols	Write or use the symbols that pertain to the concept.
Write About It	Write a definition or description in your own words.
Words	Write the words that pertain to the concept.

Meet Foldables Author Dinah Zike

Dinah Zike is known for designing hands-on manipulatives that are used nationally and internationally by teachers and parents. Dinah is an explosion of energy and ideas. Her excitement and joy for learning inspires everyone she touches.

cut on all dashed lines   fold on all solid lines   tape to page 496   FOLDABLES®

Solve Two-Step Equations

$-3x + 6 = 21$

$-4(x + 9) = 24$

cut on all dashed lines fold on all solid lines tape to page 496

FOLDABLES®

Foldables

Write About It

Write About It

page 496

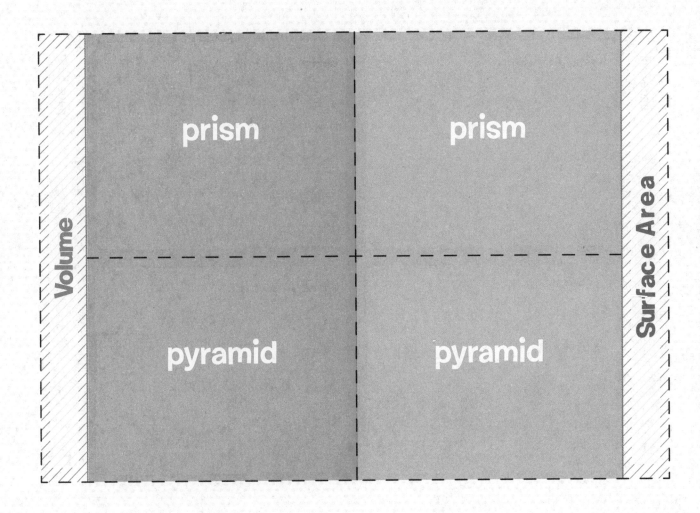

✂ - - - - - cut on all dashed lines   ⬓ fold on all solid lines   tape to page 598   **FOLDABLES**®

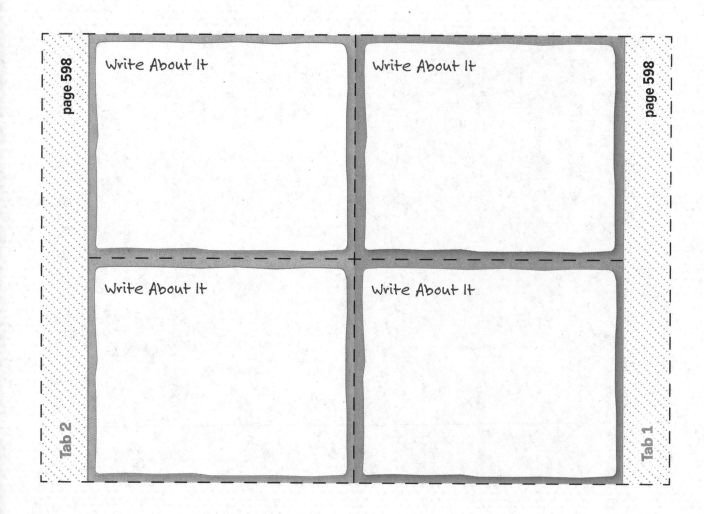

Copyright © McGraw-Hill Education

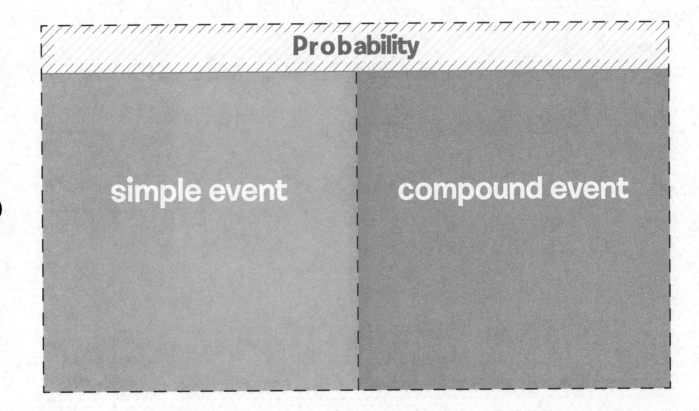

Probability

simple event

compound event

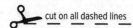 cut on all dashed lines   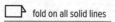 fold on all solid lines   tape to page 670

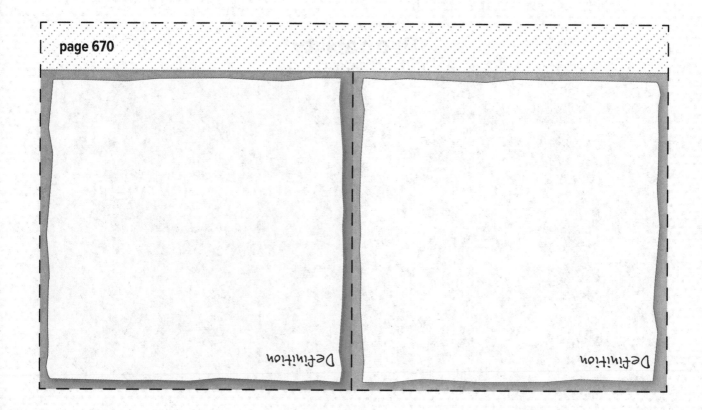

page 670

Definition

Definition

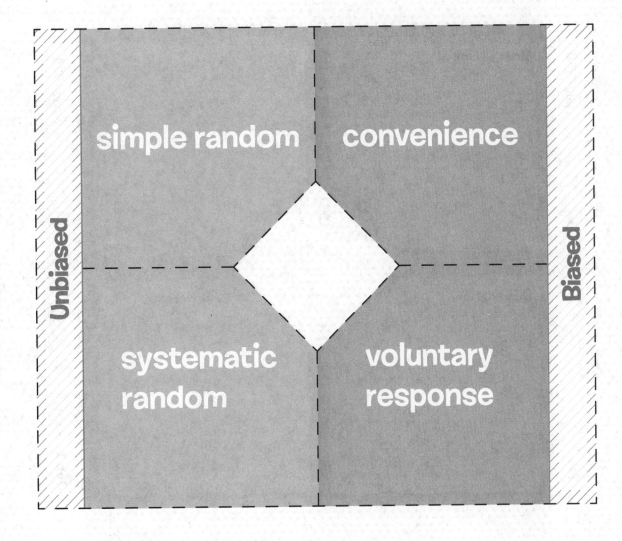

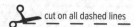 cut on all dashed lines fold on all solid lines tape to page 730

FOLDABLES®

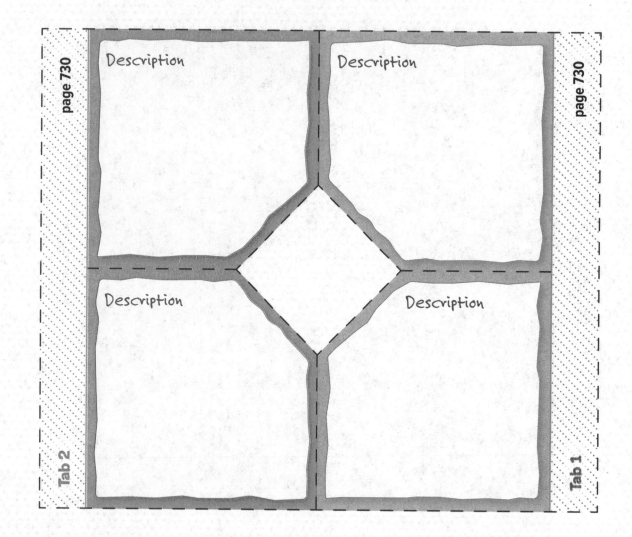

page 730

Description

Description

Description

Description

Tab 2

Tab 1

page 730